Developing Cloud Applications with Windows Azure™ Storage

Paul Mehner

PUBLISHED BY
Microsoft Press
A Division of Microsoft Corporation
One Microsoft Way
Redmond, Washington 98052-6399

Library of Congress Control Number: 2012948864
ISBN: 978-0-7356-6798-3

Printed and bound in the United States of America.

First Printing

Microsoft Press books are available through booksellers and distributors worldwide. If you need support related to this book, email Microsoft Press Book Support at mspinput@microsoft.com. Please tell us what you think of this book at http://www.microsoft.com/learning/booksurvey.

Microsoft and the trademarks listed at http://www.microsoft.com/about/legal/en/us/IntellectualProperty/Trademarks/EN-US.aspx are trademarks of the Microsoft group of companies. All other marks are property of their respective owners.

The example companies, organizations, products, domain names, email addresses, logos, people, places, and events depicted herein are fictitious. No association with any real company, organization, product, domain name, email address, logo, person, place, or event is intended or should be inferred.

This book expresses the author's views and opinions. The information contained in this book is provided without any express, statutory, or implied warranties. Neither the authors, Microsoft Corporation, nor its resellers, or distributors will be held liable for any damages caused or alleged to be caused either directly or indirectly by this book.

Acquisitions and Developmental Editor: Devon Musgrave
Project Editor: Rosemary Caperton
Editorial Production: Online Training Solutions, Inc. (OTSI)
Copyeditor: Victoria Thulman
Indexer: Jan Bednarczuk
Cover: Twist Creative • Seattle

To my wife Shelley, who tolerated my many absences from family life while I worked on this book and trained and consulted on other projects. I love you! Thanks to my son Austin and my daughter Taryn for being the truly awesome kids that they are! I love you both, too! Thanks to our pet Rotsky (Rottweiler/Husky) Bella, our deceased black lab Codey (RIP), and our Bearded Dragon Uri, who made their own loving and memorable contributions.

Thanks to my friend and mentor Jeffrey Richter for the many hours of assistance that he gave me with this book, and for allowing me to use the source code from Wintellect's Windows Azure class as the basis for most of the code samples provided.

—PAUL MEHNER

Contents at a glance

Contents

PART I   ARCHITECTURE AND USE

What do you think of this book? We want to hear from you!

Microsoft is interested in hearing your feedback so we can continually improve our
books and learning resources for you. To participate in a brief online survey, please visit:

microsoft.com/learning/booksurvey

Chapter 4   Accessing Windows Azure data storage   53

PART II   BLOBS, TABLES, AND QUEUES

Chapter 5   Blobs   71

Chapter 6   Tables   119

What do you think of this book? We want to hear from you!

Microsoft is interested in hearing your feedback so we can continually improve our
books and learning resources for you. To participate in a brief online survey, please visit:

microsoft.com/learning/booksurvey

Foreword

To my fellow Data Lover,

The most important part of any application is its data. Data is used for user accounts, orders, game scores, news items, status updates, documents, photos, music, images—the list goes on and on. It used to be that data was all about bytes stored on a hard disk and how quickly our applications could access these bytes. But for today's modern cloud-based applications, topics related to data now include:

- The geo-location of the data center storing the data, which impacts latency and geopolitical boundaries.

- Security and confidentiality of the data.

- Redundancy and high availability of the data.

- Performance and scalability when accessing the data.

- Optimistic concurrency patterns, transactions, and atomicity.

- Historical copies, or versioning of the data.

- Pricing (of course) related to all of the above.

Yes, data and everything associated with it has become a complex web of topics and issues that many applications must manage today. Fortunately, Microsoft has built a world-class, cloud-based data storage service that can easily be incorporated into many existing applications. This system addresses all of the issues I just mentioned and more. This book helps you understand what this service can do and how to use the service effectively. The book offers guidance, design patterns, and tips and tricks along the way.

And, dear reader, you are quite lucky to have Paul Mehner as the author of this book. I met Paul at a .NET user group meeting many years ago and was immediately impressed with him. I watched in admiration as he presented complex topics to the audience in such a way that they immediately grasped what he was saying. In fact, I was so impressed with Paul that I asked him to be a part of my company, Wintellect, and he has been working with us for many years now.

Furthermore, Paul has been working with Windows Azure long before it officially shipped. Through Wintellect, he teaches various Windows Azure topics (including storage) to Microsoft's own employees. And, he has also worked on many consulting engagements related to Windows Azure. This book is filled with insight from Paul's real-world experiences.

Today, just about everyone is interested in learning the best ways possible to manage their data, and this book is the best place to start on your journey.

— *Jeffrey Richter (http://Wintellect.com/)*

Introduction

Windows Azure storage provides independent data management services to your application, that is, data storage for any application, on any platform capable of making an HTTP request, written in any programming language, and deployed to the cloud or hosted in your own data center. Windows Azure storage provides a rich set of features that your applications can take advantage of to achieve operating characteristics that might otherwise be unobtainable because these characteristics were too complex, cumbersome, time-consuming, or expensive to implement. Not every application will require this set of features offered by the data management service; however, most will benefit from at least a few of them. It's hard to imagine an application that would not benefit from improved data reliability.

Developing Cloud Applications with Windows Azure Storage provides detailed information about the Windows Azure data management services platform. The book approaches the subject from the perspective of an open and RESTful data storage platform that can be used independent of any other Microsoft technology. The book focuses on the RESTful API of Windows Azure data management services to provide you with a much deeper understanding of how the storage platform works. Each REST example is also supplemented with an example that uses the Windows Azure client library (also referred to as Windows Azure storage library), which is available on many platforms, including the Microsoft .NET Framework. The Windows Azure client library eases some of the mundane and repetitive tasks such as attaching security and other custom HTTP headers to your storage requests. This gives you a much more complete, top-to-bottom understanding of the technology.

Who should read this book

This book will help existing Microsoft Visual Basic and Microsoft Visual C# developers understand the core concepts of Windows Azure data management services and related technologies. It is especially useful for programmers looking to manage database-hosted information in their new or existing .NET applications. Although most readers will have no prior experience with Windows Azure data management services, the book is also useful for those familiar with building applications against a relational database such as Microsoft SQL Server.

Assumptions

This book is written with the assumption that you have a minimal understanding of the HTTP protocol in addition to .NET development and object-oriented programming concepts for the Windows Azure client library code samples. Although the Windows Azure client library is available for many platforms and languages, this book includes examples in C# only. You should also have a basic understanding of database concepts, and perhaps some experience with relational database systems such as SQL Server.

Who should not read this book

Because the focus of this book is on software development on the Windows Azure platform, it is not intended for the information technology (IT) professional. It is also not intended for novice developers, because you will need intermediate software development experience.

Organization of this book

This book is divided into three parts:

- **Part I: Architecture and use**   This part covers the architecture and use of Windows Azure data management services and how they are accessed.

- **Part II: Blobs, tables, and queues**   This part covers specifics about blob, table, and queue storage and the scenarios that lend themselves to their use.

- **Part III: Analytics**   This part focusses on how to collect and analyze Windows Azure data management service consumption logs and metrics for blobs, tables, and queues.

Conventions and features in this book

This book presents information using conventions designed to make the information readable and easy to follow:

- Boxed elements with labels such as "Note" provide additional information or alternative methods for completing a step successfully.

- A plus sign (+) between two key names means that you must press those keys at the same time. For example, "Press Alt+Tab" means that you hold down the Alt key while you press the Tab key.

System requirements

You will need the following hardware and software to complete the practice exercises in this book:

- One of the following: Windows 7, Windows 8, Windows Server 2003 with Service Pack 2, Windows Server 2003 R2, Windows Server 2008 with Service Pack 2, or Windows Server 2008 R2

- Microsoft Visual Studio 2012, any edition (multiple downloads may be required if using Express Edition products)

- SQL Server 2008 R2 Express Edition or later, with SQL Server Management Studio 2008 Express or later (included with Visual Studio; Express Editions require separate download)

- Windows Azure client library appropriate for your client application platform (the book assumes you are using the .NET Framework)

- Microsoft Internet Information Services (IIS) or IIS Express version 7.5 or newer.

- Computer that has a 1.6 gigahertz (GHz) or faster processor (2 GHz recommended)

- 1 gigabyte (GB), 32-bit; or 2 GB (64-bit) RAM (add 512 MB if running in a virtual machine or SQL Server Express Editions, more for advanced SQL Server editions)

- 3.5 GB of available hard disk space

- 5400 RPM hard disk drive

- DirectX 9 capable video card running at 1024 x 768 or higher resolution display

- DVD-ROM drive (if installing Visual Studio from DVD)

- Internet connection to download software or chapter examples

Depending on your Windows configuration, you might require Local Administrator rights to install or configure Visual Studio 2010 and SQL Server 2008 R2 products.

Code samples

Most of the chapters in this book include examples that let you interactively try out new material learned in the main text. All sample projects can be downloaded from the following page:

http://aka.ms/DevCloudApps/files

Follow the instructions to download the DevCloudApps_667983_CompanionContent.zip file.

 Note In addition to the code samples, your system should have Visual Studio 2010 and SQL Server 2008 R2 (any edition) installed to support the Windows Azure storage emulator. Alternatively, you can run all examples against Windows Azure data management services without using the storage emulator.

Installing the code samples

Follow these steps to install the code samples on your computer so that you can use them with the exercises in this book.

1. Unzip the DevCloudApps_667983_CompanionContent.zip file that you downloaded from the book's website.

2. If prompted, review the displayed end user license agreement. If you accept the terms, select the accept option, and then click Next.

3. Install the Wintellect Windows Azure Power Library NuGet package. You can do this from the NuGet Package Manager by searching for **Wintellect**, clicking Wintellect.WindowsAzure.dll (Wintellect Power Azure Library), and then clicking Install, as shown in the following figure.

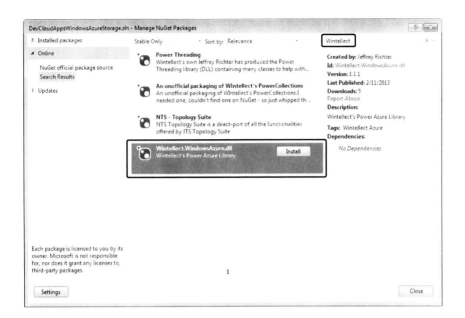

 Note If the license agreement doesn't appear, you can access it from the same webpage from which you downloaded the DevCloudApps_667983_CompanionContent.zip file.

4. You'll be prompted for the project that you want to add the Wintellect Power Azure Library to. Click the Wintellect.DevCloudAppsAzureStorage project and click OK, as shown in the following figure.

5. After the library is installed, you may need to close the package manager by clicking Close.

Note You can also download the Wintellect Windows Azure Power Library package directly from the following URL: *https://nuget.org/packages /Wintellect.WindowsAzure.dll.*

Using the code samples

Locate the AzureSecrets.txt file in the root directory of the folder you expanded the zip file into. Modify this file with your own Windows Azure subscription, management certificate thumbprint, the name of your storage account, and its key.

```
# The projects in this solution require the use of your personal Azure account
# information which you supply below.
# You do not need to enter all the values; you only need to enter values for the
# projects that require the specific information.
# If you run a project that requires a value that you did not supply, an exception
# will be thrown and this file will open automatically in Notepad so that you can
# add the missing value. After adding the value, you must re-run the
# project so that it picks-up the new value.

ManagementSubscriptionId=
ManagementCertificateThumbprint=

# http://msdn.microsoft.com/en-us/library/windowsazure/gg432983.aspx
```

```
StorageAccountName=devstoreaccount1
StorageAccountKey=
Eby8vdM02xNOcqFlqUwJPLlmEtlCDXJ1OUzFT5OuSRZ6IFsuFq2UVErCz4I6tqeksoGMGw==
```

The unzipped contents will contain a Visual Studio 2012 solution file named Dev-
CloudAppsWindowsAzureStorage.sln and a project folder. Load the DevCloudApps-
WindowsAzureStorage.sln solution into Visual Studio 2012, and go to the Storage-
Patterns.cs. file located in the Wintellect.DevCloudAppsAzureStorage project folder.
All examples shown in this book are located in this file. The *Main()* routine in the
following code calls five categories of examples: the code examples beginning with
AzureManagement are for Chapter 3, "Windows Azure data storage"; *BlobPatterns* are
for Chapter 5, "Blobs"; *TablePatterns* are for Chapter 6, "Tables"; *QueuePatterns* are for
Chapter 7, "Queues"; and *AnalyticPatterns* are for Chapter 8, "Analytics, logging, and
transaction metrics."

```
public static class AzureBookStoragePatterns {
    private static readonly Boolean c_SpawnStorageKiller = false;
    private static CloudStorageAccount m_account = null;
    private static CloudStorageAccount Account {
        [DebuggerStepThrough]
        get {
            if (m_account != null) return m_account;
            // Chose the default account to execute these demos against:
            m_account =
            //GetStorageAccount(FiddlerPrompt(StorageAccountType.DevStorage, true));
            //GetStorageAccount(FiddlerPrompt(StorageAccountType.DevStorageWithFiddler,
true));
            GetStorageAccount(FiddlerPrompt(StorageAccountType.AzureStorage, true));
            return m_account;
        }
    }

    private const String c_tableName = "Demo";

    static string s_storageAccountLabel1 =

"StagingAAAStagingAAAStagingAAAStagingAAAStagingAAAStagingAAAStagingZZZABCDE";
    static string s_storageAccountDesc1 = "Wintellect Demo Staging";
    static string s_storageAccountLocation1 = "West US";

    static string s_storageAccountName1 = "contosocohovinyard";
    static string s_storageAccountName2 = "contosotailspintoys";

    static string s_subscriptionId = AzureSecrets.ManagementSubscriptionId;
    static string s_certThumbprint = AzureSecrets.ManagementCertificateThumbprint;
    static string s_MsVersion = "2011-06-01";

    public static void Main() {
        Management.Rest();
```

```
        StorageAccountsEndpoints();

        AzureManagement.CreateAccount(s_storageAccountName1, s_storageAccountLabel1,
            s_storageAccountDesc1, null, s_storageAccountLocation1);
        AzureManagement.GetAccountProperties(s_storageAccountName1);
        AzureManagement.GetAccountKeys(s_storageAccountName1);
        AzureManagement.RegenerateAccountKeys(s_storageAccountName1, "Primary");
        AzureManagement.UpdateAccount(s_storageAccountName1, Convert.ToBase64String(
            Encoding.UTF8.GetBytes(s_storageAccountName2)), "Label Changed");
        AzureManagement.GetAccountProperties(s_storageAccountName1);
        AzureManagement.DeleteAccount(s_storageAccountName1);

        BlobPatterns.Basics(Account);
        BlobPatterns.RootContainer(Account);
        BlobPatterns.Attributes(Account);
        BlobPatterns.ConditionalOperations(Account);
        BlobPatterns.SignedAccessSignatures(Account);
        BlobPatterns.BlockBlobs(Account);
        BlobPatterns.PageBlobs(Account);
        BlobPatterns.Snapshots(Account);
        BlobPatterns.Leases(Account);
        BlobPatterns.DirectoryHierarchies(Account);
        BlobPatterns.Segmented(Account);

        TablePatterns.Basics(Account);
        TablePatterns.OptimisticConcurrency(Account);
        TablePatterns.LastUpdateWins(Account);
        TablePatterns.QueryFilterStrings(Account);
        TablePatterns.Segmented(Account);
        TablePatterns.MultipleKinds(Account);

        QueuePatterns.Basics(Account);
        QueuePatterns.Segmented(Account);

        AnalyticPatterns.AnalyticsLogs(Account);
        AnalyticPatterns.AnalyticsBlobMetrics(Account);
        AnalyticPatterns.AnalyticsCapacityBlob(Account);


        Console.WriteLine("===== finished =====");
        Console.ReadLine();
    }

    [DebuggerStepThrough]
    private static StorageAccountType FiddlerPrompt(StorageAccountType accountType,
        Boolean prompt = true) {
        const MessageBoxOptions MB_TOPMOST = (MessageBoxOptions)0x00040000;
        if (prompt && (accountType == StorageAccountType.DevStorage)) {
            if (MessageBox.Show(
                "Drag Fiddler's Process Filter cursor on this window.\n" +
                "Are you using Fiddler?",
                "Wintellect's Windows Azure Data Storage Demo",
```

```
                MessageBoxButtons.YesNo, MessageBoxIcon.Information,
                MessageBoxDefaultButton.Button1, MB_TOPMOST) == DialogResult.Yes)
                    accountType = StorageAccountType.DevStorageWithFiddler;
        }
        return accountType;
    }

    public enum StorageAccountType {
        AzureStorage,
        DevStorage,
        DevStorageWithFiddler
    }

    [DebuggerStepThrough]
    private static CloudStorageAccount GetStorageAccount(StorageAccountType
accountType) {
        switch (accountType) {
            default:
            case StorageAccountType.DevStorage:
                return CloudStorageAccount.DevelopmentStorageAccount;
            case StorageAccountType.DevStorageWithFiddler:
                return CloudStorageAccount.Parse(
    "UseDevelopmentStorage=true;DevelopmentStorageProxyUri=http://ipv4.fiddler");
            case StorageAccountType.AzureStorage:
                String accountName = AzureSecrets.StorageAccountName;
                String accountKey = AzureSecrets.StorageAccountKey;
                return new CloudStorageAccount(new StorageCredentials(accountName,
                    accountKey), false);
        }
    }

    private static void StorageAccountsEndpoints() {
        Console.Clear();

        Console.WriteLine("Azure storage endpoints:");
        String accountName = AzureSecrets.StorageAccountName;
        String accountKey = AzureSecrets.StorageAccountKey;
        CloudStorageAccount account = new CloudStorageAccount(
            new StorageCredentials(accountName, accountKey), true);
        Console.WriteLine("   BlobEndpoint:  " + account.BlobEndpoint);
        Console.WriteLine("   TableEndpoint: " + account.TableEndpoint);
        Console.WriteLine("   QueueEndpoint: " + account.QueueEndpoint);
        Console.WriteLine();

        Console.WriteLine("Storage emulator endpoints:");
        account = CloudStorageAccount.DevelopmentStorageAccount;
        Console.WriteLine("   BlobEndpoint:  " + account.BlobEndpoint);
        Console.WriteLine("   TableEndpoint: " + account.TableEndpoint);
        Console.WriteLine("   QueueEndpoint: " + account.QueueEndpoint);
        Console.WriteLine();
    }
```

To use the samples, set a breakpoint on the line AzureManagement *CreateAccount* method and run the sample with your debugger attached. When the debugger stops on the breakpoint, you can set the next line to execute by clicking Set Next Statement from the context menu (or the hotkey sequence Ctrl+Shift+F10) in Visual Studio to set the next statement to execute to the example you want to see, and then pressing F11 to step into the code.

Acknowledgments

I'd like to thank Jeffrey Richter for the sample code included in this book, and the Wintellect Windows Azure Power Library, which the code uses heavily. The code and the library are part of Wintellect's training class materials for Windows Azure. Jeffrey also reviewed several chapters and provided a lot of useful suggestions.

I'd also like to thank Victoria Thulman for her editorial review and suggestions, and Marc Young for his technical review. I could not have completed this endeavor without their care and dedication to this project. Scott Seely, Julie Lerman, and Sharyn Mehner also reviewed various chapters, and I would like to thank them as well.

Errata & book support

We've made every effort to ensure the accuracy of this book and its companion content. Any errors that have been reported since this book was published are listed on our Microsoft Press site at *oreilly.com*:

http://aka.ms/DevCloudApps/errata

If you find an error that is not already listed, you can report it to us through the same page.

If you need additional support, email Microsoft Press Book Support at *mspinput@ microsoft.com*.

Please note that product support for Microsoft software is not offered through the preceding addresses.

We want to hear from you

At Microsoft Press, your satisfaction is our top priority, and your feedback our most valuable asset. Please tell us what you think of this book at:

http://www.microsoft.com/learning/booksurvey

The survey is short, and we read every one of your comments and ideas. Thanks in advance for your input!

Stay in touch

Let's keep the conversation going! We're on Twitter: *http://twitter.com/MicrosoftPress*

Architecture and use

Understanding data storage

This chapter provides an overview of the kinds of data storage options that are available to help you gain an understanding of how Windows Azure data management services fits in. The chapter begins with a short review of data storage history, which is necessary to provide you with context for data storage in the cloud.

Database types

For the past 20 years, relational databases have dominated the information technology landscape. Software developers learn the skills of data normalization and how to write efficient queries to join tables to create results that are suitable for consumption by an application or human. These skills have become so ingrained in the development community and have been with us for so long now, that it is almost impossible to imagine that there are other types of databases with different characteristics from relational databases. The advent of cloud computing and the need for data storage that is massively scalable has changed this trend, and the relational database model, which has held such a powerful dominance, is now losing ground to other alternatives. It is not that the relational database model is flawed in any way; it's just that the relational database model is better suited than other models for some types of data storage. In the interest of commonality and speed of application development, it has been advantageous for the developer community to approach a wide variety of data storage requirements by using the relational database model, primarily because it has been so ubiquitously available and also because it has proven itself to be quite adaptable to scenarios where an alternative might have provided a better set of characteristics such as scalability, cost, or maintainability.

In this chapter, you explore some of the data storage options that have been available over the past few decades and address which ones are making a comeback in storage account applications.

Flat file

The most basic of all database structures is a simple flat file. In this kind of database, precise positioning of data within the file may be used to delineate the fields of an entity. In the following example, every line in the file represents an entity, and the fields of that entity are identified by their character position within the line. The last name occupies characters 00 through 19; the first name occupies characters 20 through 39; the middle initial occupies characters 40 through 42, and so on. The meaning of the data is inferred entirely off the position at which the data exists within a row. In such databases, it is necessary for the user of the data to possess its own copy of the schema to properly consume it.

```
LastName_____FirstName_____MI_Address_____City_____St_Zip____
00000000001111111111222222222233333333334444444444555555555566666666667777777777
01234567890123456789012345678901234567890123456789012345678901234567890123456789
```

Another popular approach to the flat file database is to use delimiters to separate fields from one another. In the 1980s, many popular spreadsheet and database programs such as VisiCalc, Lotus 1-2-3, and Microsoft Excel popularized the use of the *CSV* format (which stands for comma-separated values), which turned the comma into the most widely used delimiter. Of course, commas exist naturally in some of your data (a single name field comprising Last, First, MI for example). In such cases, the pipe symbol (|) has been a popular alternative to the comma. The same personal information would be stored as follows in a CSV file.

```
LastName, FirstName, MI, Address, City, State, Zip
```

Although arguably a little easier to consume than the fixed field length method because the user does not have to have knowledge of the field boundary locations, the user still has to possess knowledge about the meaning of each field of data to make use of it.

Software Arts, the makers of the popular VisiCalc spreadsheet program, created an alternative called Data Interchange Format (DIF). DIF successfully put metadata into the same file as the data so that the data could more easily be consumed by a user without requiring the kind of positional knowledge that the preceding techniques required.

Everything in a DIF file is stored as ASCII text to provide cross-platform compatibility suitable to that generation of application platform. This format is still useful for certain interoperability scenarios. A DIF file has a header segment and a data segment, where each item is represented by two or three lines of information (see Table 1-1). A header is three lines constituting a text identifier, a second line that is a comma-separated pair of numbers, and a third line containing a quoted string (see Table 1-2). The data is all represented in two lines, with the first line being a pair of quoted numbers identifying the type of data, and the next line containing the quoted data value (see Table 1-3).

TABLE 1-1 DIF format segments

Segment	Segment purpose	Example
TABLE	A numeric value follows the version; the second line of value contains a generated comment.	TABLE 0,1 "COMMENT"
VECTORS	The number of columns follows in the next line as a numeric value.	VECTORS 0,2 ""
TUPLES	The number of rows follows in the next line as a numeric value.	TUPLES 0,3 ""
DATA	After a placeholder numeric value of 0, the data for the table follows. Each row is preceded by a BOT (Beginning of Tuple) directive. The table is terminated by an EOD (End of Data) directive.	DATA 0,0 "" -1,0

TABLE 1-2 Second line data descriptors

Property	Meaning	Examples/description
−1	Directive: BOT-Beginning of Tuple EOD-End of Data	-1,0 BOT
0	Numeric value: The value after the comma is a numeric; or ■ valid ■ *NA* – not available ■ *ERROR* – error ■ *TRUE* – true Boolean value ■ *FALSE* – false Boolean value *V*	1,0 "Cost" 0,56 V
1	String value	Second number is ignored; quoted string on the next line is the value

TABLE 1-3 Data to be serialized in DIF format

Property	Value
Cost	56
Price	79

When the data shown in Table 1-3 is serialized into the DIF format, it appears as follows.

```
TABLE
0,1
"COMMENT"
VECTORS
0,2
""
TUPLES
0,3
""
DATA
0,0
""
-1,0
BOT
1,0
"Property"
1,0
"Value"
-1,0
BOT
1,0
"Cost"
0,56
V
-1,0
BOT
1,0
"Price"
0,79
V
-1,0
EOD
```

File-based relational databases

In the 1980s, during the early age of the microcomputer, a plethora of file-based database systems emerged. They all built upon the principles of the flat file database but added features such as built-in support for relationships, querying languages to perform efficient database operations (such as create, read, update, delete), indexes to improve the performance of retrieving data, filters to constrain the data retrieved, and ordering semantics to sort data for viewing and reporting. Many of these database packages such as Access, Clipper, FoxPro, and Profile had so-called 4GL support (4GL stood for fourth-generation programming language) built into them, which could be used to build entire business applications. A few of the popular packages include the following:

- Btrieve

- Clipper

- dBase

- FoxPro

- Lotus Notes

- Microsoft Access

- Profile and filePro

These file-based database packages and the business applications that were developed by using them dominated much of the 1980s and a good stretch of the 1990s.

Relational

The predominant database model in information technology for the past two decades has been the relational database model. It was first defined in June of 1970 by Edgar Codd during his employment with IBM's San Jose Research Laboratory.

Relational databases are composed of tables that represent entities, where each row in the table represents an instance of an entity, and every column in the table represents an attribute of those instance entities.

The definition of a *relational database table* is the set of attributes that make up the entity and the type of data that each property is composed of. Figure 1-1 shows a table of suppliers to a business enterprise. Each supplier has characteristics such as a unique identifier (a supplier number), a name, a status (active or inactive in this case), a city, and a state.

Id	Supplier Name	Status	City	State
S1	Tailspin Toys	A	Olympia	WA
S2	Contoso, Ltd.	A	Seattle	WA
S3	Fourth Coffee	A	Olympia	WA

FIGURE 1-1 Table of suppliers.

In Figure 1-1, which depicts a table of data, redundant information is being stored. The City and State information is duplicated for every row of the table. In the preceding example, the city of Olympia, Washington appears twice, once for Tailspin Toys and again for Fourth Coffee. One of the objectives of the relational database model is to eliminate data redundancy. Doing this makes data easier to maintain and prevents embarrassing business mistakes, such as a software defect that updates a supplier's address in a table full of purchase orders but misses updating the address in a purchasing table, the result of which is orders going to one address but payments to the same supplier going to another. A change to information about a supplier's address should be able to be made in one location so that every application that needs to know a supplier's address can gain access to the most recent address by reference.

In Figure 1-2, which depicts a table of data, the city data is factored out into its own table of cities. Each row in the city table is assigned a unique identifier, which is used as a key to uniquely locate that city. The supplier table is modified to have the key of the city that the supplier is located in instead of the actual city name. The state information is factored out in a similar manner, but in this example, the state abbreviation was already a natural key, so we used it to link the city table to the state table where supplementary data about each state may be kept, such as the full state name.

Id	Supplier Name	City		Id	City Name	State		State	State Name
S1	Tailspin Toys	C1		C1	Olympia	WA		WA	Washington
S2	Contoso, Ltd.	C2		C2	Seattle	WA		KS	Kansas
S3	Fourth Coffee	C1		C3	Tacoma	WA		FL	Florida
				C4	Topeka	KS		CA	California

FIGURE 1-2 Tables of suppliers, cities, and states with references.

Windows Azure table storage provides storage for tabular data, as you will see in Chapter 6, "Tables"; however, table storage in the cloud is not the same as the tables of a relational database depicted here. Although there may be relationships between various tables in data storage, such relationships must be managed by the consuming user or application, because they are not provided by the database.

In Windows Azure, Microsoft offers its relational database server for the cloud under the name of SQL Azure. The service comprises Windows Azure Virtual Machines running a special build of SQL Server 2008 R2. Most features of the on-premise product are available in SQL Azure. This book is focused on building cloud applications with Windows Azure data management services, and not with SQL Azure. For the most part, building cloud applications that use a SQL Azure database are very similar to building applications for on-premise deployment. The software developer's biggest hurdle is ensuring that that applications are written with enough resilience to be able to detect and recover from common environmental deficiencies and errors such as loss of connectivity, timeouts, and delayed data transmissions. It is not safe to assume that your on-premise application that uses a SQL Server database can be transplanted to the cloud without review of the error-handling code in your data access layer.

Hierarchical

Hierarchical databases are composed of distinct nodes of information organized into an inverted tree structure. They are used to present information in parent-child relationships, where a single parent node can have any number of child nodes, and each child can itself be a parent to its own children. Nodes in a hierarchical database can have only one parent. The entire database begins with a single root node. A hierarchical database may be considered as a special case of the network, a case in which every child node has exactly one parent node.

Figure 1-3 depicts a customer database where each customer contains a collection of orders, invoices, and receipts, and each invoice node in this example contains a collection of service invoices, product invoices, and maintenance invoices.

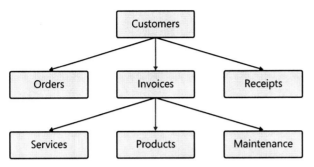

FIGURE 1-3 Hierarchical databases organize information in a tree-like structure with a root node at the top branching into *n*-number of child-nodes, with each node having exactly one parent.

An XML document is a very popular form of hierarchical database. The XML document itself may be stored in a variety of different mediums such as volatile memory (for example, RAM), the file system on a computer's hard drive, or a blob in Windows Azure blob storage (as discussed in Chapter 5, "Blobs"). The storage medium has no impact upon the internal structure of the database, so it is useful to think of XML documents in an abstract form. The structure shown in Figure 1-3 might be represented in an XML document similar to the following.

```xml
<Customers>
  <Orders></Orders>
  <Invoices>
    <Service>
       <ServiceInvoice id="1" .../>
       <ServiceInvoice id="2" .../>
       <ServiceInvoice id="3" .../>
    </Service>
    <Products>
       <ProductInvoice id="1" .../>
       <ProductInvoice id="2" .../>
       <ProductInvoice id="3" .../>
    </Products>
    <Maintenance>
       <MaintenanceInvoice id="1" .../>
       <MaintenanceInvoice id="2" .../>
       <MaintenanceInvoice id="3" .../>
    </Maintenance>
  </Invoices>
  <Receipts></Receipts>
</Customers>
```

Network

Network databases are composed of distinct nodes of information that are organized into a mesh structure. They are often used to represent many-to-many relationships. Unlike the hierarchical database, the network database does not have a single parent node, and nodes are not constrained to having only one parent. Instead, all nodes are treated as peers, and every node can have relationships with 1 to as many as all of the other nodes.

Figure 1-4 depicts a customer database where each customer contains a collection of local, national, and international customers. Each type of customer can have service, product, and maintenance invoices.

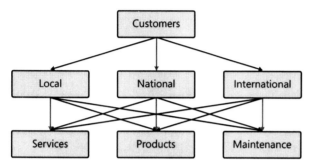

FIGURE 1-4 Network databases organize information in a mesh structure where any node can connect with *n*-number of other nodes.

Federated

Federated databases are composed of many distinct instances of smaller relational databases that are woven together through the use of a meta-database, which provides the illusion of a single database to the user. The constituent database may be geographically distributed or centrally located, which can aid in geo-locating data to where it is needed most, while still maintaining referential integrity. Federated databases are an alternative to merging the data contained in multiple databases. More information about Federating SQL Azure databases in the cloud can be found here:

http://msdn.microsoft.com/en-us/library/ms190381(v=sql.105).aspx

NoSQL (Not Only SQL)

The term *NoSQL* database (short for *Not Only SQL*) is used to describe several database platforms that are not built on relational tables and do not offer Structured Query Language (SQL) as their means of performing data operations.

Major internet companies such as Microsoft, Google, Amazon, Twitter, and Facebook faced many performance and maintenance challenges dealing with massively large data stores using relational database solutions. Beginning in 2009, NoSQL databases were designed specifically to address the problems that were encountered in behemoth data stores. Data in NoSQL storage does not necessarily follow a fixed schema, and to meet performance goals and to stay within the hardware constraints of a single machine, data is partitioned across multiple machines. Horizontal scalability was essential in achieving these objectives, but the distributed nature of using multiple machines makes ACID-style transactions (ACID stands for atomicity, consistency, isolation, durability) impractical for certain kinds of operations (specifically those involving data spread across multiple machines). In Chapter 6, you will be introduced to the Entity Group Transaction (EGT) and the rules for ACID semantics associated with Windows Azure table storage. Some NoSQL databases use an eventually consistent model for transactions, where there is a window of time that data may be referentially inconsistent but over time, as the transaction propagates throughout distributed database nodes, the data will eventually become fully consistent again. Many NoSQL architectures, including Windows Azure data storage, redundantly store data across multiple servers in a seamless fashion to provide high reliability and fault tolerance.

NoSQL databases are useful when working with very large data stores when the nature of the data to be stored does not require a relational model. Often this is a compromise between the benefit of the features of a relational database and the cost of those features. The data stored in a NoSQL database such as Windows Azure table storage may be structured, but strict adherence to a schema is not required as it is for SQL databases.

Data storage types

NoSQL databases leave us at Windows Azure storage, which is an implementation of a NoSQL-styled database. To understand some of the features of Windows Azure storage in context, you must first have an understanding of the types and characteristics of the data you will be storing. Windows Azure storage provides three major storage types. In Chapters 5 and 6, and in Chapter 7, "Queues," you will delve into blobs, tables, and queues, respectively, and learn when to use each one and the value that each of them brings to our applications. The following is a short and high-level description of the three major data storage types.

Blobs

Blob storage is used to store unstructured data such as images, documents, video, and other data frequently used as content in websites. You will learn more about blobs in Chapter 5.

Tables

Table storage is used to store *semi-structured data*, or data that loosely adheres to a schema in high-volume scalability scenarios. You will learn more about tables in Chapter 6.

Queues

Message queue storage provides a reliable means to asynchronously transmit messages between the tiers of your application. You will learn more about message queues in Chapter 7.

Conclusion

In this chapter, you reviewed the kinds and history of data storage options that are available and gained an understanding of where Windows Azure data storage fits in. The rest of this book will focus entirely on Windows Azure data management services and will build upon information presented in this chapter.

Windows Azure data storage overview

The objective of this chapter is to provide you with an infrastructural understanding of Windows Azure data storage to facilitate strategic and architectural decisions regarding its use in your applications. A primary byproduct of achieving this objective is establishment of the versatility of Windows Azure storage for use as an autonomous data management service independent of your application's platform or your deployment choices.

Feature-rich data storage for almost any application

Windows Azure storage provides independent data management services to your application, that is, data storage for *any* application, on *any* platform capable of making an HTTP request, written in *any* programming language, and deployed to the cloud or hosted in your own data center. Windows Azure storage provides a rich set of features that your applications can take advantage of to achieve operating characteristics that might otherwise be unobtainable because these characteristics were too complex, cumbersome, time-consuming, or expensive to implement. Not every application will require this set of features offered by the data management service; however, most will benefit from at least a few of them. It's hard to imagine an application that would not benefit from improved data reliability.

Before exploring what Windows Azure storage is, it is useful to clearly identify what it is not. Windows Azure storage is *not* a relational database. Relational databases eliminate (or significantly reduce) redundant data through a process called *normalization*. A single entity is stored in the database one time, where it is indexed by a unique identifier (called a *primary key*), which is used to make reference to that single entity wherever duplication of that information would occur in other entities. This is a powerful feature because data needs to be updated in only one place. Data stored in relational databases is also strongly typed and constrained to ensure that only strictly conformant data can be inserted into entities, reducing the collection of bogus data and the numerous bugs encountered when processing unanticipated data. If you need the features of a relational database, you likely need Windows Azure SQL Database. In Chapter 6, "Tables," you tackle the problem of how to structure your data for transactional storage in Windows Azure table storage. If you're a developer who has worked with Microsoft SQL Server (or other relational databases) most of your career, it's enough to simply state that Windows Azure table storage is significantly different from what you're likely familiar with.

The following list describes a few of the high-level Windows Azure storage features that your application might use and that you delve into in this chapter:

- **Independence and interoperability**   Windows Azure storage is a service designed to be used independent of the applications that might utilize it. Because access to data management services is done with a simple REST API, Windows Azure storage can be used independent of your application's platform, programming language, or deployment model.

- **Geo-location**   An application might use the geo-location feature of Windows Azure storage to store and retrieve data local to where it is being most used. Sometimes there are legal requirements for data storage as well. For example, some types of data must be stored in data centers that are physically located in a particular country.

- **Replication**   Windows Azure storage maintains three replicas of your data at all times, providing a high degree of confidence in the safety of your data. Replication also improves the scalability of reading data, because data being read can be served from all replicas simultaneously.

- **Geo-replication**   Windows Azure data is replicated from the data center that you select as your primary data to a secondary data center within the same geographical region but hundreds of miles away, further increasing your confidence in the safety of your data in the event of data center disaster.

- **The illusion of infinite storage**   A sudden increase in storage capacity for your application or service can be accommodated without costly infrastructural changes to your own data center. Data storage capacity is allocated on demand in units of logical servers called *storage nodes*.

- **Automatic and on-demand scalability**   A sudden increase in demand for your data will be automatically accommodated by Windows Azure storage without costly infrastructural changes to your own data center. The scalability capabilities of Windows Azure are truly astounding. Windows Azure will dedicate an entire storage node to a single partition of data if that's what is required to meet Microsoft's scalability objectives, which are introduced later in this chapter.

- **Data consistency** Windows Azure storage maintains a fully consistent data model. When a write operation completes, all subsequent read operations will return the updated value. This is different from other eventually consistent data models such as Amazon's S3, where data is eventually consistent. In the *eventually consistent* model, read operations that happen after a write operation may or may not return the updated value. All read operations will eventually return the updated value.

- **ISO 27001 certification** Windows Azure storage received ISO 27001 certification, which may be useful in helping your own application meet certification requirements for sensitive data. The Windows Azure core services of Cloud Services, data management services, Virtual Network, and Virtual Machines are all covered by this certification, which was conducted in 2011 by BSI Americas. A copy of this certification can be found online at the following URL:

  http://www.bsigroup.com/en/Assessment-and-certification-services/Client-directory /CertificateClient-Directory-Search-Results/?searchkey=companyXeqXmicrosoft

- **Pay as you go and pay only for what you need** No upfront expenditures to purchase equipment, space, and bandwidth are necessary to meet peak demand in your data center. You pay as you go and only for what you consume today. As your storage capacity and scalability needs change, so does your bill. This helps to keep your fixed costs in alignment with your revenues.

That's a very compelling list of features. The following sections explore what you need to know to use and have confidence in these capabilities.

Data storage abstractions

To provide context for some of the features of Windows Azure storage, you must first have an understanding of the types and characteristics of the data you will be storing. Windows Azure storage provides three major storage types. In Chapter 5, "Blobs," Chapter 6, and Chapter 7, "Queues," you will delve into these three types and learn when to use each one as well as the value that each brings to your applications. For the purposes of this chapter, a short and high-level description of the three major data storage types is adequate.

The abstractions of Windows Azure storage are considered forms of NoSQL data storage. The characteristics of NoSQL are that the database does not use the Structured Query Language (SQL), and the ACID-style transaction guarantees (*ACID* stands for atomicity, consistency, isolation, and durability) are either not supported or are supported only in a limited way. They may employ techniques such as *eventual consistency*, which is the notion that the data will eventually arrive at a consistent state across all storage nodes, but that brief periods of data inconsistency are anticipated and tolerable. NoSQL database management systems are useful when working with extremely large data stores because they improve performance and high availability of data. The emphasis in NoSQL database systems is on the ability to store and retrieve large quantities of data quickly rather than on the relationships between elements of data.

Blobs

The Windows Azure Blob service provides a simple RESTful API for storing and retrieving unstructured data (for example, documents, pictures, videos, and music), including a small amount of metadata about the contents. Blobs are organized into containers (which are very similar to directories), and you can store several hundred gigabytes (GB) in a single blob. Blobs and blob containers are accessible as unique URLs, and they can be created, read, updated, and deleted using simple HTTP verbs against their URLs. Blob containers may be set to allow public accessibility, allowing anonymous read-only access to the blob's contents. Blobs are ideal for the storage of web content. The primary purpose of publicly accessible read-only containers is to allow direct consumption of such content by unauthenticated web browsers. This is a convenient way of augmenting your on-premise web servers with content delivered from Windows Azure storage. This not only saves you the cost of making additional upfront capital investments, but it also allows you some flexibility in not having to purchase server and network capacity for planned peaks in advance of demand. In the real world, the demand may never materialize; or potentially even worse, the demand might materialize but your resources are inadequate to meet the demand and you miss opportunities. You'll learn more about the Blob service in Chapter 5.

Tables

The Windows Azure Table service provides a simple RESTful API for storing massive amounts of semi-structured data. Windows Azure tables are not at all like relational database tables, and you should avoid making such a correlation. Rows, which are called *entities*, consist of properties, which are like columns.

Different rows stored in the same table can often have different sets of properties. You can perform queries on individual tables just as you might do with a relational database, but queries cannot span tables. Of course, relationships are what a relational database is all about, and queries that span multiple tables are the bread and butter of what relational databases do, and how normalized data becomes denormalized for consumption by your applications and reports. You should therefore avoid making any kind of direct correlation between relational database tables and Windows Azure tables. You'll learn more about the Table service in Chapter 6.

Queues

Unlike blobs and tables, queues do not provide permanent storage of the messages they handle. In fact, messages are quietly deleted from queues if they are not processed within seven days. Windows Azure queues are a means of transmitting messages between different server roles and instances when your application runs on Windows Azure Cloud services. Like all of Windows Azure storage, queues are exposed through a RESTful API that could potentially be used by on-premise and non-Microsoft platforms. The queued message data management service provides durable fire-and-forget message storage and reliable delivery to your applications. You'll learn more about the Windows Azure Queue service in Chapter 7.

Windows Azure data centers

Windows Azure data centers are located in three major geographic regions: the United States, Europe, and Asia. Each geographic region is further subdivided into subregions. As depicted in the world map in Figure 2-1, the United States is divided into South Central, North Central, East, and West. Europe is divided into North and West, and Asia is divided into Southeast and East. You select the primary subregion where you want to store your data.

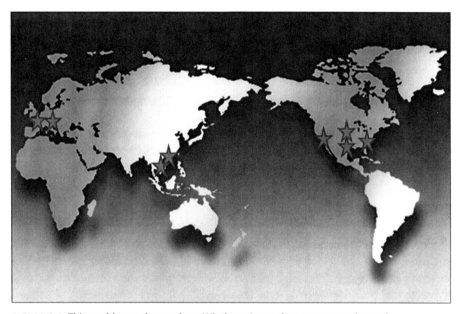

FIGURE 2-1 This world map shows where Windows Azure data centers are located.

Inside each data center are shipping containers packed full of servers with appropriate cooling and electrical supplies. You can take an interesting tour of one of the Microsoft data centers by visiting the following YouTube link, which was created by the Microsoft Cloud Infrastructure Team (MSGFST):

http://www.youtube.com/watch?v=hOxA1l1pQlw

You can then continue the tour to facilitate a more detailed view of the assembly of the individual shipping containers that house the servers by going to this MSGFST-prepared YouTube link:

http://www.youtube.com/watch?v=nIliMskAHro

Your data in one data center will be replicated again to another data center within the same geo-graphical region. For example, if your data is stored in the North Central US data center, that data will be replicated to the South Central US data center. Having three replicas of your data stored in two distinct data centers means that there will be at least six copies of your data, making the specter of cataclysmic data loss because of a natural disaster extremely unlikely.

Microsoft publishes a dashboard (shown in Figure 2-2) to allow convenient monitoring of the health of the data centers worldwide at the following URL:

http://www.windowsazure.com/en-us/support/service-dashboard/

Status	Service [Sub-Region]	Description	RSS
⊘	Windows Azure Storage [East Asia]	Service is running normally.	⬓
⊘	Windows Azure Storage [East US]	Service is running normally.	⬓
⊘	Windows Azure Storage [North Central US]	Service is running normally.	⬓
⊘	Windows Azure Storage [North Europe]	Service is running normally.	⬓
⊘	Windows Azure Storage [South Central US]	Service is running normally.	⬓
⊘	Windows Azure Storage [Southeast Asia]	Service is running normally.	⬓
⊘	Windows Azure Storage [West Europe]	Service is running normally.	⬓
⊘	Windows Azure Storage [West US]	Service is running normally.	⬓

FIGURE 2-2 Windows Azure Service dashboards enable monitoring of data management service health.

Each Windows Azure service has a convenient RSS feed for each geographical subregion. This allows you an opportunity to provide custom notification implementations or create automated adjustments to your application based on the health of any particular part of Windows Azure.

Storage topology

As depicted in Figure 2-3, the Windows Azure storage architecture consists of a front-end Virtual IP and three basic layers: a front-end (FE) layer, a partition layer, and a Distributed File System (DFS) layer. In this chapter, you're going to drill down into these three layers to gain a clear understanding of and confidence in exactly how this architecture is used. Doing so will help you achieve the 99.9 percent level of reliability in your applications that Microsoft guarantees in its Service Level Agreement (SLA).

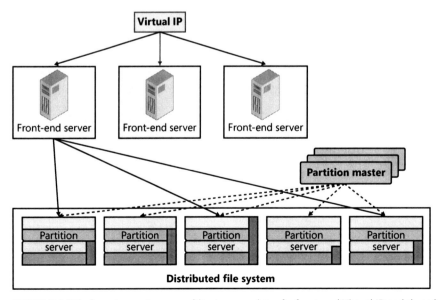

FIGURE 2-3 Windows Azure storage architecture consists of a front-end Virtual IP and three basic layers.

The following list describes the Windows Azure architecture:

- **Virtual IP** Requests for data storage operations enter through a Virtual IP (VIP) address, where they are routed to an available server in the front-end layer. The VIP balances the load of incoming requests by evenly distributing these requests to the front-end servers.

- **Front-end layer** The front-end (FE) layer accepts incoming requests and routes them to an appropriate partition server in the partition layer based on a partition map. It maintains this map to keep track of which servers are servicing which partitions.

- **Partition layer** The partition layer manages the partitioning of blob, table, and queue data. A data object belongs to a single partition identified by a partition key, and each partition is served by only one partition server. The partition layer manages what partition is served on what partition server and provides automatic load balancing of partitions across servers to meet the traffic requirements. A single partition server can serve the data for many partitions at one time.

- **Distributed File System layer** The DFS layer stores the data on disk and distributes and replicates the data across many servers. Data is stored by the DFS layer, but all data stored in servers managed by the DFS layer are accessible from any of the partition servers in the partition layer.

  The DFS layer provides Windows Azure storage with redundant durability because all data is replicated multiple times. The DFS layer spreads your data out over potentially hundreds of storage nodes. All of the replicas of your data are accessible from all the partition servers as well as from other DFS servers.

Failure management and durability

Hardware failure management and recovery is handled by the storage system according to the layer it occurs on. The following sections describe how failures are mitigated at each of the three layers.

Front-end layer failure mitigation

The load balancer monitors the responsiveness of each of the front-end servers. If one of the servers becomes unresponsive, the load balancer removes it from the available server pool so that incoming requests are no longer dispatched to it. This ensures that requests arriving at the VIP get sent only to healthy front-end servers.

Partition layer failure mitigation

If one of the partition servers is unavailable, the storage system immediately reassigns any partitions it was serving to other available partition servers and updates the front-end server partition maps to reflect this change. This allows the front-end servers to continue to correctly locate the partitioned data. When this reassignment is made, no data is moved on disk because all of the partition data is stored in the DFS layer and is accessible from any partition server. The storage system ensures that data partitions are always available to be served.

Distributed File System layer failure mitigation

If the storage system determines that one of the DFS servers is unavailable, the partition layer will direct the request instead to one of the other available DFS servers containing replicas of the data. The partition layer will resume usage of the DFS server when it is available again, but if a DFS server remains unavailable too long, the storage system generates an additional replica of the data to ensure an adequate number of durable replicas are maintained.

Data is stored in the DFS in basic units of storage called *extents*, which range in size from 100 MB to 1 GB in size. Each extent is spread randomly and replicated multiple times over multiple DFS servers. Data in a blob, entities in a table, or messages in a queue are all stored in one or more of these extents. A 10-GB blob may be stored across 10 1-GB extents, with three replicas for each extent, which potentially means that storage of this single blob is spread out over 30 DFS servers. The spreading and duplication of the data over multiple extents is what gives the DFS such resiliency against failure, and its inherent parallelism significantly increases the number of I/O operations that can be performed.

Each extent has a primary server and multiple DFS secondary servers. All writes to the extent are routed through the extent's primary DFS server. The writes are then forwarded to the secondary servers and success is returned back from the primary DFS server to the requestor once the data has been written to at least three DFS servers. If one of the DFS servers is unreachable, the DFS layer will select different DFS servers to write to until the data for the extent has been written at least three times. Once the third write has occurred, success is returned from the primary DFS server to the requestor. The other replicas will be updated asynchronously resulting in them being *eventually consistent*. When a subsequent read occurs on the same extent, the DFS layer will serve that data from any up-to-date extent replica.

To ensure high availability, no two replicas for an extent are ever placed on the same fault domain or upgrade domain (defined in the next section). If one fault domain goes down, or when an upgrade is occurring, there will always be healthy replicas from which the data can be accessed from. The data storage system automatically keeps the number of available replicas at a healthy level by replacing unavailable extent replicas. It does this by re-replicating to healthy servers when necessary.

Dynamic replication reduces the mean-time-to-recovery of healthy data extents when failures occur. If a DFS server fails for any reason, all extents that had a replica on that server are re-replicated to another server as quickly as possible; thus, a healthy number of replicas of every extent are always available. While re-replication is taking place, the other healthy replicas are used to service data requests and are used as data sources for re-replication. Because the extents are distributed randomly, network availability is also spread out to prevent hotspots.

The DFS layer also provides detection and repair of random errors (so-called *bit-rot*). It does this by computing and storing a checksum with the extent data. When data is read, this checksum is recomputed and verified against the stored checksum. In the rare event that the checksums do not match (indicating bit rot has occurred), the DFS discards the replica and re-replicates to another DFS server to bring the extent back to a healthy level of replication.

Fault and upgrade domains

As mentioned earlier in the chapter, the Microsoft Service Level Agreement guarantees that Windows Azure storage will successfully process add, update, read, and delete requests 99.9 percent of the time. Imagine the planning and expense necessary to achieve this level of reliability for your application within your own data center. To achieve your 99.9 percent objective, you would need to keep your downtime for all hardware, network access, electricity, HVAC, and software to fewer than nine hours per year! That's a pretty daunting task when you consider that even a single hardware failure, network outage, or software defect could exceed your entire SLA for the year. Achieving a 99.9 percent level of reliability for your application would require considerable investment in infrastructural software and redundant hardware, and so is yet another compelling argument for how cloud computing benefits your application.

To achieve the level of reliability promised in its SLA, Microsoft configures their hardware and software assets into two arrangements called *fault domains* and *upgrade domains*. These configurations boost the reliability to the promised level in ways that you will learn about in more detail later in this chapter, but first you need to learn exactly what these configurations are.

Fault domains

The term *fault domain* describes a unit of hardware components that share a single point of failure. One technique for maintaining high availability of your data during hardware failures is to spread your data out across multiple fault domains, thereby limiting the impact of a single hardware component failure. Windows Azure applies fault domain strategies to three layers of hardware in each data center: the server rack, the network switch, and the power supply. The Windows Azure SLA guarantees that at least two fault domains will be utilized at all three of these layers, meaning that if one rack, network switch, or power supply fails, at least one of these components will still be operating. The data stored on each storage node is replicated onto two other storage nodes across two or more fault domains at all hardware layers.

Upgrade domains

Upgrade domains represent another form of potential outage because storage nodes may not be available during application upgrades or operating system patches. To minimize the impact of upgrades, servers for each of the three layers (for example, the front-end layer, partition layer, and DFS layer) are spread evenly across upgrade domains in a similar fashion to the way data is spread over fault domains. Upgrades are performed through a *rolling upgrade* process, where only a small percentage of available servers are taken offline for upgrades to the data management service. Once upgraded, storage nodes are brought back up and then checked for health before being rolled back online.

Replication, geo-replication, and reliability

There are three replicas within the same data center in three separate racks, giving you robust resilience against hardware failures within a single data center. To add an even higher margin of safety against data loss, your data in your primary data center is replicated to another data center within the same geographical location. This provides you with one original and five current backups of your data in six separate server racks located in two separate geographical locations.

At the time of this writing, the geo-location displayed in the Windows Azure Management Portal, which you will see more of in the next chapter, is your primary geo-location. According to the September 15, 2011, post on the Windows Azure Storage Team Blog (*http://blogs.msdn.com/b /windowsazurestorage*), the secondary location will eventually be shown in a future version of the Management Portal (described a bit later in this book).

Geo-replication is included at no additional charge and is on by default. You can turn the feature on or off from the storage account's configuration pane of the Windows Azure portal. There is no cost savings in turning off the geo-replication. Replication to your secondary data center is handled asynchronously so that there is no load or performance impact on your applications.

When you perform data-modifying updates or deletes on your data, these changes are fully replicated on three separate and distinct storage nodes across three fault domains and upgrade domains within that data center.

After the transaction has been committed, a successful status is returned to the caller and the changes are asynchronously replicated to the secondary data center. The transaction is made durable in that data center by replicating itself across three storage nodes in different fault and upgrade domains. Because the updates are asynchronously geo-replicated, there is no impact on performance.

Microsoft's goal is to keep the data durable at both the primary and secondary locations. They accomplish this goal by keeping enough replicas in both locations to ensure that each location is capable of recovering itself from common failures such as a hard drive failure, storage node failure, rack failure, Top of the Rack (TOR) switch failure, and so on, without having to talk to the other location. The two locations talk to each other only to recover data in the event of common failures. If you had to failover to a secondary storage account then all the data that had been committed to the secondary location would already be there.

At the time of this writing, there was no SLA for how long it takes to asynchronously geo-replicate the data, but transactions are typically geo-replicated within a matter of a few minutes after the primary location has been updated.

Dynamic scalability

A significant factor to Microsoft in meeting the SLA obligations for data storage is scalability. The data service must scale so that 99.9 percent of the data operations can be executed successfully. In addition, Microsoft has established scalability targets per storage accounts. At the time of this writing, the following targets are in place:

- **Capacity**   Up to 100 terabytes

- **Transactions**   Up to 5,000 entities, messages, or blobs per second

- **Bandwidth**   Up to 3 GB per second

At the time of this writing, all objects stored in Windows Azure storage have a partition key, which the data management service uses in allocating resources. One or more storage nodes will be allocated to your data dynamically. The partition key is your way of indicating your preferences for how this allocation is performed. A single partition key can have an entire storage node devoted to it if the data management service determines that is what is necessary to meet these scalability targets.

Every storage object (blobs, table entities, and queue messages) has a partition key that is used to locate the object in the data management service. The partition key is also used to load balance and dynamically partition the objects across storage nodes to meet storage request traffic in accordance with the scalability objectives. The partition keys used by storage type are given in Table 2-1.

TABLE 2-1 Storage types and partition keys

Storage type	Full partition key
Blobs	Container name + blob name
Table entities	Table name + partition key
Queue messages	Queue name

As you might infer from the differences in full partition keys shown in Table 2-1, the scalability characteristic of the three data storage types is significantly different. Blobs use the name of the blob within a container, but the partition level for queues is at the queue name level (not at the individual message level). Table entities are special in the sense that the data for the partition key is part of the data being stored, where blobs and queues are at the level of name (regardless of the data contained in the blob or message).

A blob always lives in one partition; two blobs could be on separate partitions. A queue also lives on one partition; two queues may live on separate partitions. A set of entities from a table could live on one partition; different sets from the same table could be on different partitions. Of course, different tables could be on separate partitions.

RESTful APIs

The data management services are exposed through an open and RESTful API, which can be used from any platform (including many non-Microsoft platforms). The RESTful API is covered throughout the book. These APIs are accessible from anywhere on the public Internet, allowing you to use the data management services from any kind of application, even applications not written using Microsoft technologies. Your applications might be running on-premises but storing and retrieving data from Windows Azure storage in order to take advantage of its multiple geographical locations, reliability, redundancy, and dynamic scalability characteristics. You might even have your application deployed to a competitive cloud platform but use Windows Azure storage instead of the competitor's equivalent. The reasons for hybrid configurations are abundant, but certainly the features offered by storage platforms such as performance, location, reliability, and their pricing structure are almost always going to be factors.

Software development kits

The RESTful API of Windows Azure storage requires the use of HTTP verbs against the Windows Azure storage endpoints. This includes repetitively populating the required HTTP headers and providing security credentials. Of course, this pattern quickly emerges to any application developer making use of data management services. Most application developers tend to work at a higher layer of abstraction than the HTTP transport layer by using object oriented programming paradigms. To formalize these patterns, Microsoft has provided several client library software development kits (SDKs) for Microsoft .NET languages, Node.js, Java, and PHP. There is also an oddly named "other" SDK which contains the storage and compute emulators as well as package and deployment tools for developers running on a Windows machine.

Storage library ports are available on other platforms as well, including Python, Ruby, Perl, and JavaScript. Steve Marx published a blog on many of these libraries that you can find at this URL:

http://blog.smarx.com/posts/windows-azure-storage-libraries-in-many-languages

There is also source code available on the Windows Azure site, which might prove useful in developing ports to other platforms:

https://www.windowsazure.com/en-us/develop/downloads/

In the chapters that follow, you will see many transcripts of HTTP traffic that were gathered using a diagnostic tool called Fiddler. *Fiddler* is a free tool for inspecting, diagnosing, and replaying HTTP web traffic. It is installed as an HTTP proxy that runs on port 8888 of your development workstation. WinINET-based applications such as Windows Internet Explorer will automatically use Fiddler as an HTTP Proxy when the Capture Traffic check box is selected on Fiddler's File menu. You can debug the traffic of any application that is capable of being configured to use an HTTP Proxy. It is highly recommended that you download and install a copy of Fiddler on your own development machine, because this tool will likely save you hours of diagnostic time by allowing you to directly monitor and debug your own application's requests against the Windows Azure data management service. You can read more about Fiddler and download a free copy from *http://www.fiddler2.com*.

Pricing

In the world of cloud computing and storage, it is impossible to not take pricing into account when making architectural decisions. Unfortunately, specific prices for Windows Azure are under constant review and adjustment based on a wide variety of factors. Variable prices that can change rapidly are a result of the commodification of computing and storage resources. The latest pricing information is available online at:

> *http://www.microsoft.com/windowsazure/pricing/*

Although subject to change, at the time of publication, the following statements were true:

- Data storage utilized (including metadata) is 12.5 cents per gigabyte per month.

- Data transfer into a data center is free, but outbound data egress is billable at 12.5 cents per gigabyte per month. Transfer within the same subregion is free.

- Transactions are billable based on the number of I/O transactions completed at 1 cent per 10,000 per month.

If you are using a client library to assist you with development, you should be aware that some client library methods make multiple I/O requests to the data center to complete a single logical call.

Analytics and metrics

Windows Azure Storage Analytics provides metrics and logging of your storage account activity. Logs provide tracing of requests, and metrics provide capacity and request statistics. This information can be very useful in analyzing usage trends and in diagnosing storage account issues. Logging and metrics are controlled independently of one another and target each type of storage: blobs, tables, and queues. You will be introduced to the specifics of each in Chapters 5, 6, and 7, respectively.

Conclusion

The purpose of this chapter was to acquaint you with the Windows Azure storage platform. In particular, the chapter familiarized you with the features of the platform, which add valuable data availability, reliability, and protection assurances to your applications, as well as the tools for gathering analysis and metrics.

Although Windows Azure is built on Windows servers, it should be apparent that this data management service is sold piecemeal and may be used in any heterogeneous application that requires NoSQL type storage. In Chapter 4, "Accessing Windows Azure data storage," you will explore the Windows Azure SDKs for leveraging Windows Azure storage from Microsoft and non-Microsoft platforms.

Windows Azure data storage accounts

This chapter will familiarize you with all of the core concepts necessary to set up and manage storage accounts in Windows Azure, including security and the relationships between key data storage components, by using the Service Management API. The Service Management API is platform-agnostic and language-agnostic. However, in case you're developing on the Microsoft platform, you will learn about the Windows Azure storage emulator, which simulates blob, table, and queue storage, making testing your application locally very simple and convenient. Later in the chapter, you will become familiar with strategies for multi-tenancy in the cloud.

Set up your Windows Azure subscription

Windows Azure provides a convenient and centralized website portal for deploying and managing all of your Windows Azure cloud services and resources. The chapter discussion starts with this portal, because it is the most convenient and approachable way to set up and manage storage in Windows Azure. I touch on only the parts of the portal that you'll need to manage your data storage service deployments, but it's important to be aware that the scope of the portal extends far beyond just managing data storage. From the portal, you can manage Windows Azure Virtual Machines, the Windows Azure Service Bus, Windows Azure SQL Database instances, data synchronization, and myriad other Microsoft cloud-based services that are available with Windows Azure.

Windows Azure is sold on a subscription basis, where you select individual services from a menu of services that you want to have included in your subscription. Monthly fees are based on your feature selections and service resource usage.

To get started, you will find the Windows Azure Management Portal here:

https://manage.windowsazure.com/

Follow the instructions on the screen to create your subscription and associate your Windows Live account with it. If necessary, you can use links on the site to create a new Windows Live account. A single Windows Live ID can be used to manage multiple subscriptions, so you do not have to create new Windows Live accounts for each subscription unless you need to as a matter of convenience or internal organization security. For example, it might be desirable to use a separate Windows Live account for development and production subscriptions as a means of providing concrete separation of environmental authorization. In a smaller organization, though, managing development and production subscriptions with a single Windows Live account might prove to be far more convenient.

After you successfully create your subscription and log on for the first time, you will see the portal screen in Figure 3-1.

FIGURE 3-1 You see this screen after you log on to the Windows Azure Management Portal.

All actions performed in the portal may be performed programmatically from other software and platforms using the RESTful Windows Azure Service Management API, which you'll see shortly. The Management Portal uses this API to perform all of its functions.

IDs, subscriptions, and storage accounts

Your Windows Azure subscription provides high-level access to the complete suite of computational and data storage services offered on the Windows Azure platform. Your subscription is created and secured using a Windows Live ID account, as illustrated in Figure 3-2. The Windows Live ID that you choose when you set up your Windows Azure subscription will become the subscription's service administrator. You are also allowed to assign other Windows Live IDs as co-administrators, thereby allowing you to delegate authority to appropriate personnel without sharing the user name and password of the Windows Live account used to create the subscription.

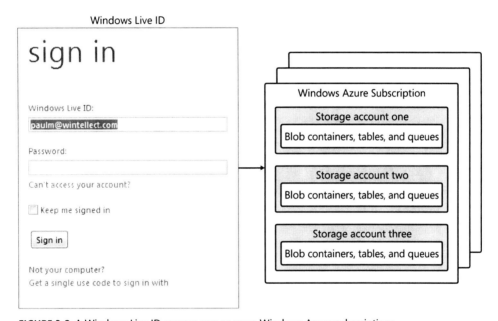

FIGURE 3-2 A Windows Live ID secures one or more Windows Azure subscriptions.

Your subscription will be assigned an identifier that is used to uniquely identify your subscription within the Windows Azure infrastructure. The subscription ID is just a simple GUID that must be passed as an argument throughout the Service Management API. All resources that can be operated upon via the Service Management API, which you'll learn about shortly, are organized beneath the subscription ID. URLs in the Service Management API adhere to the following pattern:

https://management.core.windows.net/<subscriptionId>/services/storageservices/<storageservice>

The *subscriptionId* of the URL is the GUID assigned as your subscription ID, and the *storageservice* is the globally unique name that you selected for your storage account.

By default, you are allowed to create up to five storage accounts within a single Windows Azure subscription, but you can contact Microsoft to raise this limit in order to meet your needs. You can store up to 100 terabytes of data in each of your storage accounts. You might partition your application's data by using separate storage accounts based on business or organizational separation rules. An independent software vendor (ISV) hosting their customer's data in Windows Azure might use separate storage accounts for each of their customers to ensure physical data separation and separate data access keys for each customer. You'll explore a few multi-tenancy scenarios later in this chapter.

Each storage account that you create must be named in lowercase letters and be globally unique within all of Windows Azure. At the time you create your storage account, you must also select the geographical subregion that you would like your data to be stored in. After you select the geographical subregion, you are stuck with your choice—a storage account created in a location cannot be moved to another, so make your choice carefully.

At the time of this writing, data transfer was free within the same data center. If you are using storage accounts in conjunction with Windows Azure Cloud Services, you will likely want to locate your storage and cloud services within the same geographical subregion to reduce latency and costs. An easy-to-use and convenient feature built into Windows Azure called *affinity groups* will help you associate organized groups of computational and storage assets with a named geographical area. You'll explore affinity groups near the end of this chapter.

Subscription certificates for authentication

Of course it would be very awkward to require the credentials of the Windows Live account that was used to create the storage account for every request. Your Windows Live account may be used as your identity for many other personal activities, and you might not be so fond of sharing it with others. To address this issue, Windows Azure allows you to associate X.509 certificates with your subscription, and then use those certificates as a means of authenticating your storage requests. The Service Management API will use either self-signed certificates or commercially issued ones. You may want to use a commercially issued certificate for your production environment, but a self-signed certificate is reasonable and adequate for most development scenarios. There was a limit of 10 management certificates per subscription at the time of this writing, but good security practices suggest using only one or as few as possible, because each certificate is a "master key" to your subscription, providing ownership-level control over all data managed by all storage accounts in the subscription.

To associate a certificate with your subscription, log on to the portal by using your Windows Live account, click the Hosted Services, Storage Accounts & CDN tab, and click the Management Certificates folder. Upload the public portion of your certificate (.*cer* or .*der* file) to your Windows Azure subscription. Although .*cer* files may be stored as base64-encoded data instead of as binary, the Management Portal will reject base64-encoded certificates without offering much useful information beyond the format of the certificate being invalid.

> **Note** At the time of this writing, Microsoft had just published a preview of its latest Windows Azure Management Portal, shown in Figure 3-1. The new portal was used as the basis for content in this book to keep its content as current as possible; however, the preview version of the new portal did not support the ability to upload management certificates. Management certificates had to be uploaded through the original portal at *http://windows.azure.com*. It is anticipated that the ability to upload certificates will be added long before this book is published and that the procedures will be similar to those described in this book.

If your code is executing on the Windows platform, you can use the following code to retrieve a certificate from your machine's local certificate store using the certificate's thumbprint. You'll use this routine to manage your data storage account via the RESTful Service Management API a little later in this chapter.

```
public static X509Certificate FindCertificate(String thumbprint) {
    X509Store store = null;
    X509Certificate2 cert = null;
    try {
        store = new X509Store(StoreName.My, StoreLocation.CurrentUser);
        store.Open(OpenFlags.ReadOnly);
        var certificate = store.Certificates.Find(X509FindType.FindByThumbprint, thumbprint,
false)[0];
        //return certificate;
        cert = store.Certificates.OfType<X509Certificate2>().FirstOrDefault(
            c => String.Equals(c.Thumbprint, thumbprint, StringComparison.OrdinalIgnoreCase));
        store.Close();
    }
    finally { if (store != null) store.Close(); }
    return cert;
}
```

On the Windows platform, you'll find a certificate's thumbprint on the Details tab when viewing a certificate, as shown in Figure 3-3.

FIGURE 3-3 In Windows, a certificate's thumbprint is located on the Details tab.

Primary and secondary access keys

When you set up your storage account, Microsoft will generate a base64-encoded 256-bit random primary and secondary key for your account. These two keys are equivalent, and either can be used to make authenticated create, read, update, and delete operations on your data. You are provided with two keys instead of one to enable the convenient enforcement of password rotation policies. The two-key scheme allows you a little breathing room when migrating applications using the primary access key to the secondary access key. When all applications using the primary key have been migrated, you can change the value of the primary key. The primary key then becomes the new secondary key, and you can begin another cycle of password rotation without experiencing any downtime.

Service management API

The Service Management API allows you to create new storage accounts, and to retrieve, update, or delete existing ones. You can also retrieve and generate new storage account keys through the API. The complete documentation for the RESTful Service Management API can be found at:

http://msdn.microsoft.com/en-us/library/windowsazure/ee460790.aspx

The Service Management API also allows you to create and delete cloud services (Virtual Machines), manage X.509 certificates, create affinity groups, create locations, and interact with the Windows Azure Traffic Manager. This chapter focuses solely on the data storage features of the Service Management API.

For many application scenarios, creating a new storage account is easily accomplished through the portal. Toward the end of the chapter, though, you will explore some real-world business use-cases where multi-tenancy will be an important consideration. In one multi-tenant use case, a high degree of data isolation is achieved for your customers by creating separate storage accounts for each customer. In such a scenario, it is very likely that there would be a requirement for a new customer provisioning feature that would create the storage account behind the scenes. The Service Management API provides you with the interface that you might require to create software that can seamlessly bring new customers on board and provide very high separation.

Data storage service management URL

Data storage operations with the Service Management API are performed against resources that begin with the base Microsoft data storage URL (*http://management.core.windows.net*).

The base URL for your data storage subscription is computed by appending your subscription ID to the Microsoft base data storage management URL. The subscription is followed by the path element *services* and the name of the service to be managed (*storageservices* in this case). Except for the operation of creating a new storage account, the storage account name follows, giving you a management URL that looks like this:

```
https://management.core.windows.net/<subscription-id>/
    services/storageservices/<storage-account-name>
```

HTTP request headers

Two HTTP headers are used extensively by the Storage Management API, described in Table 3-1. The x-ms-version header is required for all operations, and the Content-Type header is required only for HTTP *POST* and *PUT* data storage operations. The Content-Type header is ignored if present for other types of storage operations. You will add these two headers as appropriate in the code that follows.

TABLE 3-1 HTTP request headers

Header	When required	Description
Content-Type	For all *POST* and *PUT* data storage operations	Set to *application/xml*.
x-ms-version	For all operations	Specifies the version of the operation to use for this request. The value of this header must be set to 2011-06-01 or later. For more information about the x-ms-version versioning header, see *Versioning for the Blob, Queue, and Table services in Windows Azure*, which can be found at: *http://msdn.microsoft.com/en-us /library/windowsazure/dd894041.aspx*.

Certificate authentication

The Service Management API uses a self-signed X.509 certificate to authenticate your request. Of course, you may want to use a commercially issued certificate for your production environment, but a self-signed certificate is adequate for most development scenarios.

You must first upload the public portion of your certificate (.cer or .der file) to your Windows Azure subscription. The easiest way to do this is through the Management Portal. Although .cer files may be stored as base64-encoded data instead of binary, the Management Portal will reject base64-encoded certificates without offering much useful information beyond the format of the certificate being invalid.

> **Note** Microsoft Certificate Manager will export DER binary-encoded certificates and base64-encoded certificates to the same file name extension of .cer. This can be confusing because the Windows Azure Management Portal will reject a base64-encoded certificate. If you open the file with Notepad before attempting to upload, it will become quickly apparent that the contents are either nicely formatted base64-encoded characters or unprintable binary data.

You can use the code shown previously in this chapter to retrieve a certificate from your machine's local certificate store using the certificate's thumbprint.

Create a new storage account

To create a new storage account, execute to your subscription's *storageservices* endpoint URL an HTTP *POST* of an XML payload that matches the following schema with values from Table 3-2.

```
POST https://management.core.windows.net/bd8a8c41-fd7e-42a2-a00a-7ca0ada3474d/
        services/storageservices HTTP/1.1
x-ms-version: 2011-06-01
Content-Type: application/xml
Host: management.core.windows.net
<?xml version="1.0" encoding="utf-8"?>
<CreateStorageServiceInput xmlns="http://schemas.microsoft.com/windowsazure">
    <ServiceName>contosocohovinyard</ServiceName>
    <Description>Wintellect Demo Staging</Description>
    <Label>
        U3RhZ2luZ0FBQVNOYWdpbmdBQUFTdGFnaW5nQUFBVU3RhZ2luZ0FBQVNOYWdpbmd
            BQUFTdGFnaW5nQUFBVU3RhZ2luZ1paWkFFCQORF
    </Label>
  <Location>West US</Location>
</CreateStorageServiceInput>
```

TABLE 3-2 Schema for creating a new storage account request

Element	Required?	Format	Description
ServiceName	Required	3 and 24 characters in length. Use numbers and lower-case letters only.	A name for the storage account that is unique within Windows Azure
Description	Optional	1024 characters or fewer.	Description of the storage account
Label	Required	75 clear text characters or fewer (before base64 encoding); 100 base64-encoded characters or fewer.	Specifies the name that identifies your storage account as a base64-encoded string
AffinityGroup	Required if Location not specified	Either a Location or an AffinityGroup element in the request body, but not both.	The name of an existing affinity group in the specified subscription
Location	Required if AffinityGroup not specified	Either a Location or an AffinityGroup element in the request body, but not both.	The location where the storage account is created

The following code creates a new Windows Azure storage account using the required storage account name, a label, a description, and either an affinity group name or a location.

```
public static void CreateAccount(String storageAccountName, String label, String description,
    String affinityGroupName, String location) {

    Console.WriteLine("******************** Create Storage Account ********************\n");

    if ((affinityGroupName == null && location == null) ||
      (affinityGroupName != null && location != null)) {
        throw new ArgumentException("affinityGroupName or location must be supplied (but not
both).");
    }

    String subscriptionId = AzureSecrets.ManagementSubscriptionId;
    String operationName = "storageservices";
    String uriTemplate = "https://management.core.windows.net/{0}/services/{1}";
    var requestUri = new Uri(String.Format(uriTemplate, subscriptionId, operationName));
    var encodedLabel = Convert.ToBase64String(Encoding.UTF8.GetBytes(label));

    Console.WriteLine("Length of encoded label is: " + encodedLabel.Length);

    XmlWriterSettings wSettings = new XmlWriterSettings();
    wSettings.Indent = true;
    MemoryStream ms = new MemoryStream();
    XmlWriter xw = XmlWriter.Create(ms, wSettings);
```

```
      xw.WriteStartDocument();
      xw.WriteStartElement("CreateStorageServiceInput", @"http://schemas.microsoft.com/
windowsazure");
          xw.WriteStartElement("ServiceName"); xw.WriteString(storageAccountName);
xw.WriteEndElement();
          xw.WriteStartElement("Description"); xw.WriteString(description); xw.WriteEndElement();
          xw.WriteStartElement("Label"); xw.WriteString(encodedLabel); xw.WriteEndElement();
          if (null != affinityGroupName) {
              xw.WriteStartElement("AffinityGroup");
              xw.WriteString(affinityGroupName);
              xw.WriteEndElement();
          }
          if (null != location) {

              xw.WriteStartElement("Location");
              xw.WriteString(location);
              xw.WriteEndElement();
          }
      xw.WriteEndElement();
      xw.WriteEndDocument();
      xw.Flush();

      byte[] bodyBytes = ms.ToArray();

      HttpWebRequest request = (HttpWebRequest)HttpWebRequest.Create(requestUri);

      request.Headers.Add("x-ms-version", s_MsVersion);
      request.Method = "POST";
      request.ContentType = "application/xml";

      Stream dataStream = request.GetRequestStream();
      dataStream.Write(bodyBytes, 0, bodyBytes.Length);

      var requestStream = new MemoryStream();
      requestStream.Write(bodyBytes, 0, bodyBytes.Length);
      requestStream.Position = 0;

      PrintStreamToConsole("---Request---", request.Method, requestUri.ToString(),
          String.Empty, request.Headers, requestStream);
      HttpWebResponse response;
      // attach credentials used to authenticate the request
      request.ClientCertificates.Add(AzureManagementClient.FindCertificate(
          (AzureSecrets.ManagementCertificateThumbprint)));
      try {
          response = (HttpWebResponse)request.GetResponse();
          PrintStreamToConsole("--Response--", String.Empty, String.Empty,
              response.StatusDescription, response.Headers, response.GetResponseStream());
      }
      catch (Exception ex) {
          Console.WriteLine(ex.Message);
      }
}
```

A successful storage account creation request will result in an HTTP Status Code of 202 (Accepted) and an x-ms-request-id response header, which contains an ID that uniquely identifies a request made against Windows Azure Storage.

```
HTTP/1.1 202
x-ms-request-id: 82c1fba8491548fcbe7ad50d7f27f532
Content-Length: 0
Cache-Control: no-cache
Date: Wed, 23 Jan 2013 05:47:44 GMT
Location: https://management.core.windows.net/subscriptions/bd8a8c41-fd7e-42a2-a
00a-7ca0ada3474d/storage/contosocohovinyard
Server: 33.0.6198.3 (rd_rdfe_stable.130115-1822) Microsoft-HTTPAPI/2.0
```

The most common failure to receive is a 409 (Conflict), which occurs when your storage name is already in use. As you may recall, your storage account names must be unique, not just across all of your own application's customers (if applicable) but across all of Windows Azure. There is no provision for subdomains or special characters such as a hyphen or period that can be used as a delimiter. With that in mind, if you were using the Service Management API to provision new customers to have their own storage accounts for your application, you will very likely want to have a universal prefix that you appended to the front of every storage account name that you generate to reduce the frequency of conflicts. For example, if Contoso, Ltd. was offering software as a service, it might choose to use contoso as a prefix. Contoso's customer and tenant Coho Vineyard might therefore be named *contosocohovinyard*, and Contoso's other customer and tenant, Tailspin Toys, might be named *contosotailspintoys*, and so on. You will also want to capture HTTP Status Code 400 (Bad Request), with logic to vary the storage account name either by adding a suffix, modifying the prefix, or both, because this is generally indicative of a violation of the rules surrounding storage account names (such as the name already being in use).

Retrieve account properties

A new customer provisioning system would need to allow a customer's storage account information to be retrieved and updated. To retrieve storage account information, issue an HTTP *GET* with the x-ms-version HTTP header to your storage service's endpoint URL.

```
GET https://management.core.windows.net/bd8a8c41-fd7e-42a2-a00a-7ca0ada3474d/
    services/storageservices/contosocohovinyard HTTP/1.1
x-ms-version: 2011-06-01
Content-Type: application/xml
```

The following code creates and submits the request just shown against your storage account and retrieves the properties in the body of the corresponding response.

```
public static void GetAccountProperties(String storageAccountName) {
    Console.WriteLine("\n******************** Get Storage Account Properties
********************\n");

    string operationName = "storageservices";

    String uriTemplate = "https://management.core.windows.net/{0}/services/{1}/{2}";
    var requestUri = new Uri(String.Format(uriTemplate, s_subscriptionId, operationName,
storageAccountName));


    // Create the request and specify attributes of the request.
    HttpWebRequest request = (HttpWebRequest)HttpWebRequest.Create(requestUri);

    // Define the required headers to specify the API version and operation type.
    request.Headers.Add("x-ms-version", s_MsVersion);
    request.Method = "GET";
    request.ContentType = "application/xml";

    PrintStreamToConsole("---Request---", request.Method, requestUri.ToString(), String.Empty,
request.Headers, null);
    HttpWebResponse response;
    // attach credentials used to authenticate the request
    request.ClientCertificates.Add(AzureManagementClient.FindCertificate((AzureSecrets.
ManagementCertificateThumbprint)));
    try {
        response = (HttpWebResponse)request.GetResponse();
        PrintStreamToConsole("--Response--", String.Empty, String.Empty, response.
StatusDescription, response.Headers, response.GetResponseStream());
    }
    catch (Exception ex) {
        Console.WriteLine(ex.Message);
    }
}
```

The storage account properties are returned to you as an XML document in the response body, similar to the following example. The schema for this response is described further in Table 3-3.

```
HTTP/1.1 202
x-ms-request-id: 82c1fba8491548fcbe7ad50d7f27f532
Content-Length: 0
Cache-Control: no-cache
Date: Wed, 23 Jan 2013 05:47:44 GMT
Location: https://management.core.windows.net/subscriptions/bd8a8c41-fd7e-42a2-a
00a-7ca0ada3474d/storage/contosocohovinyard
Server: 33.0.6198.3 (rd_rdfe_stable.130115-1822) Microsoft-HTTPAPI/2.0
```

Of the storage account properties that are returned, only the *Description* and the *Label* properties may be updated, and you'll learn how to do that next.

TABLE 3-3 Windows Azure storage account properties schema

Element	Description
Url	URL for storage account requests.
ServiceName	The storage account name. This is the unique storage account name that you provided when you created the account. You will use this value when constructing the fully qualified URI to the resource.
Description	The storage account's description (as provided when the storage account was created or updated).
AffinityGroup	The affinity group that this storage account is a member of (if applicable). Either *AffinityGroup* or *Location* will be populated (but not both).
Location	The *Location* that this storage account has been deployed to. Either *AffinityGroup* or Location will be populated (but not both).
Label	A base64-encoded string of the label you assigned to this storage account. This is sometimes used to assign a human-readable purpose to the account (such as "staging" or "production").
Status	The current human-readable status of this storage account. The values for this field are *Creating*, *ResolvingDns*, *Created*, and *Deleting* (which are self-explanatory).
Endpoints	A list of data endpoints corresponding to the three different types of storage: blob, table, and queue. These three topics are covered in Chapter 5, "Blobs," Chapter 6, "Tables," and Chapter 7, "Queues."

Update account properties

Occasionally, it may be necessary to update the storage account's *Description* or *Label* properties. These are the only two properties that Windows Azure storage allows you to change after the storage account is created, and upon careful examination, you will quickly see why that is true. The *Status* is outbound information, the *Endpoints* are calculated from the storage account name, and the *Location* and *AffinityGroup* are much more than just properties, because they control which data center your storage physically exists in. If you needed to change one of these other properties, for example, the *Location* or the *AffinityGroup*, you would need to create a new storage account with the new property values, and then copy all of the data from the original account into the new account before deleting the original account. There is currently no *rename* functionality offered that might allow your storage account name to be changed without copying all of its data.

To update the *Description* or *Label* account properties, you send an HTTP *PUT* request to your storage service's endpoint URL with an XML payload that conforms to the following schema. The request must also have the appropriate *x-ms-version* HTTP header (as shown in Table 3-1).

```
PUT https://management.core.windows.net/bd8a8c41-fd7e-42a2-a00a-7ca0ada3474d/
    services/storageservices/contosocohovinyard HTTP/1.1
x-ms-version: 2011-06-01
Content-Type: application/xml
Host: management.core.windows.net
<?xml version="1.0" encoding="utf-8"?>
<UpdateStorageServiceInput xmlns="http://schemas.microsoft.com/windowsazure">
  <Description>Label Changed</Description>
  <Label>Y29udG9zb3RhWxzcGludG95cw==</Label>
</UpdateStorageServiceInput>
```

The following code creates and submits the preceding request against your storage account.

```csharp
public static void UpdateAccount(String storageAccountName, String label, String description) {
    Console.WriteLine("\n******************** Update Storage Account ********************\n");

    String operationName = "storageservices";
    String uriTemplate = "https://management.core.windows.net/{0}/services/{1}/{2}";
    var requestUri = new Uri(String.Format(uriTemplate, s_subscriptionId,
        operationName, storageAccountName));

    XmlWriterSettings wSettings = new XmlWriterSettings();
    wSettings.Indent = true;
    MemoryStream ms = new MemoryStream();
    XmlWriter xw = XmlWriter.Create(ms, wSettings);

    xw.WriteStartDocument();
    xw.WriteStartElement("UpdateStorageServiceInput", @"http://schemas.microsoft.com/
windowsazure");
    xw.WriteStartElement("Description"); xw.WriteString(description); xw.WriteEndElement();
    xw.WriteStartElement("Label"); xw.WriteString(label); xw.WriteEndElement();
    xw.WriteEndElement();
    xw.WriteEndDocument();
    xw.Flush();

    byte[] bodyBytes = ms.ToArray();

    HttpWebRequest request = (HttpWebRequest)HttpWebRequest.Create(requestUri);

    request.Headers.Add("x-ms-version", s_MsVersion);
    request.Method = "PUT";
    request.ContentType = "application/xml";

    Stream dataStream = request.GetRequestStream();
    dataStream.Write(bodyBytes, 0, bodyBytes.Length);

    var requestStream = new MemoryStream();
    requestStream.Write(bodyBytes, 0, bodyBytes.Length);
    requestStream.Position = 0;

    PrintStreamToConsole("---Request---", request.Method, requestUri.ToString(),
        String.Empty, request.Headers, requestStream);
    HttpWebResponse response;
    // attach credentials used to authenticate the request
request.ClientCertificates.Add(
        AzureManagementClient.FindCertificate((AzureSecrets.ManagementCertificateThumbprint)));
    try {
        response = (HttpWebResponse)request.GetResponse();
        PrintStreamToConsole("--Response--", String.Empty, String.Empty, response.
StatusDescription,
            response.Headers, response.GetResponseStream());
    }
    catch (Exception ex) {
        Console.WriteLine(ex.Message);
    }
}
```

```
        wSettings);
        xw.WriteStartDocument();
        xw.WriteStartElement("UpdateStorageServiceInput", @"http://schemas.microsoft.com/
        windowsazure");
        xw.WriteStartElement("Description"); xw.WriteString(description); xw.WriteEndElement();
        xw.WriteStartElement("Label"); xw.WriteString(label); xw.WriteEndElement();
        xw.WriteEndElement();
        xw.WriteEndDocument();
        xw.Flush();
        byte[] bodyBytes = ms.ToArray();
        HttpWebRequest request = (HttpWebRequest)HttpWebRequest.Create(requestUri);
        request.Headers.Add("x-ms-version", s_MsVersion);
        request.Method = "PUT";
        request.ContentType = "application/xml";
        Stream dataStream = request.GetRequestStream();
        dataStream.Write(bodyBytes, 0, bodyBytes.Length);
        var requestStream = new MemoryStream();
        requestStream.Write(bodyBytes, 0, bodyBytes.Length);
        requestStream.Position = 0;
        PrintStreamToConsole("---Request---", request.Method, requestUri.ToString(),
        String.Empty, request.Headers, requestStream);
        HttpWebResponse response;
        // attach credentials used to authenticate the request
        request.ClientCertificates.Add(
        AzureManagementClient.FindCertificate((AzureSecrets.ManagementCertificateThumbprint)));
        try {
            response = (HttpWebResponse)request.GetResponse();
            PrintStreamToConsole("--Response--", String.Empty, String.Empty, response.
            StatusDescription,
            response.Headers, response.GetResponseStream());
        }
        catch (Exception ex) {
            Console.WriteLine(ex.Message);
        }
}
```

Windows Azure storage will respond with an HTTP status code of 200 (OK) and a few HTTP headers upon successful update. Your response should look similar to the following.

```
HTTP/1.1 200
x-ms-request-id: 86d49bf0b8d24b9e991b136966bf79b3
Content-Length: 0
Cache-Control: no-cache
Date: Wed, 23 Jan 2013 05:47:52 GMT
Server: 33.0.6198.3 (rd_rdfe_stable.130115-1822) Microsoft-HTTPAPI/2.0
```

Retrieve storage account keys

You append your storage account to the end of the following base address followed by the specific resource that you are operating on. For example, you would do the following to request the current account key for a storage account.

```
GET https://management.core.windows.net/bd8a8c41-fd7e-42a2-a00a-7ca0ada3474d/
    services/storageservices/contosocohovinyard/keys HTTP/1.1
x-ms-version: 2011-06-01
```

Windows Azure returns a response payload like this one.

```
HTTP/1.1 200
x-ms-request-id: 6d42a7b7705a4ec3a77f62aea7bbdb48
Content-Length: 521
Cache-Control: no-cache
Content-Type: application/xml; charset=utf-8
Date: Wed, 23 Jan 2013 23:30:55 GMT
Server: 33.0.6198.3 (rd_rdfe_stable.130115-1822) Microsoft-HTTPAPI/2.0
<StorageService xmlns=http://schemas.microsoft.com/windowsazure
    xmlns:i="http://www.w3.org/2001/XMLSchema-instance">
<Url>https://management.core.windows.net/bd8a8c41-fd7e-42a2-a00a-7ca0ada3474d/
    services/storageservices/contosocohovinyard
</Url>
<StorageServiceKeys>
  <Primary>
    N38NOozTbl93TnniXgyGWKRReEJI/US5wFQy3AYAWzxyvGFh5kyJzBUoPkWVsg...==
  </Primary>
  <Secondary>
    hPpO5a7D6GKI5dAXfOUEGAfIW+zw+OzdmIlG7vVy7WXLcSdOHwEXr4Q3VKQA...==
  </Secondary>
</StorageServiceKeys>
</StorageService>
```

Regenerate storage account keys

As part of your password rotation strategy, you will probably want to rotate your storage account keys, and the Service Management API provides a convenient way for you to perform this action. Typically, this action is performed by modifying your application configuration files to use the secondary key and then rotating the primary key. When the next rotation cycle occurs, modify your application configuration to use the primary again, and then regenerate the secondary.

To generate a new storage password, you *POST* a message to the key's resource of your data storage service's base URL. The body of the message contains the type of key you are regenerating (*Primary* or *Secondary*).

```
POST https://management.core.windows.net/bd8a8c41-fd7e-42a2-a00a-7ca0ada3474d/
    services/storageservices/contosocohovinyard/keys?action=regenerate HTTP/1.1
x-ms-version: 2011-06-01
Content-Type: application/xml
Host: management.core.windows.net
<?xml version="1.0" encoding="utf-8"?>
<RegenerateKeys xmlns="http://schemas.microsoft.com/windowsazure">
  <KeyType>Primary</KeyType>
</RegenerateKeys>
```

The body of the response will contain both the *Primary* and the *Secondary* keys, which you can parse out to use in programmatically updating the configuration files of your applications that are accessing data storage. The reason that both keys are returned (instead of just the one that was regenerated) is to support key rotation without the need for a separate request to get the alternative key. Stated differently, the key you rotate is not the key that you use. The key you rotate is the one you will use on the next password rotation cycle. The code that follows illustrates how the code that you rotate becomes the next available password for the rotation cycle.

```
HTTP/1.1 200
x-ms-request-id: a851959cf47942c2878dcce235ed52a4
Content-Length: 521
Cache-Control: no-cache
Content-Type: application/xml; charset=utf-8
Date: Wed, 23 Jan 2013 23:30:57 GMT
Server: 33.0.6198.3 (rd_rdfe_stable.130115-1822) Microsoft-HTTPAPI/2.0
<StorageService xmlns="http://schemas.microsoft.com/windowsazure" xmlns:i="http://www.
w3.org/2001/XMLSchema-instance">
<Url>https://management.core.windows.net/b

d8a8c41-fd7e-42a2-a00a-7ca0ada3474d/services/storageservices/contosocohovinyard<

/Url>
  <StorageServiceKeys>
    <Primary>
      r13FQzjRTx81DmODCbuHcrZ748oef/nl1l3O2rCs6UORp95ZdYu9OOj9KfTihBkOcFVW511pXebA...==
    </Primary>
    <Secondary>
      hPp05a7D6GKI5dAX+EBUBqfOUEGAfIW+zw+OzdmIlG7vVy7WXLcSdOHwEX1H+8VbHUUcCKqsDKQA...==
    </Secondary>
  </StorageServiceKeys>
</StorageService>


--Response--

HTTP/1.1 200
x-ms-request-id: 64abbbc996134bfca0f3ed87762beae6
Content-Length: 810
Cache-Control: no-cache
Content-Type: application/xml; charset=utf-8
Date: Wed, 23 Jan 2013 05:47:45 GMT
Server: 33.0.6198.3 (rd_rdfe_stable.130115-1822) Microsoft-HTTPAPI/2.0
<StorageService xmlns=http://schemas.microsoft.com/windowsazure
    xmlns:i="http://www.w3.org/2001/XMLSchema-instance">
    <Url>https://management.core.windows.net/
        bd8a8c41-fd7e-42a2-a00a-7ca0ada3474d/services/storageservices/contosocohovinyard</Url>
    <ServiceName>contosocohovinyard</ServiceName>
    <StorageServiceProperties><Description>Wintellect Demo Staging</Description>
    <Location>West US</Location>

    <Label>U3dpbmdmdBQUFTdGFnaW5nQUFBU3RhZ21uZ0FBQVN0YWdpbmdBQUFTdGFnaW5nQUFBU3RhZ21uZ1paWkFkFCQQRF</
Label>
    <Status>Creating</Status>
    <Endpoints>
      <Endpoint>http://contosocohovinyard.blob.core.windows.net/</Endpoint>
      <Endpoint>http://contosocohovinyard.queue.core.windows.net/</Endpoint>
      <Endpoint>http://contosocohovinyard.table.core.windows.net/</Endpoint>
    </Endpoints>
  </StorageServiceProperties>
</StorageService>
```

Delete storage accounts

To delete your storage account, simply send an HTTP DELETE verb to the Service Management API URI for your service account with an appropriately set x-ms-version HTTP header.

```
DELETE https://management.core.windows.net/bd8a8c41-fd7e-42a2-a00a-7ca0ada3474d/
    services/storageservices/contosocohovinyard HTTP/1.1
x-ms-version: 2011-06-01
```

The following code demonstrates how to delete a storage account using the RESTful Service Management API.

```
public static void DeleteAccount(String storageAccountName) {
    Console.WriteLine("\n********** Delete Storage Account **********\n");

    string operationName = "storageservices";
    String uriTemplate = "https://management.core.windows.net/{0}/services/{1}/{2}";
    var requestUri =
        new Uri(String.Format(uriTemplate, s_subscriptionId, operationName,
storageAccountName));

    // Create the request and specify attributes of the request.
    HttpWebRequest request = (HttpWebRequest)HttpWebRequest.Create(requestUri);

    // Define the required headers to specify the API version and operation type.
    request.Headers.Add("x-ms-version", s_MsVersion);
    request.Method = "DELETE";

    PrintStreamToConsole("---Request---", request.Method, requestUri.ToString(),
        String.Empty, request.Headers, null);
    HttpWebResponse response;

    // attach credentials used to authenticate the request
    request.ClientCertificates.Add(
        AzureManagementClient.FindCertificate((AzureSecrets.ManagementCertificateThumbprint)));
    try {
        response = (HttpWebResponse)request.GetResponse();
        PrintStreamToConsole("--Response--", String.Empty, String.Empty,
            response.StatusDescription, response.Headers, response.GetResponseStream());
    }
    catch (Exception ex) {
        Console.WriteLine(ex.Message);
    }
}
```

The result of successful deletion is the following very short acknowledgement.

```
HTTP/1.1 200
x-ms-request-id: f0c65a4281c24692a7ddbc7dd23a06ba
Content-Length: 0
Cache-Control: no-cache
Date: Wed, 23 Jan 2013 23:31:04 GMT
Server: 33.0.6198.3 (rd_rdfe_stable.130115-1822) Microsoft-HTTPAPI/2.0
```

All data stored in the storage account is deleted. There are no second chances because your data cannot be recovered after you delete it. Your disaster recovery plan might want to cover programmer and application errors, as well as the proverbial volcano or meteor wiping out your data center.

HTTP and data storage return codes

In the body of the response, the Service Management API returns both an HTTP Status Code as defined in the HTTP 1.1 specification and supplemental error information.

```xml
<?xml version="1.0" encoding="utf-8"?>
<Error>
  <Code>error code</Code>
  <Message>human readable error message</Message>
</Error>
```

The *Code* element supplies a more precise identification of the error condition and is useful in writing robust applications that can gracefully recover from failures or identify failure causes. Table 3-4 lists HTTP and Service Management error return codes.

TABLE 3-4 HTTP and service management API return codes

HTTP error return codes and Service Management API return codes	Error description
Bad Request (400)	
MissingOrIncorrectVersionHeader	The versioning header was missing or invalid.
InvalidXmlRequest	The message body was invalid.
MissingOrInvalidRequiredQueryParameter	A required query parameter was missing or invalid.
InvalidHttpVerb	The HTTP verb was invalid or not valid for the requested resource.
BadRequest	One or more request parameters were invalid.
Forbidden (403)	
AuthenticationFailed	The request could not be authenticated.
SubscriptionDisabled	The Azure Subscription has been disabled.
Not Found (404)	
ResourceNotFound	The resource requested does not exist.
Conflict (409)	
ConflictError	A conflict occurred, which prevented the operation from being completed.
Internal Error (500)	
InternalError	Server error. The operation may be retried.
OperationTimedOut	The operation did not complete within the permissible amount of time.
Service Unavailable (503)	
ServerBusy	The service or one of its dependencies is currently unavailable to service this request.

Affinity groups

When using storage accounts in conjunction with Cloud Services, it is often desirable that the two be deployed to the same data center. This can reduce latency and improve performance as well as reduce your costs, because data transfer within the same data center is not charged. Each affinity group is associated with the subscription it was created under and can be used by multiple storage accounts and hosted services for the same subscription. You can use an affinity group only in the subscription that it was created under.

Your affinity group choices at the time of this writing are West Europe, Southeast Asia, East Asia, North Central US, North Europe, South Central US, West US, and East US.

Storage emulator

Windows Azure was designed from the very beginning to be a language-agnostic and platform-agnostic data storage service. Of course, Microsoft built into their own set of tools such as Microsoft Visual Studio conveniences that make using the cloud as easy as possible for the Microsoft developer. To facilitate convenience of development and testing of your application on the Windows platform, the Windows Azure Software Development Kit (SDK) provides a storage emulator and integration with Visual Studio. The storage emulator can be used to simulate nearly every operation on blobs, tables, and queues, which are the focus of Chapters 5, 6, and 7, respectively. At the time of this writing, there were a few minor bugs and a couple of inconsistencies between the storage emulator and the actual cloud—such as blobs being limited in the storage emulator to 2 GBs—but overall, the storage emulator provides reasonable fidelity in emulation of the actual services for most applications, and it's a superb tool for development and validation of cloud storage when you're developing on the Microsoft platform.

Because of the architectural separation between data storage and application functionality, even development using a non-Microsoft language such as Java can make use of the storage emulator when the development is performed on a Windows box and the Windows Azure SDK is installed.

On a developer's workstation, the storage emulator is implemented as a set of RESTful web services that operate against a collection of SQL Express tables. You may also configure the workstation to work against standard Microsoft SQL Server if you prefer. As a result of the multiple layers of abstraction, the storage emulator will not scale very well or handle a high volume of simultaneous connections. It is also not useful for gathering metrics when attempting to measure performance and throughput. You will need to deploy to the actual cloud in order to address these kinds of scenarios and gather metrics for production capacity planning.

The first time you run the storage emulator, the emulator will initialize storage for you by creating the underlying SQL database. You can manually perform the data storage initialization using the command-line tool DSInit, which ships with the Windows Azure SDK. The DSInit tool can be most easily run from the Windows Azure command prompt found on the Windows Azure SDK under the All Programs menu. To get the complete syntax of the **DSInit.exe** command, run it with the /? argument.

```
C:\Program Files\Windows Azure Emulator\emulator\devstore\DSInit.exe /?

Syntax:
DSInit [/sqlinstance:<DatabaseInstanceName> | /server:<Machine name>] [/silent] [/forcecreate]

Description:
        The DSInit Command-Line Tool (DSInit.exe) initializes Windows Azure storage
        emulator in the local environment. This tool runs automatically the first
        time storage emulator is started. You can also run DSInit explicitly. After
        you initialize the local environment, it is not necessary to call DSInit again.

Options:
        sqlInstance : Use the name of the SQL Server instance without the server
                      qualifier (for example, MSSQL instead of .\MSSQL) to refer
                      to a named instance. Use "." to denote an unnamed or default
                      instance of SQL Server. Not compatible with /SERVER.

                      You can run DSInit at any time to configure the storage emulator
                      to point to a different instance of SQL Server.

        server : Specifies the name of the machine that is running the instance
                 of SQL Server to use for Windows Azure storage emulator in the
                 local environment. Use <Machine Name>\<Instance Name> to specify
                 the SQL instance to run on machine. Not compatible with
                 /SQLINSTANCE.

        silent : Automatically dismisses the Development Storage Initialization dialog
                 box once the initialization is complete. If you do not include this
                 parameter, you must manually dismiss the dialog.

        forcecreate : Recreates the database and causes all existing data in the local Blob
                      and Queue services to be removed.
```

The dialog box shown in Figure 3-4 is displayed upon execution of the **DSInit.exe** command (unless the *silent* parameter was selected). The **DSInit.exe** command will also take reservations on the ports used for the Blob, Table, and Queue services, which provide an emulated Open Data Protocol (OData) interface to data storage.

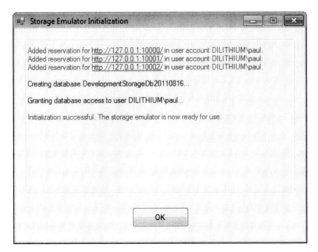

FIGURE 3-4 The Storage Emulator Initialization dialog box is displayed when **DSInit.exe** is executed.

After the storage emulator is initialized, it must be started before use. Visual Studio can perform this action for you automatically when you set the Start Windows Azure storage emulator value to True on the Development tab of your cloud application project, as shown in Figure 3-5.

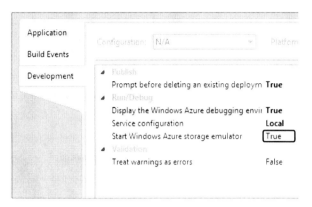

FIGURE 3-5 The storage emulator must be started before use. Visual Studio will do this for you automatically by setting the Start Windows Azure Storage Emulator property to True.

You can also start the storage emulator from the command line by using the **CSRun.exe** command. You may need to do this if you're working with the storage emulator using a non-Microsoft editor on your development box, or you're working with it as part of a build and deployment scenario where certain tests require the storage emulator to be running.

```
C:\Program Files\Microsoft SDKs\Windows Azure\Emulator\CSRun.exe /devstore:start
```

The storage emulator may be shut down in a similar fashion by using the */devstore:shutdown* parameter.

After the storage emulator is run, you can start and stop it from the system tray by right-clicking the Windows Azure icon and selecting either Start or Shutdown Developer Storage. (You can also start and shut down the Compute Emulator in the same manner.)

Also available on the same system tray context menu are options to Show Storage Emulator UI and Show Compute Emulator UI. When you select the Show Storage Emulator UI, a dialog box similar to the one depicted in Figure 3-6 is displayed, allowing you to see and change the status of the various types of storage emulation: blob, table, and queue. This is useful as a verification that things are running, but it can also be useful for testing your error recovery code for failure (for example, you might want to test what happens when blob storage requests are successful, but table storage requests fail).

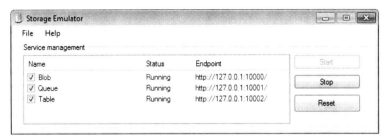

FIGURE 3-6 Use the storage emulator user interface to change the status of storage emulation types.

Multi-tenancy

ISVs often have hundreds, thousands, or perhaps even millions of customers using the same software application. The data for these software applications can often be sensitive or strategic in nature. In order to take advantage of the ISV's software offering in the cloud, the customer must give up control and trust that the ISV will protect their data from unauthorized access or fraudulent use. Customers generally demand assurances about how their data will be protected against these threats. Windows Azure provides a wide range of choices to achieve varying levels of tenant data isolation.

There are many factors to consider when planning your multi-tenancy strategy, which range from the potential for legal liability for data breach, to your customer's perception of how your firm respects the confidentiality and integrity of their data.

> **Note** Data confidentiality may be an important consideration for your application. You should be aware that no data encryption is provided natively by Windows Azure. If confidentiality through data encryption is important to your application, your application will need to encrypt the data before storage and decrypt it upon retrieval. Chapter 5 covers this topic more.

Separate Windows Azure subscription per tenant

In a scenario in which there is one separate subscription per tenant, each customer obtains their own Windows Azure subscription, and within this subscription, they create a separate storage account, as shown in Figure 3-7. The storage account keys are then shared with the ISV's application to allow data operations to be performed. This model provides the greatest level of isolation because data isolation is enforced by Windows Azure and each customer of the ISV holds their own set of access keys. The ISV must take steps to protect their customer's storage account keys, but because these keys grant permission to only a single storage account, the damage caused by the keys' compromise would be limited solely to the data stored in the one storage account. Even though such a compromise might be bad, it is not as bad as if all the data stored in the ISV's customers Windows Azure subscriptions were compromised. The extent of damage is most likely contained to a single ISV customer.

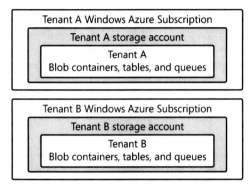

FIGURE 3-7 Tenant isolation is accomplished by requiring each tenant to have their own Windows Azure subscription.

Because of the dangers, you might want to avoid storing all of the storage access keys in a single centralized location. If your application is a desktop or mobile application, you might distribute the storage access keys and allow them to be transmitted as part of the authentication process.

When centralized storage of the tenant storage access keys is required, as is the case with Web applications, you might consider storing an encrypted copy of the tenant's storage access key in each user's profile. The tenant storage access key can then be decrypted upon successful logon and used to perform the necessary data storage operations. This kind of a scheme requires writing a little plumbing code to re-encrypt the tenant's storage access key whenever a user changes their password. Rotating the storage access keys is also a bit more complex, because it requires all users to change their passwords upon their next logon. As with most "change of password" screens, the user must be prompted for their current password as well as their new password. The current password is used to decrypt the tenant storage access key and the new password is used to re-encrypt it for storage in the user's profile.

You might wonder why you should encrypt the storage access key with the user's password. The reason is predicated upon the assumption that decentralizing the storage access keys will reduce the scope of a successful attack. If it is impractical to store the storage access keys in a distributed fashion, you can use something that is already distributed: the user's password.

One subscription, separate storage accounts per tenant

In the scenario in which there is one subscription and separate storage accounts per tenant, the ISV obtains a single Windows Azure subscription and then provisions individual storage accounts for use with each tenant's data, as shown in Figure 3-8. At the time of this writing, there was a default limit of five storage accounts per subscription, but Microsoft will increase this limit for you upon request to a maximum of 20. This model provides the maximum amount of isolation possible without requiring your customers to purchase their own Windows Azure subscription. As with the "separate subscription" model, each storage account will have its own unique storage access keys, which must be carefully guarded. As with the *separate subscription* strategy for tenant isolation, a compromise of the collection of tenant storage access keys would essentially provide unlimited access to the data stores of all of an ISV's customers. When using this strategy, you may want to consider encrypting the tenant's storage access keys with the user's password and storing the encrypted key in the user's profile to reduce the likelihood that a successful compromise of one tenant's data might spread to all tenants.

As with the separate Windows Azure subscription per tenant model, you may want to avoid centralized storage of the storage access keys, or encrypt them with decentralized keys such as the user's password.

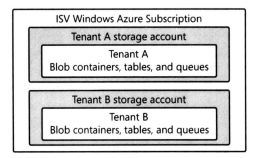

FIGURE 3-8 Tenant isolation is accomplished by provisioning a separate storage account for each tenant within a single subscription.

One subscription, one storage account, separate blob containers, tables, and queues per tenant

In the scenario in which there is one subscription, one storage account, and separate blob containers, tables, and queues per tenant, the ISV obtains a single Windows Azure subscription and then creates a single storage account for the application. Tenant separation is provided by provisioning separate blob containers, tables, and queues when bringing a new tenant onboard. (See Figure 3-9.) The creation of unique blob containers, tables, and queues per tenant is generally accomplished by following a naming convention to tie the name of the blob container, table, or queue to a specific tenant. A hashed customer name or ID can often be good name candidates.

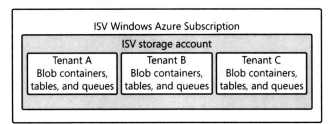

FIGURE 3-9 Tenant isolation is accomplished by provisioning separate blob containers, tables, and queues for each tenant.

One subscription, one storage account, shared blob containers, tables, and queues

The scenario in which all tenant's data is stored in the same blob containers, tables, and queues is the easiest to set up and administer when data confidentiality is not a high concern. (See Figure 3-10.) This strategy offers you the largest degree of multi-tenancy, but it comes at the expense of tenant data isolation. In this scenario, each tenant's data is separated only by a segment of the data's *partition key*, as discussed further in Chapters 5, 6, and 7. The application ensures that one tenant cannot inadvertently (or deliberately) access another tenant's data. When using this model, great care must be taken to ensure the data being stored is not regulated or confidential, and that potentially sensitive information is encrypted with keys and salts that are unique to each tenant. You may also want to rigorously test your software for penetration and closely watch for the potential for a tenant to inadvertently or deliberately store regulated or confidential data in your application's data storage. Although you may or may not be legally responsible, the ramifications of a data breach in the cloud can be large, and the damage to your company's reputation may be expensive and hard to recover from. Because the application operates as the sentry to protect one tenant's data from another, security vulnerabilities in your application potentially compromise the data of all of your tenants.

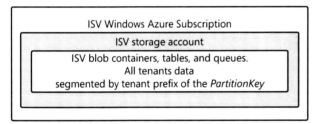

FIGURE 3-10 Tenant isolation is accomplished by utilizing a segment of the partition key of blobs, tables, and queues.

Conclusion

In this chapter, you set up your Windows Azure subscription and created storage accounts within that subscription. You then learned how to manage your subscription by using the RESTful Service Management API to create, update, and delete storage accounts from it, as well as manage your storage access keys. The chapter spent a little time on setup and using the local developer storage emulator, and then wrapped the discussion up with how several multi-tenant business scenarios might be approached using Windows Azure.

Accessing Windows Azure data storage

This chapter introduces features of Windows Azure Data Management Services that are applicable to all types of data storage in the cloud, such as authentication, segmented reads, and transient error recovery. Many of these higher-level features follow repetitive patterns or require code to implement as opposed to what would be required with a higher level of abstraction. It is generally desirable, therefore, to have an abstraction layer such as the Windows Azure client library to act as a façade to simplify the underlying RESTful application programming interface (API) and make the consuming software application easier to write. This chapter will cover how things work at the RESTful Windows Azure Data Management API layer; however, the examples shown for how the client participates will be performed with the Windows Azure client library for the Microsoft .NET Framework. If you were using the Windows Azure Data Management API directly (without the benefit of one of the client libraries), the procedures you would implement in your code would be similar to those discussed in this chapter.

Authentication

As you will learn in Chapter 5, "Blobs," public access can be granted to blob containers, enabling the blob containers and their contents to be read anonymously over the Internet. All other storage operations require authentication. Windows Azure storage authenticates your request using the *Authentication* HTTP header, which adheres to the following format.

```
Authorization: <SharedKey|SharedKeyLite> <accountname>:<signature>
```

Constructing the signature

Constructing this header is a clear enough procedure, but getting the algorithm assembled manually can be tedious the first time you do it. Fortunately, the Windows Azure client library removes this burden; however, it is still important for you to understand the procedures involved so that you have confidence in the security of your data.

To compute the signature, begin by using the uppercased HTTP verb being used for the request (*GET, PUT, POST, DELETE*, or *HEAD*) followed by a newline character.

Next, add an optional MD5 hash of the data being uploaded to ensure that the data is not corrupted during upload, and then follow it with a newline character. If an MD5 hash is not used, the value is just an empty string followed by a newline character. The MD5 hash is useful when you want the extra level of reliability during data transmission that results from verifying a hash of the sent data against a hash of the received data. In many scenarios, the MD5 hash offers only marginal reliability improvements when using HTTPS.

After the optional MD5 hash, you add the *Content-Type* value (MIME type) of the data being uploaded followed by a newline character.

Add the date and time of the request in ISO 8601 format (*YYYY-MM-DDTHH:MM:SSZ*) and follow this date with a newline character. (See the W3C note on this specification, located at *http://www.w3.org/TR/NOTE-datetime*.)

Next, you include a canonicalized collection of the value of the custom headers (those that begin with the *x-ms-* prefix), sorted lexicographically using the header name, with any duplicate headers removed.

Append the canonicalized resource to the end of the header. The *canonicalized resource* is a string that represents the storage being targeted by the request, encoded exactly as it is in its URI. To compute the *CanonicalizedResource* for the signature, begin by using the slash character (/) and appending the storage account name, and then add the resource's encoded URI path. Trim off any query parameters from the URI path.

Next, you need to convert any uppercase parameters into lowercase and sort them lexicographically in ascending order by parameter name. Each query parameter name and value must be URL-decoded and then reformatted so that the name and value are separated by a colon (*<name>:<value>*). For parameters that have more than one value, the values must be separated with commas (*<name> :<value>,<value>,<value>*). Append a newline character after each name-value pair to complete the *CanonicalizedResource* used by the signature algorithm.

 Note You'll find additional information about Windows Azure authentication schemes at *http://msdn.microsoft.com/en-us/library/windowsazure/dd179428.aspx*.

The Windows Azure SDK for the .NET Framework

As introduced in Chapter 2, "Windows Azure data storage overview," many storage account client libraries target different platforms and languages, including the .NET Framework, PHP, and Java. These libraries are designed to reduce the code necessary to write client-side code against the RESTful API of Windows Azure storage service. You will review the .NET client library in this chapter, but the client libraries available on the Windows Azure site are ports of the same codebase, so your experience on other platforms will be similar.

To use the Windows Azure storage client library after installing the Windows Azure software development kit (SDK) for the .NET Framework, add a reference to the *Microsoft.WindowsAzure.StorageClient.dll* assembly. This assembly is home to many types, which are located in three namespaces:

- **Microsoft.WindowsAzure**   Contains types related to your storage accounts and credentials.

- **Microsoft.WindowsAzure.StorageClient**   Contains types for object-oriented data access and the types most frequently used by application developers.

- **Microsoft.WindowsAzure.StorageClient.Protocol**   Contains types for direct RESTful data access and are more "plumbing" related, that is, a lower level of abstraction over the API to support the higher level types in the *StorageClient* namespace. Types in this namespace are not frequently used by application developers.

Connection string formats

The Windows Azure SDK Storage Client code places an abstraction over the RESTful authentication mechanism by emulating the familiar ADO.NET database connection string pattern, where a database connection string is provided as a delimited string that is usually stored in a configuration file. When using the Windows Azure client library, the *Authorization* header is constructed at run time by the classes in the client library using the data that you supply in your connection string.

If you're accessing data management services from a cloud application on Windows Azure, the typical location where connection strings are stored is the *ServiceConfiguration.cscfg* file. Connection strings are made as individual *Setting* subelement nodes located under the *Role* node to which the setting applies. This file is part of the Windows Azure deployment package for Windows Azure Cloud Services and is global to all of your computational instances. Its contents may be modified without redeploying your application. This is largely a feature of the cloud service, but is introduced here only for completeness and clarity.

The following example shows the configuration of a connection string for a web role named *PS_WebRole* of a cloud service deployed on Windows Azure. In the example, the name of the setting used to store the connection string information is *DataConnectionString*, but the name you choose is not very important; whatever name you choose will be used in your application code to access the value. The following code shows the typical contents of a *ServiceConfiguration.cscfg* file. Notice the placement of the *Setting* node containing *DataConnectionString*. (In this example, it has a value of *UseDevelopmentStorage=true*.)

```xml
<?xml version="1.0" encoding="utf-8"?>
<ServiceConfiguration serviceName="PhotoShare"
      xmlns=http://schemas.microsoft.com/ServiceHosting/2008/10/ServiceConfiguration
      osFamily="1" osVersion="*">
  <Role name="PS_WebRole">
    <Instances count="1" />
    <ConfigurationSettings>
      <Setting name="DataConnectionString" value="UseDevelopmentStorage=true" />
    </ConfigurationSettings>
    <Certificates>
      <Certificate name="SSLCertificate"
          thumbprint="F8ACE24A36F93B006BFAF495F6C14FB827AC61A3" thumbprintAlgorithm="sha1" />
    </Certificates>
  </Role>
  <Role name="PS_WorkerRole">
    <Instances count="1" />
    <ConfigurationSettings>
      <Setting name="DataConnectionString" value="UseDevelopmentStorage=true" />
    </ConfigurationSettings>
  </Role>
</ServiceConfiguration>.
```

Like an ADO.NET database connection string, the data management service account connection string format is a semicolon-delimited set of well-known name-value pairs, with each name and value being further delimited by an equal sign. The parameters for the connection string are as follows:

- **DefaultEndpointsProtocol** This value of this parameter is the protocol being used by the endpoint. It is either *http* or *https*. This parameter is optional and if not specified, its default is *http*.

- **AccountName** The value of this mandatory parameter is the account name for your data management service account. When using the data management service emulator, the *AccountName* is set to the well-known value of *devstoreaccount1*. It is generally preferred that you use the alternative of setting the *UseDevelopmentStorage* connection string parameter to *true*.

- **AccountKey** The value of this mandatory parameter is the account key for your data management service account. When using the data management services emulator, the *Account-Key* is set to a well-known value of the following:

    *Eby8vdM02xNOcqFlqUwJPLlmEtlCDXJ1OUzFT50uSRZ6IFsuFq2UVErCz4I6tq
    /K1SZFPTOtr/KBHBeksoGMGw==*

    It is generally preferred that you use the alternative method of setting the *UseDevelopment-Storage* connection string parameter to *true*, but in certain situations the symmetry of using a full-fledged account key for the emulator and the cloud is desired.

- **UseDevelopmentStorage** The value of this optional Boolean parameter indicates whether the local development data management service emulator is being used. When using the data management service emulator, this parameter is used in lieu of the *AccountName* and *AccountKey* parameters as a convenient alternative. The value of this parameter is set to *true* when using the data management services emulator, and *false* when using the actual data management services in the cloud.

- ***DevelopmentStorageProxyUri***   The value of this optional parameter is the URI of the HTTP proxy that will be used with the development data management service emulator. This parameter is especially useful for debugging your data management services because it allows you to substitute a man-in-the-middle proxy such as *Fiddler* into the request-response process. This substitution allows you to fully monitor all data management traffic. By default, the data management service emulator uses the loopback adapter IP address of *127.0.0.1*. *Fiddler* ignores traffic on the loopback adapter but provides a special proxy address of *http://ipv4.fiddler*, which allows *Fiddler* to hook itself into the loopback traffic. When working locally using the Windows Azure storage emulator, you can instruct the Windows Azure client library to use this proxy by adding the optional *DevelopmentStorageProxyUri* parameter to the connection string with a value of *http://ipv4.fiddler*.

- ***BlobEndpoint***   The value of this optional parameter is the endpoint URI to be used to access blobs. It's frequently used to override the default data management URI with a custom domain.

- ***TableEndpoint***   The value of this optional parameter is the endpoint URI to be used to access tables. It's frequently used to override the default data management URI with a custom domain.

- ***QueueEndpoint***   The value of this optional parameter is the endpoint URI to be used to access *queues*. It's frequently used to override the default data management URI with a custom domain.

- ***SharedAccessSignature***   The value of this optional parameter is the shared access signature used to perform authorized data operations against the resource specified by the request's URI. You'll learn more about Shared Access Signatures (SAS) in Chapter 5, Chapter 6, "Tables," and Chapter 7, "Queues."

These connection string parameters are combined in various ways to meet the requirements of different use-cases, such as these:

- Development storage emulator

```
UseDevelopmentStorage=true;
```

- Development storage emulator over HTTP with *Fiddler*

```
UseDevelopmentStorage=true;DevelopmentStorageProxyUri=http://ipv4.fiddler
```

- Data management services over Secure Sockets Layer (SSL) with default endpoints

```
DefaultEndpointsProtocol=https;AccountName=nnn;AccountKey=kkk
```

- Data management services over SSL with custom domain name endpoints

```
BlobEndpoint=https://customdomain.com/;QueueEndpoint= https://customdomain.com/;
TableEndpoint= https://customdomain.com/;AccoutName=Nnn;AccountKey=Kkk
```

Segmented reads

The dynamic scalability provided by Windows Azure adds a small but manageable amount of complexity. When consumption of your data resources is high, to maintain or exceed its delivery performance targets, Windows Azure storage reallocates data across storage nodes, thereby balancing the workload. As a side effect of the dynamic scalability features of Windows Azure storage, requests for some kinds of data under certain conditions may result in an incomplete fulfillment. To retrieve all of your data from the data management service, you must execute a series of consecutive data segment reads and aggregate the result.

When segmented reading is necessary, a supplemental piece of data called a *continuation token* will be returned with your data. The continuation token is used to construct your next data retrieval request. It is possible that subsequent data requests will also be incomplete and that you will be provided a new continuation token with your data that you must use to obtain your next segment of data. It is important to note that the continuation token changes with every request. The continuation token is an opaque value that bookmarks the location in your data where reading should resume.

To capture all of the results of your query, you must continuously execute retrieval requests from inside of a loop. You can exit the loop when the response no longer contains a continuation token. Of course, you might also exit this loop when any of your application's limits for data retrieval have been met or exceeded (for example, you download more data than your application is capable of handling at one time).

A client's request for data retrieval may take longer than Windows Azure allows for a single request. For example, a table query that takes more than five seconds to execute will result in a response containing a portion of the data requested plus a continuation token.

Your client might make a request for a large quantity of data. A table query returning more than a thousand rows will result in the return of your data plus a continuation token, which must be used to retrieve the next thousand rows.

Continuation tokens may be received as a response to the following types of Windows Azure requests:

- Retrieving table rows across storage nodes
- Retrieving more than 1,000 table rows in a single request
- Retrieving more data than can be returned in five seconds
- Enumerating blobs in a blob container
- Enumerating more than 1,000 tables in an account
- Enumerating more than 5,000 queues in an account

Any of these scenarios could result in a portion of your data being returned with a continuation token for use in retrieving the next segment of data. In some cases, it is even possible to receive a continuation token without receiving any data. This can occur when Windows Azure storage has recently moved your data to a new storage node, in which case, reissuing your request with the storage token returns data from the appropriate storage node. This is usually inconsequential as long as your code does not make any assumptions that your first read will result in data to process.

Many of these conditions are outside of your control, so robust client code should always assume the existence of a continuation token and provide code to process it when it occurs. Ignoring the existence of continuation tokens can often result in a loss of data, which is a serious condition for most applications. Because loss of data from these conditions will generally be rare and intermittent, this kind of defect can also be hard to find later and even harder to diagnose in production.

Continuation tokens for retrieving lists of data are implemented differently from continuation tokens for retrieving rows of data in tables. Tables, which will be explored further in Chapter 6, use a pair of HTTP response headers, whereas operations that return lists of data regarding blobs, queues, and tables in your account return an element called *NextMarker* as the continuation token. Despite the implementation difference between these two techniques, both serve the purpose of providing you with the information required to retrieve the next segment of your data.

Blob container list continuation tokens

In the following code sample, you can see the *Marker* and *NextMarker* elements (bolded), located within the enumerable results of a query, requesting a list of the contents of a blob container.

```xml
<?xml version="1.0" encoding="utf-8"?>
<EnumerationResults AccountName="http://azureinsiders.blob.core.windows.net">
  <Prefix>string-value</Prefix>
  <Marker>string-value</Marker>
  <MaxResults>int-value</MaxResults>
  <Containers>
    <Container>
      <Name>container-name</Name>
      <URL>container-address</URL>
      <Properties>
        <Last-Modified>date/time-value</Last-Modified>
        <Etag>etag</Etag>
      </Properties>
      <Metadata>
        <metadata-name>value</metadata-name>
      </Metadata>
    </Container>
  </Containers>
  <NextMarker>marker-value</NextMarker>
</EnumerationResults>
```

Queue list continuation tokens

A request for a list of queues may also return a segmented result. As shown in the following code, the presence of a *NextMarker* element in the response requires the consumer to make subsequent read requests and aggregate the results of all responses for a complete list.

```xml
<?xml version="1.0" encoding="utf-8"?>
<EnumerationResults AccountName="http://azureinsiders.queue.core.windows.net">
  <Prefix>string-value</Prefix>
  <Marker>string-value</Marker>
  <MaxResults>int-value</MaxResults>
  <Queues>
    <Queue>
      <Name>string-value</Name>
      <Url>queue-address</Url>
      <Metadata>
      <metadata-name>value</metadata-name>
    <Metadata>
    </Queue>
  <NextMarker>marker-value</NextMarker>
</EnumerationResults>
```

Blob storage continuation

A request for a list of all the blobs in a container with a large population may result in a segmented result being returned, as shown in the following example. The presence of a *NextMarker* element indicates a segmented response, which means that retrieving the entire list will require the requester to make repeated read requests as well as aggregate the results of each response.

```
HTTP/1.1 200 OK
Transfer-Encoding: chunked
Content-Type: application/xml
Server: Windows-Azure-Blob/1.0 Microsoft-HTTPAPI/2.0
x-ms-request-id: 466d1c04-25df-41ca-ba70-e30dce7ff8ae
x-ms-version: 2011-08-18
Date: Tue, 05 Jun 2012 00:43:22 GMT

3A7DD
<?xml version="1.0" encoding="utf-8"?>
<EnumerationResults ContainerName="http://azureinsiders.blob.core.windows.net/manyblobs">
<MaxResults>5000</MaxResults>
<Delimiter>/</Delimiter>
<Blobs>
  <Blob>
    <Name>00000</Name>
    <Url>http://azureinsiders.blob.core.windows.net/manyblobs/00000</Url>
    <Properties>
      <Last-Modified>Tue, 05 Jun 2012 00:14:00 GMT</Last-Modified>
      <Etag>0x8CF10C73DA9D05E</Etag>
      <Content-Length>0</Content-Length>
      <Content-Type>application/octet-stream</Content-Type>
      <Content-Encoding /><Content-Language />
      <Content-MD5 /><Cache-Control />
      <BlobType>BlockBlob</BlobType>
```

```
      <LeaseStatus>unlocked</LeaseStatus>
    </Properties>
  </Blob>
  <Blob>
    <Name>00001</Name>
    <Url>http://azureinsiders.blob.core.windows.net/manyblobs/00001</Url>
    <Properties>
      <Last-Modified>Tue, 05 Jun 2012 00:14:00 GMT</Last-Modified>
      <Etag>0x8CF10C73DB0600E</Etag>
      <Content-Length>0</Content-Length>
      <Content-Type>application/octet-stream</Content-Type>
      <Content-Encoding /><Content-Language />
      <Content-MD5 />
      <Cache-Control />
      <BlobType>BlockBlob</BlobType>
      <LeaseStatus>unlocked</LeaseStatus>
    </Properties>
  </Blob>
</Blobs>
<NextMarker>2!68!MDAwMDA1ITA1MDATk5LTEyABCDEFGHIJKLMNOPQRSTUVWXYZk5OTk5OTlaIQ--</NextMarker>
</EnumerationResults>
```

Table storage continuation HTTP headers

The HTTP response for table storage uses two headers for entity continuation: *x-ms-continuation-NextPartitionKey*, which indicates the *PartitionKey* to be used for the next operation; and *x-ms-continuation-NextRowKey*, which indicates the next *RowKey*. In Chapter 6, you'll learn more about *PartitionKey* and *RowKey*. In short, every row in a data management service table can be uniquely identified by a composite of its *PartitionKey* and its *RowKey*.

```
HTTP/1.1 200 OK
Cache-Control: no-cache
Content-Type: application/atom+xml;charset=utf-8
Server: Windows-Azure-Table/1.0 Microsoft-HTTPAPI/2.0
x-ms-version: 2011-08-18
x-ms-continuation-NextPartitionKey: 1!4!UEs-
x-ms-continuation-NextRowKey: 1!12!Q3VzdDAyMDAw
Date: Mon, 04 Jun 2012 22:57:15 GMT
Content-Length: 935604
. . . message body . . .
```

When these two HTTP headers are present in the response, you use them to construct a query string modifier and then repeat your HTTP *GET* request against the resource URI as follows.

```
GET http://azureinsiders.table.core.windows.net/demoSegmented()
    ?NextPartitionKey=1!4!UEs-&NextRowKey=1!12!Q3VzdDAxMDAw HTTP/1.1
```

You should check after each response for the existence of continuation token headers. If these headers are present and your application cares about more than the first page of data, you must construct a query string and supply the *NextPartitionKey* and *NextRowKey* parameters with the values from the headers of your last request to retrieve the next segment of data. You should repeat this process until you have either found the row of data that you were searching for or acquired all of the data that completes the query.

When retrieving tables in your account, you may encounter a third type of continuation response header: *x-ms-continuation-NextTableName*. This header name is relatively self-explanatory: it represents the next table name in the sequence to be retrieved. You'll learn more about this header in Chapter 6.

Windows Azure client library support for continuation tokens

The concept of continuation was implemented using HTTP headers for table row retrievals and a *NextMarker* element for lists of items. Although the implementation details are different, their purpose of acting as a bookmark is the same. Handling continuation tokens is repetitive and follows a pattern. The Windows Azure storage client library of the Windows Azure SDK abstracts the implementation details of how continuation tokens are implemented and makes them simpler to deal with.

The following code from the Windows Azure client library shows the public members of the *ResultSegment<T>* class, which allows you to see that a continuation token of type *ResultContinuation* is surfaced to the storage consumer as a property. The *HasMoreResults* property allows efficient checking of whether there are more results to process, and the *Results* property returns an *IEnumerable<T>* for convenient iteration over the returned data.

```
namespace Microsoft.WindowsAzure.StorageClient {
    // Summary:
    //     Represents a result segment that was retrieved from the total set of possible
    //     results.
    //
    // Type parameters:
    //   TElement:
    //     The type of the element.
    public class ResultSegment<TElement> {
        // Summary:
        //     Gets a continuation token to use to retrieve the next set of results with
        //     a subsequent call to the operation.
        public ResultContinuation ContinuationToken { get; internal set; }
        //
        // Summary:
        //     Gets a value indicating whether there are additional results to retrieve.
        public bool HasMoreResults { get; }
        //
        // Summary:
        //     Gets an enumerable collection of results.
        public IEnumerable<TElement> Results { get; }

        // Summary:
        //     Begins an asynchronous operation to retrieve the next result segment.
        //
        // Parameters:
        //   callback:
        //     The callback delegate that will receive notification when the asynchronous
        //     operation completes.
        //
        //   state:
        //     A user-defined object that will be passed to the callback delegate.
        //
```

```
      // Returns:
      //      An System.IAsyncResult that references the asynchronous operation.
      public IAsyncResult BeginGetNext(AsyncCallback callback, object state);
      //
      // Summary:
      //      Ends an asynchronous operation to retrieve the next result segment.
      //
      // Parameters:
      //    asyncResult:
      //      An System.IAsyncResult that references the pending asynchronous operation.
      //
      // Returns:
      //      The next result segment.
      public ResultSegment<TElement> EndGetNext(IAsyncResult asyncResult);
      //
      // Summary:
      //      Gets the next result segment.
      //
      // Returns:
      //      The next result segment.
      public ResultSegment<TElement> GetNext();
   }
}
```

The *ResultContinuation* class is defined as an *IXmlSerializable* type, which is simply a convenient way to deserialize the continuation token for use, as the following code shows.

```
namespace Microsoft.WindowsAzure.StorageClient {
    // Summary:
    //      Manage continuation information for various listing operation.  Can be serialized
    //      using XmlSerialization.
    [Serializable]
    public sealed class ResultContinuation : IXmlSerializable {
    }
}
```

Because *ResultSegment* can be null (even when there is more data to process), you must first establish that it is a populated instance before attempting to access the *ContinuationToken* property. Otherwise, a *NullReferenceException* will be thrown when the property is accessed. The redundant code that must check the instance for use before accessing the property will negatively impact code readability. You can improve the readability of your code and cut down on the amount of code that you have to write by adding a couple of extension methods (*SafeHasMoreResults<T>* and *SafeContinuationToken<T>*), as shown in the next bit of code. These methods are from the Wintellect Power Azure Library available as a *NuGet* package.

```
namespace Wintellect.WindowsAzure.CloudStorage {
    public static class CloudStorageExtensions {

        // Methods that apply to Blobs, Tables, and Queues
        public static Boolean SafeHasMoreResults<T>(this ResultSegment<T> rs) {
            return (rs == null) ? true : (rs.SafeContinuationToken() != null);
        }
```

```
        public static ResultContinuation SafeContinuationToken<T>(this ResultSegment<T> rs) {
            return (rs == null) ? null : rs.ContinuationToken;
        }
    }
}
```

These extension methods allow you to write consistently simple code when handling segmented reads for blobs, tables, and queues. (The extension method technique will be used more in Chapters 5, 6, and 7.) The following code example uses this technique to demonstrate a segmented read of 6,000 blobs in a blob container. Because the Windows Azure storage limits allow only 5,000 items per request to be returned, the following code, which requests 6,000 items, results in a segmented read. The *SafeHasMoreResults()* and *SafeContinuationToken()* extension methods provide a very clean and simple coding paradigm.

```
// Enumerate containers & blobs in segments
for (ResultSegment<CloudBlobContainer> rsContainer = null; rsContainer.SafeHasMoreResults(); ) {
    rsContainer = client.ListContainersSegmented(null,
        ContainerListingDetails.None, 6000, rsContainer.SafeContinuationToken());

    foreach (var c in rsContainer.Results) {
        for (ResultSegment<IListBlobItem> rsBlob = null; rsBlob.SafeHasMoreResults(); ) {
            rsBlob = c.ListBlobsSegmented(6000, rsBlob.SafeContinuationToken(), null);
            foreach (var b in rsBlob.Results) {
                // perform work with each blob
            }
        }
    }
}
```

Cloud reliability concerns

The dynamic scalability characteristic of Windows Azure introduces new reliability challenges. In particular, the chances that data operations will fail is higher in the cloud than with on-premise solutions. It is a best-practice to always write your code defensively with the assumption that failures will happen.

Some errors are caused by conditions that are expected to be temporary, such as a network outage, a service being unavailable, or a service being too busy to respond. These kinds of conditions are considered *transient errors*. Recovery from transient errors is possible in many situations by simply retrying an operation. Often, by the time the operation is performed again, the error condition that caused the failure is no longer present and the operation succeeds.

Performance targets

Whenever you make a network request for a data operation, failure is a possibility. Failures are returned as HTTP status codes. Some status codes represent potentially transient conditions from which recovery may be possible by simply retrying the operation, whereas other status codes are terminal to the operation. For example, none of the HTTP status codes in the 400 range are recoverable by retrying the operation, nor are HTTP status codes 501 (Not Implemented) and 505 (HTTP Version Not Supported).

Windows Azure storage has several performance targets:

- **Single account**   5,000 I/O operations per second and 3 gigabits per second

- **Single blob**   60 MB per second

- **Single table partition**   500 entities per second

- **Single queue**   500 messages per second

When your application's processing demands approach or exceed these performance targets, it becomes increasingly likely that you will receive an HTTP status code response of 503 (Service Unavailable).

Failure conditions and strategies for recovery

When a failure occurs, the code on your client must detect the kind of error received and attempt to retry the operation when the error is transient. The Windows Azure client library provides an implementation to help your application facilitate the necessary handling of transient error conditions. Any HTTP status code received from a request that is in the 400 range is an error condition that cannot be tried again, and your application should handle the error as a failure. The same is true for HTTP status codes 501 (Not Implemented) and 505 (HTTP Version Not Supported). Other error conditions indicated by an HTTP status code that is not in the 200 range may be considered transient and retried.

When an error condition can be tried again, you have options as to how you handle the timing of the retries. The Windows Azure client library provides two implementations that allow the retries to be either linear or exponential. In a linear retry, a fixed amount of specified delay between each request is injected to allow adequate time for the transient condition to potentially dissipate. In an exponential retry, the time between retries increases exponentially.

Generally speaking, linear retry strategies are preferred for applications where a user is waiting directly for an operation to be performed, but the exponential technique is the most robust technique and has a higher probability of recovery. Retrying an operation several times in a short span of time (even with delays) is not as likely to result in success because some transient faults may last for a longer duration, and the exponential technique accommodates the larger time window required for recovery of these kinds of transient failures.

Recovery code

The Windows Azure client library provides a *RetryPolicy* delegate to aid you in writing recovery code. When evaluated, the *RetryPolicy* delegate returns a *ShouldRetry* delegate, which is used to provide a custom implementation to tell the calling code whether it should attempt to retry the operation. This scaffolding provides a lightweight method of injecting custom retry logic into your application. When each data management operation is performed, the *RetryPolicy* delegate is evaluated, which results in a state object being created by the .NET runtime to track the parameters of the policy. The following code shows a typical linear retry policy implementation.

```
// typical linear Retry policy
public static RetryPolicy LinearRetry(int count, TimeSpan interval) {
  return () => {
    return (int curCount, Exception ex, out TimeSpan retryInterval) => {
      // Add any custom handling here
      retryInterval = interval;
      // if we have exceeded our count then return false, otherwise return true to continue
      return curCount < count;
    };
  };
}
```

The following code shows a typical exponential retry policy implementation. Because some kinds of failures can be time-dependent, a random time tweak is introduced to vary the delay between each retry event by a small margin.

```
public static RetryPolicy RetryExponential(int retryCount, TimeSpan minBackoff
      , TimeSpan maxBackoff, TimeSpan backoffChg) {
    return () => {
      return (int count, Exception ex, out TimeSpan retryDelayMs) => {
          if (count < retryCount) {
              // increment is exponential,
              // but tweaked +/- 20% to avoid timing-related failures
              Random r = new Random();
              int tweak = r.Next((int)(backoffChg.TotalMilliseconds * 0.8),
                  (int)(backoffChg.TotalMilliseconds * 1.2));
              double increment = (Math.Pow(2, count) - 1) * tweak;
              // calcluate delay between retry attempts
              // but trimmed to min and max values to ensure we stay within range
              double retryDelay = (double)Math.Min(minBackoff.TotalMilliseconds +
                  increment, maxBackoff.TotalMilliseconds);
              retryDelayMs = TimeSpan.FromMilliseconds(retryDelay);
              return true;
          }
          retryDelayMs = TimeSpan.Zero;
          return false;
      };
    };
}
```

Failure mitigation strategies

When frequent failures are occurring, you may want to look at various strategies to reduce the failure rate.

The Content Delivery Network (CDN) may be used to strategically cache copies of your data closer to where it is being used. The CDN provides maximum bandwidth to consumers of your content at geographical nodes in the United States, Europe, Asia, Australia, and South America. Because the list of CDN locations is always changing, a complete and current list may be found at *http://msdn.microsoft.com/en-us/library/windowsazure/gg680302.aspx*.

The lowest common denominator for dynamically scaling resource availability is the *PartitionKey*, and you will learn more about this key in Chapters 5, 6, and 7. The Windows Azure data management service will attempt to maintain its performance targets by automatically migrating to other storage node partitions that are in high demand, and by adding new storage nodes as it deems necessary to keep itself within compliance of the performance targets. The *PartitionKey* is used as the basis for decisions about data migration across storage nodes. An individual *PartitionKey* can have as much as an entire storage node dedicated solely to service it. This is where your strategy of selecting a *Partition-Key* scheme comes into play, and the whole spectrum of strategies is available to you. On one end of the spectrum, you could have all your data share a single *PartitionKey* (meaning that it would be mandatory for all data to be stored on a single storage node). On the other end of the spectrum, you could assign every blob, every row of a table, or every queue its own *PartitionKey*, thereby enabling (in extreme circumstances) every item to potentially be assigned its own storage node. Rethinking and restructuring your *PartitionKey* scheme, and applying it to your data, can have a large impact on scalability.

You might also consider grouping sets of messages together in batches to make your application more "chunky" instead of "chatty," which cuts down on unnecessary consumption of network bandwidth, or you might add additional queues to enable parallel message processing.

The transient fault handling application block

The Transient Fault Handling Application Block embodies out-of-the-box and custom error detection strategies to identify known transient error conditions when you use the following Windows Azure services in your application:

- Windows Azure SQL Database

- Windows Azure Service Bus

- Windows Azure storage

- Windows Azure caching service

The goal of the Transient Fault Handling Application Block is to make your application more robust and resilient to failure by providing a straightforward and easy means of applying consistent retry behaviors against transient faults that might have a negative impact on your application.

You can find additional information and download links for the Transient Fault Handling Block at the following link: *http://msdn.microsoft.com/en-us/library/hh680934(v=pandp.50).aspx*.

Conclusion

This chapter familiarized you with features of Windows Azure data management services that are applicable to all types of data storage in the cloud, such as authentication, segmented reads, and transient error recovery. You are now ready to learn the specifics of blobs, tables, and queues, which are covered in the next three chapters.

Blobs, tables, and queues

Blobs

In this chapter:

In this chapter, you learn about Windows Azure blob storage. First you examine the characteristics of this kind of data storage, including the kinds of real-world data and storage scenarios that lend themselves well to blob storage. You then learn about the organizational structure of this storage type, including the naming conventions and other rules that must be followed. This chapter discusses how to perform common create, read, update, and delete (CRUD) operations on blobs and their containers. To deepen your understanding, you tackle the advanced and valuable but often overlooked features of blobs, such as metadata, snapshots, and granular security access, which allow CRUD operations to be performed only by authorized parties. Finally, you learn how to write applications for robustness and resiliency in the cloud.

Blob basics

BLOB is an acronym for *Binary Large Object*, but the uppercase convention is generally ignored in favor of the more colloquial lowercase *blob*, which I use throughout the book. A *blob* holds arbitrarily structured data, which the blob has no knowledge of. To the blob, the data it contains is just a bunch of random bytes that may be read or written to either sequentially or in randomly accessed chunks (called *blocks*, or *pages*). Although the data contained in a blob may have a structure and may even adhere to a schema, the blob itself, as just mentioned, has no knowledge of what this structure might be. Blobs are often used to store documents such as Microsoft Word, Microsoft Excel, and XML documents; pictures; audio clips; videos; and backups of file systems. Files that might be stored on your computer's hard drive, or content that you might publish on a website, can alternatively be stored in blob storage.

In addition to the data contained within a blob, a blob also stores its own name, a small amount of metadata—8 kilobytes (KB) at the time of this writing—and an MD5 hash that can be used to validate a blob's integrity.

The cloud fabric manages the dynamic scaling of your data to meet demand. If a particular set of blobs are receiving a high volume of traffic, the cloud fabric will move those blobs to their own storage node. In a more extreme circumstance, an individual blob could potentially be on its own storage node. An individual blob cannot float around on its own anywhere it pleases, however; it must be stored in a structure called a *blob container*, which you will learn about later in this chapter. Windows Azure storage provides two distinct types of blob: the block blob and the page blob. You'll examine the block blob first.

Block blobs

Block blobs are useful in sequential access scenarios when storage and consumption of the data can begin at the first byte and end at the last. These blobs can be uploaded in equal-sized chunks referred to as *blocks*. This characteristic makes them well suited for applications requiring recovery from transmission failures, because transmission can be simply resumed from the last successfully transmitted block. Blocks in a blob may also be uploaded in parallel to increase throughput. An individual block blob can be any size up to 200 gigabytes (GB). When on-demand access to arbitrary locations within a blob is required, a better option may be the page blob, which is covered next.

Page blobs

Page blobs are useful when storage and consumption of the data may occur in any order. When on-demand access to arbitrary locations within a blob is required, the page blob is often the best option. An individual page blob can be any size up to 1 terabyte. Page blobs may also be sparsely populated, which is useful when implementing certain kinds of data structures and algorithms. Microsoft uses the sparsely populated page blob as the basis for *drive storage*, which is a virtual VHD—and for those paying careful attention, that would be a *Virtually Virtual Hard Drive*! Microsoft charges only for the pages that are occupied, so if you had a 1-terabyte blob with only 2 GB of population, you would pay only for the 2 GB of actual storage space used. This cost does not include fees for egress out-of-data-center and transaction fees, which are not impacted by a page blob's ability to be sparsely populated.

Blob containers

The structures used to store blobs are called *blob containers*. Blob containers provide a unit of organization and also of privacy sharing. By default, all blobs stored in a container share the same level of sharing, either private or public. Private containers require credentials to perform operations, whereas public containers allow anonymous read-only access to all blobs stored in the container. Creation, deletion, and update of the blobs stored in a container always require an authenticated request, irrespective of the privacy settings you assigned to the container.

An individual blob container can hold anywhere from zero to an infinite number of individual blobs. There is a limit, of course, on the total amount of storage capacity available with your account (not to mention the likely constraints you have on the money available to pay for your storage), but the limit is placed on your storage capacity, not on the number of blobs that can be placed in a single blob container. Because the capacity restrictions on an account are so large, in most situations, this number is virtually limitless.

No limit is placed on the number of containers that you can have in a single Windows Azure storage account, but just like individual blobs, the actual numerical limit is determined indirectly by the storage capacity of your Windows Azure storage account.

Blob containers allow access policies to be applied, which control access and operations performed against the individual blobs that the containers encapsulate. You'll learn more about access policies later in this chapter.

Blob addressing

Blob resources are located in data storage via URLs that match this pattern: *http://<account>.blob. core.windows.net/<container>/<blobname>*. The *<account>* placeholder is the Windows Azure account name, *<container>* is the blob's container name, and *<blobname>* is the name of the blob (for example, *http://wintellect.blob.core.windows.net/pictures/Employee.jpg*).

When using the local development storage emulator, the URL pattern is slightly different. The hostname becomes the IP address of the loopback adapter (that is, 127.0.0.1), to which the port number *10000* and the hardcoded literal account name *devstorageaccount1* are appended to form the complete base address, as depicted in the Storage Emulator window shown in Figure 5-1. The container name and blob name are appended to this base address to form the full URL of a resource (for example, *http://127.0.0.1:10000/devstorageaccount1/pictures/Employee.jpg*).

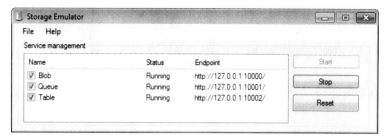

FIGURE 5-1 The IP address is shown in the Windows Azure Storage Emulator window.

Business use cases

Much of the nontextual content displayed by web browsers is blob data. This kind of content tends to be significantly larger in size than the markup that references it, making it more demanding on servers and networks to deliver. Images, documents, audio, and video files are all good examples of this kind of bulky data. Because of size or demand (or both), some of this data will inevitably require greater server and network capacity to deliver, and this creates challenges for redistributing the data to meet demand.

Of course, blob data is not generally sent to the browser with the HTML markup of a website application; instead, URLs to the resources are embedded in the HTML tags that the browser receives and then uses to retrieve the referenced resources and render them locally on the user's machine. Because each resource is referenced by a URL, it makes no difference to the client's browser whether the resource is located on the same server that the HTML was retrieved from, or in another location in an entirely different domain. It is therefore quite easy to take advantage of the massive and dynamic scalability of Windows Azure blob storage to supplement on-premise and cloud-deployed applications by storing this content there. The same thing is true for other kinds of free-standing content accessed by a URL, such as Word, Excel, and PDF documents.

Blob storage structure

Figure 5-2 shows the hierarchical relationships between storage accounts, blob containers, blobs, and pages. A Windows Azure storage account encapsulates zero or more blob containers, and each blob container can in turn encapsulate a set of zero or more blobs. The final column of Figure 5-2 shows the encapsulation of the individual blocks or pages of a blob.

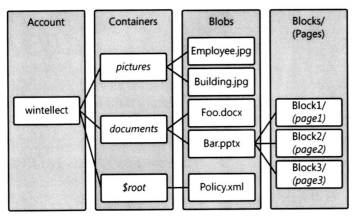

FIGURE 5-2 The blob storage structure is a hierarchical relationship between storage accounts, blob containers, blobs, and pages.

A storage account can be visualized as being similar to the root directory of your computer's hard drive, where the blob containers are like directory folders. Individual blobs can be thought of like files placed in a directory. Furthering this analogy, blobs are frequently named with common suffixes matching their content type (just as files are named with extensions that reflect their types, such as the .jpg or .png file extensions for image files, and the .docx extension for a Word file). Unlike the directory structure on your computer's hard drive, which can contain nested subfolders, blob containers cannot contain subcontainers. The way that subfolder-like behavior can be simulated is discussed a little later in this chapter.

For security and architectural reasons, there may be requirements for a blob to be physically located in the base address of a URL. For example, a cross-domain policy file is an XML document that adheres to a specification published by Adobe. This kind of file is used to grant web clients such as Microsoft Silverlight, Adobe Flash Player, and Adobe Reader permission to handle data across multiple domain boundaries. When a client running from one domain makes a request for a resource located in a secondary domain, the secondary domain must have a cross-domain policy file granting access to the requested resources in order for the web client to continue with the request. The specification requires that the file be named *policy.xml* and that it be located in the root directory of the secondary domain.

Because blobs must be stored in a blob container, a special hidden blob container named *$root* was created. The *$root* container is aliased to the base address of the domain. Any blob placed in the *$root* container will be accessible both by its physical URL (including its *$root* container name) and by its alias URL off the base address of the domain. The following two URLs are equivalent:

```
http://www.wintellect.com/$root/Policy.xml
http://www.wintellect.com/Policy.xml
```

Navigating blob container hierarchies

As suggested earlier, a rough analogy of blob storage is your file system. Actually, when developing your cloud-deployable software, your file system may be used in some circumstances as an adequate on-premise substitute for blob storage (without a few of the advanced features such as snapshots and shared access signatures). You may even consider implementing a provider model in your software to facilitate this kind of convenient on-premise abstraction.

In your file system, files are placed within directories, and those directories are stored within other directories to create an extensive organizational hierarchy. All directories can be traversed back to a single root directory that houses the entire tree structure. Blob containers are like directories that live within the root directory of blob storage, but the analogy begins to weaken at this point because blob containers may not be embedded within other blob containers. If that were the end of the story, you would be left with a very flat file system. Fortunately, this is not the case. The Windows Azure client library provides support for accessing blobs by using a simulation of a nested file system, thus allowing directory-style navigation over delimiters used in your blob names, such as the slash character.

To see how to navigate flat blob storage as if it were hierarchical, you'll first create a set of blobs in a container that uses a path delimiter. In this case, you will use the default delimiter of a slash (/).

The following code creates a container called *demo* and then populates this container with eight blobs named *FileA*, *FileB*, *Dir1/FileC*, *Dir1/FileD*, *Dir1/Dir2/FileE*, *Dir3/FileF*, *Dir3/FileG*, and *Dir4/FileH* by uploading an empty string as the content of each blob. The *UseFlatBlobListing* property of an instance of the *BlobRequestOptions* class is used as a parameter to control whether the container is navigated. You set this property to true when you want each blob in the container to be navigated without regard to the delimiter, and to false when you want navigation to behave as if the container were a file system style directory.

```
public static void DirectoryHierarchies(CloudStorageAccount account) {
    Console.Clear();
    CloudBlobClient client = account.CreateCloudBlobClient();
    Console.WriteLine("Default delimiter={0}", client.DefaultDelimiter /* settable */);
    Console.WriteLine();

    // Create the virtual directory
    const String virtualDirName = "demo";
    CloudBlobContainer virtualDir =
    client.GetContainerReference(virtualDirName).EnsureExists(true);

    // Create some file entries under the virtual directory
    String[] virtualFiles = new String[] {
                        "FileA", "FileB", // Avoid  $&+,/:=?@ in blob names
                        "Dir1/FileC", "Dir1/FileD", "Dir1/Dir2/FileE",
                        "Dir3/FileF", "Dir3/FileG",
                        "Dir4/FileH"
                };
    foreach (String file in virtualFiles) {
        virtualDir.GetBlockBlobReference("Root/" + file).UploadText(String.Empty);
    }
```

```
        // Show the blobs in the virtual directory container
        ShowContainerBlobs(virtualDir);    // Same as UseFlatBlobListing = false
        Console.WriteLine();
        ShowContainerBlobs(virtualDir, true);

        // CloudBlobDirectory (derived from IListBlobItem) is for traversing
        // and accessing blobs with names structured in a directory hierarchy.
        CloudBlobDirectory root = virtualDir.GetDirectoryReference("Root");
        WalkBlobDirHierarchy(root, 0);

        // Show just the blobs under Dir1
        Console.WriteLine();
        String subdir = virtualDir.Name + "/Root/Dir1/";
        foreach (var file in client.ListBlobs(subdir))
            Console.WriteLine(file.Uri);
}

private static void ShowContainerBlobs(CloudBlobContainer container,
        Boolean useFlatBlobListing = false, BlobListingDetails details = BlobListingDetails.None,
            BlobRequestOptions options = null, OperationContext operationContext = null) {
        Console.WriteLine("Container: " + container.Name);
        for (BlobResultSegment brs = null; brs.HasMore(); ) {
            brs = container.ListBlobsSegmented(null, useFlatBlobListing, details, 1000,
                brs.SafeContinuationToken(), options, operationContext);
            foreach (var blob in brs.Results) Console.WriteLine("   " + blob.Uri);
        }
}

private static void WalkBlobDirHierarchy(CloudBlobDirectory dir, Int32 indent) {
        // Get all the entries in the root directory
        IListBlobItem[] entries = dir.ListBlobs().ToArray();
        String spaces = new String(' ', indent * 3);

        Console.WriteLine(spaces + dir.Prefix + " entries:");
        foreach (var entry in entries.OfType<ICloudBlob>())
            Console.WriteLine(spaces + "   " + entry.Name);

        foreach (var entry in entries.OfType<CloudBlobDirectory>()) {
            String[] segments = entry.Uri.Segments;
            CloudBlobDirectory subdir = dir.GetSubdirectoryReference(segments[segments.Length - 1]);
            WalkBlobDirHierarchy(subdir, indent + 1); // Recursive call
        }
}

private static void ShowContainer(CloudBlobContainer container, Boolean showBlobs) {
        Console.WriteLine("Blob container={0}", container);

        BlobContainerPermissions permissions = container.GetPermissions();
        String[] meanings = new String[] {
                            "no public access",
                            "anonymous clients can read container & blob data",
                            "anonymous readers can read blob data only"
                    };
        Console.WriteLine("Container's public access={0} ({1})",
            permissions.PublicAccess, meanings[(Int32)permissions.PublicAccess]);
```

```
            // Show collection of access policies; each consists of name & SharedAccesssPolicy
            // A SharedAccesssBlobPolicy contains:
            //     SharedAccessPermissions enum (None, Read, Write, Delete, List) &
            //     SharedAccessStartTime/SharedAccessExpireTime
            Console.WriteLine("   Shared access policies:");
            foreach (var policy in permissions.SharedAccessPolicies) {
                Console.WriteLine("    {0}={1}", policy.Key, policy.Value);
            }

            container.FetchAttributes();
            Console.WriteLine("   Attributes: Name={0}, Uri={1}", container.Name, container.Uri);
            Console.WriteLine("   Properties: LastModified={0}, ETag={1},",
                container.Properties.LastModified, container.Properties.ETag);
            ShowMetadata(container.Metadata);

            if (showBlobs)
                foreach (ICloudBlob blob in container.ListBlobs())
                    ShowBlob(blob);
        }

        private static void ShowBlob(ICloudBlob blob) {
            // A blob has attributes: Uri, Snapshot DateTime?, Properties & Metadata
            // The CloudBlob Uri/SnapshotTime/Properties/Metadata properties return these
            // You can set the properties & metadata; not the Uri or snapshot time
            Console.WriteLine("Blob Uri={0}, Snapshot time={1}", blob.Uri, blob.SnapshotTime);
            BlobProperties bp = blob.Properties;
            Console.WriteLine("BlobType={0}, CacheControl={1}, Encoding={2}, Language={3}, 
                MD5={4}, ContentType={5}, LastModified={6}, Length={7}, ETag={8}",
                bp.BlobType, bp.CacheControl, bp.ContentEncoding, bp.ContentLanguage,
                    bp.ContentMD5, bp.ContentType, bp.LastModified, bp.Length, bp.ETag);
            ShowMetadata(blob.Metadata);
        }

        private static void ShowMetadata(IDictionary<String, String> metadata) {
            foreach (var kvp in metadata)
                Console.WriteLine("{0}={1}", kvp.Key, kvp.Value);
        }
```

Executing this code produces the following results.

```
Default delimiter=/

Container: demo, UseFlatBlobListing: False
   http://azureinsiders.blob.core.windows.net/demo/Dir1/
   http://azureinsiders.blob.core.windows.net/demo/Dir3/
   http://azureinsiders.blob.core.windows.net/demo/Dir4/
   http://azureinsiders.blob.core.windows.net/demo/FileA
   http://azureinsiders.blob.core.windows.net/demo/FileB

Container: demo, UseFlatBlobListing: True
   http://azureinsiders.blob.core.windows.net/demo/Dir1/Dir2/FileE
   http://azureinsiders.blob.core.windows.net/demo/Dir1/FileC
```

```
http://azureinsiders.blob.core.windows.net/demo/Dir1/FileD
http://azureinsiders.blob.core.windows.net/demo/Dir3/FileF
http://azureinsiders.blob.core.windows.net/demo/Dir3/FileG
http://azureinsiders.blob.core.windows.net/demo/Dir4/FileH
http://azureinsiders.blob.core.windows.net/demo/FileA
http://azureinsiders.blob.core.windows.net/demo/FileB

demo entries:
   FileA
   FileB
   Dir1 entries:
      FileC
      FileD
      Dir2 entries:
         FileE
   Dir3 entries:
      FileF
      FileG
   Dir4 entries:
      FileH

http://azureinsiders.blob.core.windows.net/demo/Dir1/Dir2/FileE
http://azureinsiders.blob.core.windows.net/demo/Dir1/FileC
http://azureinsiders.blob.core.windows.net/demo/Dir1/FileD
```

After printing the delimiter being used, the blob container named *demo* is iterated by using the *UseFlatBlobListing* property of an instance of *BlobRequestOptions* set to *false*. This option suppresses the iterator's descent into the blob names beyond the first occurrence of the delimiter character, providing you with a high-level listing of all of the simulated directories in the root of the container. The next section of code performs the same operation, with the *UseFlatBlobListing* property of an instance of *BlobRequestOptions* set to true. You'll see more on this class later in this chapter. With this option set, the container's *ListBlobsSegmented* method recursively returns the subdirectories in each directory (using the segmented technique described in Chapter 4, "Accessing Windows Azure data storage"), providing a flattened view of the blobs in the container.

Occasionally, because of business requirements, you may have to traverse all of the blobs in a container as if they were files in a file system tree. The next section of code calls the *WalkBlobDir-Hierarchy* routine, which recursively calls itself to list the contents of each segment of the delimited blob names. The *CloudBlobDirectory* class (which derives from *CloudBlob*) provides the abstraction of a blob directory. You traverse the entire tree by calling the *GetSubdirectory* method on each directory to retrieve a list of subdirectories and then use that list to recursively call back into the *WalkBlobDir-Hierarchy* routine.

In some situations, it may be desirable to locate all blobs that are contained in a single simulated directory structure. This can be accomplished using the *ListBlobsWithPrefix* method of your instance of *CloudBlobClient*, as shown in the preceding section of the code.

Storage Client library blob types

The Storage Client library provides abstractions for blobs and containers, making them easy to work with in the Microsoft .NET Framework code. The following alphabetized list explains the most important types, methods, and properties used in the topics covered later in this chapter:

■ *CloudBlob* provides a convenient object-oriented abstraction for working with an individual blob.

■ *CloudBlobContainer* provides a convenient object-oriented abstraction for working with a blob storage container.

■ *CopyFromBlob* copies an existing blob's contents, properties, and metadata to a new blob.

■ *Create[IfNotExist]* creates a blob container or optionally creates the container only if the container does not already exist.

■ *Delete* deletes a blob container and its contents.

■ *FetchAttributes* returns the container's attributes, including its system properties and any user-defined metadata.

■ *Get/SetPermissions* gets or sets the permission settings for the container.

■ *GetBlobReference* returns a reference to a blob in the container.

■ *GetSharedAccessSignature* returns a shared access signature for the container.

■ *ListBlobs[Segmented]* returns an enumerable collection of the blobs in the container, or a segmented enumerable collection of the blobs in the container.

■ *Metadata* returns the user-defined metadata for the blob or blob container.

■ *Name* returns the name of the blob or blob container.

■ *OpenWrite/Read* opens a stream for reading or writing the blob's contents.

■ *Properties* returns the blob's system properties.

■ *SnapshotTime* returns the *DateTime* value that uniquely identifies the snapshot (only when the blob is a snapshot).

■ *Upload(ByteArray/File/FromStream/Text)* uploads data from a byte array, file, stream, or string to a blob.

■ *Uri* returns the blob or container's address.

Container and blob naming rules

You should be aware of several naming rules for blobs and their containers. A blob container name must be between 3 and 63 characters in length; start with a letter or number; and contain only letters, numbers, and the hyphen. All letters used in blob container names must be lowercase. Lowercase is required because using mixed-case letters in container names may be problematic. Locating trouble in a failing application related to the incorrect use of mixed-case letters might result in a lot of wasted time and endless amounts of frustration and confusion.

To make matters a bit confusing, blob names *can* use mixed-case letters. In fact, a blob name can contain any combination of characters as long as the reserved URL characters are properly escaped. The length of a blob name can range from as short as 1 character to as long as 1024 characters.

If you inadvertently violate any of these naming rules, you receive an HTTP 400 (Bad Request) error code from the data storage service, resulting in a *StorageClientException* being thrown if you are accessing blob storage using the Windows Azure software development kit (SDK).

You are not prohibited from using mixed casing in code, though, but some irregularities may adversely impact you when you do use it. For example, if you create a container properly in lowercase, but then later attempt to use that container in mixed-cased requests, your requests will all succeed because the mixed case container name is silently matched with the lowercase container name. This silent but menacing casing coercion can lead you to really scratch your head during debugging, so I strongly urge you to commit to memory the rule that blob container names must not contain uppercase letters.

Performing create, read, update, and delete blob operations

Blobs contain many operations for saving and retrieving data to and from storage. You'll begin with the simple operation of creating a new blob container and populating it with your first blob.

Blob container security

It is useful for you to organize your blobs into storage containers by grouping data with the same security requirements into the same containers (or sets of identically secured containers, as may be appropriate). This strategy should include grouping blobs that your application requires anonymous (public) read-only access to (which is our next topic). Because each blob can be referenced directly from the Internet using its URI, delivery of anonymous public read-only content to web browsers is one of the most useful purposes of blob storage. If blobs in the same container have differing security requirements, you probably want to re-factor your design until they don't. Blob containers are full-access when the request is made with the Windows Azure account key or public read-only (where anyone with the URL to the blob or blob container can read its contents and its metadata), or they might be more granular when the request is made with a Shared Access Signature. Each of these security models is covered in this chapter.

The Windows Azure account key should generally be kept secret, because it's really the key to the entire data fiefdom controlled by a single Windows Azure data storage account. Your application using the account key is similar to Microsoft SQL Server using an account with database owner authority. This trusted application model is generally adequate for many on-premise applications and services. However, you may want to give some attention and analysis to the security ramifications of using the trusted application model in your cloud architectures. The risks go up considerably when you're no longer operating behind the safety and protection of your corporate firewall, where identities are managed and under the careful control and scrutiny of your corporate personnel department, IT staff, and infrastructure team. You may also want to give some thought to using different storage accounts for different applications (or sets of applications) in order to compartmentalize your data so that the leak of one application's credentials is not a threat to the data of other applications.

Anonymous (public) read-only blob access

In the business use-case section of this chapter, I suggested that blob web content could be placed in Windows Azure blob storage, which the markup code could simply reference. To enable this scenario, the content must be publicly accessible via an unauthenticated web request. Most content on the web is public read-only data, but by default, blob containers do not allow public access, so to enable this business use-case, you have to set your permissions on your blob containers to grant the desired level of access to anonymous users. Blob storage is the only type of data storage in Windows Azure that allows public read-only access. (Unauthenticated public access is not available for Windows Azure table or queue storage.)

By default, no public access is granted to a blob container or the blobs it encapsulates. You will learn later in this chapter how you can change this setting to Blob to allow public access to individual blobs stored in the container or to Container, which grants public read-only access to the blob container and all the blobs contained therein. It is not possible to set public read-only access on an individual blob—only on its container.

Creating the blob container

You can create a new blob container named *demo* by sending an HTTP *PUT* request to the URI of the blob container location. The following request creates a new container called *demo* in the *azureinsiders* storage account.

```
PUT http://azureinsiders.blob.core.windows.net/demo?restype=container&timeout=90 HTTP/1.1
x-ms-version: 2012-02-12
User-Agent: WA-Storage/2.0.0
x-ms-date: Mon, 17 Dec 2012 05:32:31 GMT
Authorization: SharedKey azureinsiders:+TRYhpqkDgZ6WlgG37l0qa+d/5tfvZXyYqpEKjaDs9w=
Host: azureinsiders.blob.core.windows.net
Content-Length: 0
```

The preceding code results in an HTTP status code 201 (Created) upon its successful completion.

```
HTTP/1.1 201 Created
Transfer-Encoding: chunked
Last-Modified: Mon, 17 Dec 2012 05:32:31 GMT
ETag: "0x8CFAA2F0B3FF8C8"
Server: Windows-Azure-Blob/1.0 Microsoft-HTTPAPI/2.0
x-ms-request-id: 79eea64c-7f01-4193-a6a5-1d918868dac8
x-ms-version: 2012-02-12
Date: Mon, 17 Dec 2012 05:32:31 GMT
0
```

In the Wintellect.DevCloudAppsAzureStorage project in the sample code, locate the *Blob-Patterns.Basics* method in *StoragePatterns.cs*. The *Basics* method, part of which is shown in the following code, accepts a *CloudStorageAccount*, which is a container around security credentials and storage endpoint addresses. You create a container named *demo* if one doesn't already exist.

```
// Use an OperationContext for debugging and to estimate billing
OperationContext oc = new OperationContext();
oc.SendingRequest += (Object s, RequestEventArgs e) => {
    HttpWebRequest request = e.Request;
};
oc.ResponseReceived += (Object s, RequestEventArgs e) => {
    HttpWebRequest request = e.Request;
    HttpWebResponse response = e.Response;
    RequestResult rr = e.RequestInformation;
};

CloudBlobClient client = account.CreateCloudBlobClient();

// Create a container:
CloudBlobContainer container = client.GetContainerReference("demo");
Boolean created = container.CreateIfNotExists(null, oc);
```

Listing storage account containers

After the blob container demo has been created in the storage account, you should be able to see it in storage. The following HTTP request against the *azureinsiders* storage account augments the URI with the query string parameter *?comp=list,* which in turn causes Windows Azure storage service to return a list of all blob containers for the storage account specified by the URI.

```
GET http://azureinsiders.blob.core.windows.net/?comp=list&timeout=90 HTTP/1.1
x-ms-version: 2012-02-12
User-Agent: WA-Storage/2.0.0
x-ms-date: Mon, 17 Dec 2012 05:55:22 GMT
Authorization: SharedKey azureinsiders:7QR/PWux3s6anFSQR2gSV5UPUvPInEuh+jeO8R3sflk=
Host: azureinsiders.blob.core.windows.net
```

The preceding code returns a response containing an enumeration of blob containers for the storage account.

```
HTTP/1.1 200 OK
Transfer-Encoding: chunked
Content-Type: application/xml
Server: Windows-Azure-Blob/1.0 Microsoft-HTTPAPI/2.0
x-ms-request-id: 7e1a5018-0080-472a-b817-33df3bb82f09
x-ms-version: 2012-02-12
Date: Mon, 17 Dec 2012 05:55:21 GMT

2F5
<?xml version="1.0" encoding="utf-8"?>
  <EnumerationResults AccountName="http://azureinsiders.blob.core.windows.net/">
    <Containers>
      <Container>
        <Name>demo</Name>
        <Url>http://azureinsiders.blob.core.windows.net/demo</Url>
        <Properties>
          <Last-Modified>Mon, 17 Dec 2012 05:32:31 GMT</Last-Modified>
          <Etag>"0x8CFAA2F0B3FF8C8"</Etag>
          <LeaseStatus>unlocked</LeaseStatus>
          <LeaseState>available</LeaseState>
        </Properties>
      </Container>
      <Container>
        <Name>manyblobs</Name>
        <Url>http://azureinsiders.blob.core.windows.net/manyblobs</Url>
        <Properties>
          <Last-Modified>Tue, 05 Jun 2012 00:14:02 GMT</Last-Modified>
          <Etag>"0x8CF10C73F0E2A12"</Etag>
          <LeaseStatus>unlocked</LeaseStatus>
          <LeaseState>available</LeaseState>
        </Properties>
      </Container>
    </Containers>
  <NextMarker />
</EnumerationResults>
0
```

If you're using the Windows Azure storage client, the *ListContainers* method of the storage client will return an *IEnumerable<CloudBlobContainer>*.

```
// Show this account's containers:
foreach (var c in client.ListContainers(null, ContainerListingDetails.None,
operationContext: oc))
    Console.WriteLine(c.Uri);
```

At this point, you have an empty blob container. The following code creates and populates two empty blobs in that blob container.

```
// Create 2 blobs in the container:
CloudBlockBlob blob = container.GetBlockBlobReference("SomeData.txt");
using (var stream = new MemoryStream(("Some data created at " + DateTime.Now).Encode())) {
    blob.UploadFromStream(stream, operationContext: oc);
}
```

```
using (var stream = new MemoryStream()) {
    blob.DownloadToStream(stream, operationContext: oc);
    stream.Seek(0, SeekOrigin.Begin);
    Console.WriteLine(new StreamReader(stream).ReadToEnd());    // Read the blob data back
}
```

With the blob container and blobs created, you are ready to explore permissions settings.

Setting blob container permissions

Container permissions control public read-only access (public access) to a blob container and the blobs it contains. It is not possible to set public access permission on an individual blob. This permission is applicable only to blob containers. An individual blob inherits its public access characteristic by virtue of the container's permission. To control public access to the blob container and its contents, perform an HTTP *PUT* operation against the URI of the blob container, setting the x-ms-blob-public-access header to one of three values listed in Table 5-1. (Note that the header is all lowercase letters, whereas the object model of the API depicted in Table 5-1 is Pascal-cased.) A value of *container* grants anonymous public read-only access to a blob container and its contents, a value of *blob* grants the same access but only to the blobs in the container, and a value of *off* prohibits any anonymous access.

In the following example, you are indicating that public access is being granted to the container and all of the blobs that it may contain.

```
PUT http://azureinsiders.blob.core.windows.net/demo?
    restype=container&comp=acl&timeout=90 HTTP/1.1
x-ms-version: 2012-02-12
User-Agent: WA-Storage/2.0.0
x-ms-blob-public-access: container
x-ms-date: Mon, 17 Dec 2012 06:54:11 GMT
Authorization: SharedKey azureinsiders:NYvU1XRWqZCFXhtPQu/o80FiKe8aKOlOSXAbHeyEOUY=
Host: azureinsiders.blob.core.windows.net
Content-Length: 62

<?xml version="1.0" encoding="utf-8"?><SignedIdentifiers />
```

Successful execution of the preceding HTTP *PUT* request will result in an HTTP status code 200 (OK).

```
HTTP/1.1 200 OK
Transfer-Encoding: chunked
Last-Modified: Mon, 17 Dec 2012 06:54:11 GMT
ETag: "0x8CFAA3A745859B4"
Server: Windows-Azure-Blob/1.0 Microsoft-HTTPAPI/2.0
x-ms-request-id: 54cea7b5-26b7-444c-b3a5-10a251e779ad
x-ms-version: 2012-02-12
Date: Mon, 17 Dec 2012 06:54:10 GMT
```

Public access may be granted through the Windows Azure client library, too. A *BlobContainer-Permissions* object is used to control public access to a blob container and the blobs it contains. An instance of *BlobContainerPermissions* has a *PublicAccess* property, which can be set to one of three values, as shown in Table 5-1.

TABLE 5-1 Blob container public access permission settings

Setting	Public read-only access
Off	Grant no public access to the container or the blobs stored in the container.
Blob	Grant public read-only access to all of the blobs stored in the container, but not to the container itself.
Container	Grant public read-only access to the container and all of the blobs stored in the container.

To grant public access permissions to the blob container and its blob contents, you create an instance of *BlobContainerPermissions* and set its *PublicAccess* property to *BlobContainerPublicAccessType.Container*. You then call the container's *SetPermissions* method, passing in the permission object. There are three values to the *BlobContainerPublicAccessType*: *Off* (the default) prohibits public read-only access to the container and its blobs; *Blob* grants access to the blobs in the container (but not the container itself); and *Container* grants access to read the container and the blobs it encapsulates. The next bit of code illustrates this.

```
// Change container's security to allow read access to its blobs:
BlobContainerPermissions permissions = new BlobContainerPermissions {
    PublicAccess = BlobContainerPublicAccessType.Container
};
container.SetPermissions(permissions, operationContext: oc);

// Attempt to access a blob from browser & in code (succeeds):
Process.Start("IExplore", container.Uri.ToString()).WaitForExit();
using (var stream = new MemoryStream()) {
    anonymous.GetContainerReference("demo").GetBlockBlobReference("SomeData.txt")
        .DownloadToStream(stream, operationContext: oc);
    Console.WriteLine("Download result: " + stream.GetBuffer().Decode());
    Console.WriteLine();
}

// Show the container's blobs via REST:
Process.Start("IExplore", container.Uri + "?comp=list").WaitForExit();
```

The blob container *demo* has the default public read-only permission of *off*, meaning that any attempt to read the blobs located in this container without credentials will fail. To test this assertion and prove this point, you launch a web browser to the URL of the blob you uploaded. You then attempt to access one of the blobs using code to demonstrate that this also fails.

```
// Change container's security to allow read access to its blobs:
BlobContainerPermissions permissions = new BlobContainerPermissions {
    PublicAccess = BlobContainerPublicAccessType.Container
};
container.SetPermissions(permissions, operationContext: oc);

// Attempt to access a blob from browser & in code (succeeds):
Process.Start("IExplore", container.Uri.ToString()).WaitForExit();
using (var stream = new MemoryStream()) {
    anonymous.GetContainerReference("demo").GetBlockBlobReference("SomeData.txt")
        .DownloadToStream(stream, operationContext: oc);
    Console.WriteLine("Download result: " + stream.GetBuffer().Decode());
    Console.WriteLine();
}
```

```
// Show the container's blobs via REST:
Process.Start("IExplore", container.Uri + "?comp=list").WaitForExit();
```

Now when you launch Windows Internet Explorer on the blob's URL, the contents of the blob are displayed. Because the container is now set to allow public read access, you can launch a browser directly against the blob container's URL, passing the filtration criteria (*?comp=list*) in the query string to list the contents of the blob container, as shown in Figure 5-3.

FIGURE 5-3 A list of the blob container contents is shown here.

You're going to set the *PublicAccess* property of the blob container to *BlobContainerPublicAccess-Type.Off* in the code that follows. This step may seem superfluous because *Off* is the default setting, but you want to ensure clarity of the demonstration, and you also want to ensure that the resulting access you observe is verifiably a result of the Shared Access Signature (SAS) and not a side-effect of anonymous access being granted. (You learn more about SAS in the next sections.) You use the *SetPermissions* method of the blob container to apply the *BlobContainerPermission* object to re-move public access to the blob container and its contents. As mentioned earlier, this is equivalent to executing an HTTP *PUT* operation against the URI of the blob container with the *x-ms-blob-public-access* header set to a value of *off*. Attempting to show the contents of the container or blob in a web browser after applying the permissions results in an HTTP 403 (Forbidden) error code, which proves that no anonymous access is allowed to your blob container. The following code demonstrates this.

```
container.SetPermissions(new BlobContainerPermissions {
    PublicAccess = BlobContainerPublicAccessType.Off });
CloudBlob blob = container.GetBlobReference("test.txt");
blob.UploadText("Data accessed!");
// This fails
Process.Start("IExplore", blob.Uri.ToString()).WaitForExit();
```

Shared Access Signatures and shared access policies

So what do you do when you want to grant to another party more granular control over blobs in a container without providing your private account key? This is where Shared Access Signatures are useful. A *Shared Access Signature* is a bit of cryptographic data that is appended to the query string of the URL that is used by Windows Azure storage to grant more granular control to blobs or their containers for a short period of time. After issued, an SAS is good for 60 minutes by default. This time can be extended by applying a Shared Access Policy to the Shared Access Signature, which will be introduced shortly; however, it is important to keep in mind that the shorter the duration the signature is valid, and the more minimal the authorization granted by the SAS, the stronger the effectiveness of the security the policy provides.

When you execute the following code to create a blob called *test.txt* in the blob container *demo*, and then attempt to access the contents of that blob using its address in your web browser, the attempt fails because the blob container is not public by default.

```
// Create a container (with no access) & upload a blob
```

```
// Create a container (with no access) & upload a blob
CloudBlobContainer container = account.CreateCloudBlobClient()
    .GetContainerReference("demo").EnsureExists();
container.SetPermissions(new BlobContainerPermissions {
    PublicAccess = BlobContainerPublicAccessType.Off
});
CloudBlockBlob blob = container.GetBlockBlobReference("test.txt");
blob.UploadText("Data accessed!");
Process.Start("IExplore", blob.Uri.ToString()).WaitForExit(); // This fails
```

In the following sections, you will grant granular permission to the blob for a specified period of time.

Shared Access Signature

An SAS can be thought of as a security permission filter of your blob or blob container's URI, with many segments providing the data necessary to establish the validity and duration of the signature provided in the *sig* field. The following is an example of what an SAS looks like.

```
http://account.blob.core.windows.net/container/blob
    ? st=2011-01-04T00:06:22Z
    & se=2011-01-04T01:06:22Z
    & sr=b
    & sp=r
    & si=Managers
    & sig=KKW…ldw=
```

The meaning of each segment of the SAS is described in Table 5-2.

TABLE 5-2 Shared Access Signature query string segments

Segment	Query string segment purpose
st	Signed start time (optional) provided in UTC format (for example, 2011-01-04T00:06:22Z).
se	Expiry time provided in UTC format (for example, 2011-01-04T00:06:22Z).
sr	Resource (container's blob or blobs).
sp	Permissions (r)ead/(w)rite/(d)elete/(l)ist. Permissions are supplied as single letters, and must be supplied in this order: *rwdl*. Any combination of these permissions is acceptable as long as they are supplied in the proper order (for example, *rw, rd, rl, wd, wl,* and *dl*). Specifying a permission designation more than once is not allowed.
si	Signature identifier (optional) relates an SAS to a container's shared access policies. The signature identifier must be 64 characters or fewer.
sig	Shared Access Signature. The URL parameters are signed (HMACSHA256) with the account's key.

The permissions that may be applied to a blob container using the *sp* segment are provided in Table 5-3.

TABLE 5-3 Allowable shared access signature permissions

Permission	Description
Read	Read content, properties, metadata, block list for blob (any blob in the container).
Write	Write content, properties, metadata, and block list for blob (any blob in container); copy blob is not supported.
Delete	Delete blob (any blob in the container).
List	Lists blobs in container. (This permission can be granted only to blob containers.)

It is important to note that the generation of a Shared Access Signature is a client-side cryptographic activity that makes use of the storage account key. There are no network requests made of the storage service in order to create one. To create an SAS, you simply take all of the signed query string parameter values delimited by newline characters and then hash this value using the HMACSHA256 algorithm to create the *sig* parameter. Any request received by the storage service bearing an appropriately formatted and cryptographically intact signature will be granted the access defined in the *sp* (permissions) parameter.

Because the security signature and related parameters are provided in the URL, it's very important to pay careful attention to the fact that they are subject to snooping and replay attacks if they are leaked to unintended parties, hijacked by someone sniffing traffic on the wire, or emailed to or from an employee who is ignorant of the security ramifications. You should use an SAS only in a production environment over HTTPS. You should also not use an SAS to expose blobs in a web browser, because the unexpired SAS will be cached in the browser history and hard drive of the client's machine and could be used by an unauthorized party to perform data operations. Similar precautions should be taken to keep applications from storing the SAS in a persistent data store, or from exposing the SAS directly or inadvertently in its clear text form. If the SAS must be stored, you should consider encrypting it. If a user can see the SAS, it's probably not secure enough and you may want to rethink your approach.

If you are using the Windows Azure SDK client libraries for the .NET Framework, the *GetShared-AccessSignature* method of a blob instance will ease your pain in manually constructing an SAS, saving you from having to fool around with a lot of messy URL string manipulations. The following code demonstrates how to create an SAS that is valid for a period of one hour beginning immediately, which will grant its bearer read, write, and delete permissions. You will see more on the *SharedAccess-Policy* and *SharedAccessPermission* classes shortly.

Creating a shared access policy

In the preceding code, you used an instance of a *SharedAccessPolicy* to create an SAS. The policy controls the usage characteristics of the SAS, for example, when it takes effect and how long it is valid. The policy also encapsulates, to the resource being protected, the permission set that you want to grant to the bearer of the SAS.

SharedAccessPermissions is an enumeration of bit flags that can be OR'd together to create the permission set necessary to meet your blob's permission requirements. In the following code, you select a permission set comprising the desired combination of read, write, and delete permissions.

```
Permissions perms = SharedAccessPermissions.Read |
    SharedAccessPermissions.Write |
    SharedAccessPermissions.Delete
```

There is also a *List* permission for use with blob containers.

Applying a shared access policy to a blob container

To apply a shared access policy to a blob, you first must create an instance of *SharedAccessPolicy* and then set its permissions and the effective start and end time properties (given in coordinated universal time, or UTC), as shown in the next bit of code. You can then call the blob's *GetSharedAccess-Signature* method, passing the shared access policy object as an argument to retrieve a signed shared access URL that can be used by callers to perform subsequent CRUD operations granted on the blob (as specified in the shared access policy).

```
// Create an SAS for the blob
var now = DateTime.UtcNow;
SharedAccessPolicy sap = new SharedAccessPolicy {
    // Max=1 hr after start
    SharedAccessStartTime = now,
    SharedAccessExpiryTime = now.AddHours(1),
    Permissions = SharedAccessPermissions.Read |
                SharedAccessPermissions.Write |
                SharedAccessPermissions.Delete
};
String sas = blob.GetSharedAccessSignature(sap);
String sasUri = blob.Uri + sas;
// This succeeds (in Internet Explorer, modify URL and show failure)
Process.Start("IExplore", sasUri).WaitForExit();
```

Alternatively, you can protect the blob and other blobs in the container by adding the Shared Access Policy to the container's collection of shared access policies.

Storing access policies

What if you have more stringent data access requirements than the SAS provides? For example, what if you require additional constraints on the starting or ending times that the SAS will be valid, or you require more granular control over the set of permissions being granted to a data storage item by an SAS? What if you require a means of revoking an SAS after it has been issued?

All of these tighter data access requirements can be met by augmenting a *SharedAccessSignature* with a stored access policy (SAP). Instead of being supplied as part of the query string parameters of the URL, the values that you select for your policy are stored with the data on the storage service. This decouples the SAS from the policy, thus allowing you to modify the parameters without having to re-issue another SAS. You can also revoke access granted to an SAS. The SAP is referenced by the *signedidentifier* field of the URL provided in Table 5-2. A signed identifier is a string containing 64 characters or fewer. You'll see these classes shortly, but first it's a good idea to review how to create a shared access policy through the RESTful API. In order to add new policies to the blob container, you must first retrieve the policies that are already present, as shown in the following HTTP *GET* request.

```
GET http://azureinsiders.blob.core.windows.net/demo
    ?restype=container&comp=acl&timeout=90 HTTP/1.1
x-ms-version: 2012-02-12
User-Agent: WA-Storage/2.0.0
x-ms-date: Tue, 18 Dec 2012 06:13:06 GMT
Authorization: SharedKey azureinsiders:vB79RzKYOVkhdJ9NgMonq7OU4fI9DE4OHOpxipiVQOQ=
Host: azureinsiders.blob.core.windows.net

Authorization: SharedKey azureinsiders:N6SZp4XX6NaC3ZOXHqVC94jTSnoUBQrgDV/By2+OHRU=
Host: azureinsiders.blob.core.windows.net
```

This code returns the collection of policies in the body of the response. In this case, the *SignedIdentifiers* element is empty, showing that you have no stored access policies currently assigned to this blob storage container.

```
HTTP/1.1 200 OK
Transfer-Encoding: chunked
Content-Type: application/xml
Last-Modified: Tue, 18 Dec 2012 06:09:29 GMT
ETag: "0x8CFAAFD5FEF12F7"
Server: Windows-Azure-Blob/1.0 Microsoft-HTTPAPI/2.0
x-ms-request-id: a34d3e7d-29a5-4742-8efa-7acab29aff4c
x-ms-version: 2012-02-12
Date: Tue, 18 Dec 2012 06:13:05 GMT

3E
<?xml version="1.0" encoding="utf-8"?>
<SignedIdentifiers />
0
```

To add a policy, you execute an HTTP *PUT* request against the blob container's URI with the *comp=acl* query string parameter set. The body of the request contains a payload of signed identifiers. These signed identifiers represent the policies to be applied on the Windows Azure storage service side of the network for the blob container that is specified as the target of the request, as shown in the next code. Notice the *SignedIdentifier* ID is *Managers* and the *Permission* element has a value of *rw*.

```
PUT http://azureinsiders.blob.core.windows.net/demo
     ?restype=container&comp=acl&timeout=90 HTTP/1.1
x-ms-version: 2012-02-12
User-Agent: WA-Storage/2.0.0
x-ms-date: Tue, 18 Dec 2012 06:28:02 GMT
Authorization: SharedKey azureinsiders:Oya7S8vBgOqBTBaKU3AMSL8ljnpiE9XAJrLq7kD1HYA=
Host: azureinsiders.blob.core.windows.net
Content-Length: 232

<?xml version="1.0" encoding="utf-8"?>
<SignedIdentifiers>
  <SignedIdentifier>
    <Id>Revokable-12/18/2012 6:28:00 AM</Id>
    <AccessPolicy>
    <Start />
    <Expiry />
    <Permission>rw</Permission>
    </AccessPolicy>
  </SignedIdentifier>
</SignedIdentifiers>
```

Like the preceding example, the following code snippet creates a shared access policy—with the Windows Azure client library—that grants read and write permissions on a blob container that has a signature identifier of *Managers*. The signature identifier is allowed to be any string up to 64 characters in length.

```
// Alternatively, we can add the SAP policies to the container with a name:
String signatureIdentifier = "Revokable-" + DateTime.UtcNow;
var permissions = container.GetPermissions();
// NOTE: A container can have up to 5 SAP policies
permissions.SharedAccessPolicies.Add(signatureIdentifier,
    new SharedAccessBlobPolicy {
        Permissions = SharedAccessBlobPermissions.Read |
                    SharedAccessBlobPermissions.Write
    });
container.SetPermissions(permissions);
```

Note A blob container can have a maximum of five policies assigned to it at one time. If you attempt to create more than five access policies, the sixth will result in the service returning status code 400 (Bad Request).

The *SharedAccessPolicy* cannot specify what is already present in the signature identifier.

```
// This SharedAccessPolicy CAN'T specify what is already present in the Signature Identifier
sas = blob.GetSharedAccessSignature(new SharedAccessBlobPolicy {
    SharedAccessStartTime = start,
    SharedAccessExpiryTime = start.AddYears(10)
}, signatureIdentifier);
sasUri = blob.Uri + sas;
Process.Start("IExplore", sasUri);
```

Revoking SAS permissions

After the SAS has served its useful purpose, it may be necessary or desirable (as a precautionary measure) to revoke the granted permissions. This is accomplished by simply removing the *Signature-Identifier* from the collection and performing another HTTP *PUT* operation against the blob container's URI. There is really no difference between adding or deleting a stored SAS policy because they are both accomplished in an identical fashion: by simply providing a complete list of the permissions.

```
PUT http://azureinsiders.blob.core.windows.net/demo
     ?restype=container&comp=acl&timeout=90 HTTP/1.1
x-ms-version: 2012-02-12
User-Agent: WA-Storage/2.0.0
x-ms-date: Tue, 18 Dec 2012 06:28:06 GMT
Authorization: SharedKey azureinsiders:jwtmE3xzpCu7xo/TTqJVWCZVJeO19MnXwNoPQMYdbCI=
Host: azureinsiders.blob.core.windows.net
Content-Length: 62

<?xml version="1.0" encoding="utf-8"?>
<SignedIdentifiers />
```

With the Windows Azure client library, the container's signature identifier can be used to revoke the SAS permission as follows.

```
// We can now revoke access on the container:
permissions.SharedAccessPolicies.Remove(signatureIdentifier);
container.SetPermissions(permissions);
Process.Start("IExplore", sasUri); // This fails now
```

Blob attributes and metadata

Containers and blobs support two types of ancillary data: system properties and user-defined metadata. System properties exist on every blob and blob container. Some properties are read-only, whereas others can be set. A few of them correspond to specific standard HTTP headers, which the Windows Azure SDK will maintain for you. User-defined metadata allows you to define supplementary name-value dictionary information about the blob container or the blob. As its name implies, metadata should be used to store data about your data (not the data itself). This can sometimes be a matter of perspective.

Blob containers have attributes that describe both the containers' URI and Name. Each container has two read-only properties: *LastModifiedUtc*, which is the UTC time that the blob container was last updated; and *ETag*, which is a version number used for optimistic concurrency. Blob containers also provide 8 KB of customizable metadata in the form of a name-value pair dictionary, which you can use for your own purposes. Metadata should be used to store information about the blob or the blob's container. For example, you might store the name of the person who last read the contents of a blob in its metadata, and possibly the date and time the access was made.

The following HTTP *PUT* request demonstrates how to set metadata values. The query string *comp=metadata* sets up the operation. The values for the metadata are transmitted via HTTP *x-ms-meta-<name>* headers, where *<name>* is the name you are giving your metadata, and the value of the HTTP header is the value of your named metadata. The following example shows this.

```
PUT http://azureinsiders.blob.core.windows.net/demo/ReadMe.txt?comp=metadata&timeout=90 HTTP/1.1
x-ms-version: 2012-02-12
User-Agent: WA-Storage/2.0.0
x-ms-meta-CreatedBy: Paul
x-ms-meta-SourceMachine: DILITHIUM
x-ms-date: Tue, 18 Dec 2012 07:05:23 GMT
Authorization: SharedKey azureinsiders:02TWst4Dx5Qgr0zq31w7AvENcc+0ez06+HobJ4qZMlY=
Host: azureinsiders.blob.core.windows.net
Content-Length: 0
```

The following code demonstrates how to use the Windows Azure client library to store metadata containing the person's name and the machine that person was using when they created the blob.

```
container.SetPermissions(new BlobContainerPermissions() {
PublicAccess = BlobContainerPublicAccessType.Container });
CloudBlob blob = container.GetBlobReference("ReadMe.txt");
blob.UploadText("This is some text");
blob.Attributes.Metadata["CreatedBy"] = "Paul";
blob.Metadata["SourceMachine"] = Environment.MachineName;
blob.SetMetadata();
// NOTE: SetMetadata & SetProperties update the blob's ETag & LastModifiedUtc
```

When you launch Internet Explorer on the blob's URL, the contents of the blob are displayed. Similar to what you did previously, you can launch a browser directly against the blob container's URL, passing the filtration criteria *?restype=container&comp=list&include=metadata* in the query string. The following code will launch Internet Explorer to list the contents of the blob container, including its properties and any metadata.

```
// Get blobs in container showing each blob's properties & metadata
// See http://msdn.microsoft.com/en-us/library/dd135734.aspx for more options
Process.Start("IExplore", container.Uri +
        "?restype=container&comp=list&include=metadata").WaitForExit();
```

You can also retrieve a list of blobs, including properties and metadata, programmatically using the Windows Azure client library. First, pass an instance of *BlobRequestOptions* with its *BlobListing-Details* property set to *BlobListingDetails.Metadata*. Then call the *FetchAttributes* method on the blob proxy. The *FetchAttributes* method will include properties and metadata.

```
container.ListBlobs(new BlobRequestOptions {
    BlobListingDetails = BlobListingDetails.Metadata });
blob.FetchAttributes();
```

The following code then loops through the collection of the blob's properties and metadata and displays the corresponding value for each.

```
// Read the blob's attributes (which include properties & metadata)
blob.FetchAttributes();
BlobProperties p = blob.Properties;
Console.WriteLine("Blob's metadata (LastModifiedUtc={0}, ETag={1})",
        p.LastModifiedUtc, p.ETag);

Console.WriteLine("   Content Type={0}, Encoding={1}, Language={2}, MD5={3}",
    p.ContentType, p.ContentEncoding, p.ContentLanguage, p.ContentMD5);
Console.WriteLine();
foreach (String keyName in blob.Metadata.Keys)
    Console.WriteLine("   {0} = {1}", keyName, blob.Metadata[keyName]);
```

Conditional operations

It is often desirable to perform an operation on data only when particular conditions can be satisfied. It's better still when such operations can be conditionally performed by the data storage service rather than burden the client application, because doing so reduces the time and costs associated with transporting data to the application. Filtration operations limit the consumable data to a subset of the complete set of data available, so transporting all of the data across the wire simply to discard portions of that data upon evaluation wastes time, bandwidth, and ultimately money.

Although the evaluation can often be done by the application on the client side of the wire, multiple requests may be necessary to retrieve and evaluate data. In addition to the cost and time of transmitting large volumes of unnecessary data, the elapsed time also increases the probability of a data collision when one application attempts to perform an operation on an entity, but before that operation can take place, another application performs a successful operation on it, which renders the first application's copy of the entity as stale. Most blob operations can be performed conditionally based on their date of modification, or their *ETag*.

Conditional operations using REST

Conditional operations are implemented in blob storage by including one of four optional HTTP headers in the request, including a corresponding date and time or *ETag* value, as shown in Table 5-4.

TABLE 5-4 Conditional operation HTTP headers

HTTP header	Specified value
If-Modified-Since	*DateTime*
If-Unmodified-Since	*DateTime*
If-Match	*ETag* or wildcard (*)
If-None-Match	*ETag* or wildcard (*)

Reading data conditionally using the If-Modified-Since header can save unnecessary network bandwidth and data processing time (as well as associated costs for data transmission) by only transmitting the data when it's modified. When the condition cannot be met, an HTTP status code is returned that indicates the reason the condition was not met. Table 5-5 lists these HTTP status codes.

TABLE 5-5 HTTP response codes returned for unsatisfied conditions

Conditional header	HTTP response codes when condition is not met	
If-Modified-Since	304	Not Modified
If-Unmodified-Since	412	Precondition Failed
If-Match	412	Precondition Failed
If-None-Match	304	Not Modified

Conditional operations using the Windows Azure client library

The Windows Azure client library provides a convenient programming grammar for performing conditional operations. This grammar abstracts the setting of the underlying HTTP header to give a more comfortable and intuitive programming model to the developer. To explore conditional operations, you first need a blob in storage. Given a *CloudStorageAccount* credential object, the following code snippet sets up a proxy to blob storage, creates a blob named *Data.txt*, and uploads some data (the string *"Data"*) into that blob. It also sets up a retry policy, which you will see later in this chapter, and establishes timeouts.

```
// Create a blob and attach some metadata to it:
CloudBlobClient client = account.CreateCloudBlobClient();

// No retry for 306 (Unused), 4xx, 501 (Not Implemented), 505 (HTTP Version Not Supported)
client.RetryPolicy = new ExponentialRetry();

// Time server can process a request (default = 90 secs)
client.ServerTimeout = TimeSpan.FromSeconds(90);
```

```
// Time client can wait for response across all retries (default = disabled)
client.MaximumExecutionTime = TimeSpan.FromSeconds(5);

CloudBlobContainer container = client.GetContainerReference("demo").EnsureExists();
CloudBlockBlob blob = container.GetBlockBlobReference("Data.txt");
using (var stream = new MemoryStream("Data".Encode())) {
    blob.UploadFromStream(stream);
}
```

Conditional reads

Now that your test blob has been uploaded to storage, you can create an instance of *BlobRequest-Options* and set its *AccessCondition* property to an appropriate value to try various conditional means of retrieving it. The values of this property correspond directly with the HTTP headers shown in Table 5-4. Let's say that you want to retrieve the contents of the blob but only if that content has been updated. You may have a copy of the blob you've cached, and you don't want to waste valuable resources continuously re-fetching the same data you already have. You want to expend resources only when there is something new to retrieve. You can accomplish this using the *IfModified-Since* method. First, you want to simulate what happens when the blob has not been updated by another party, so you pass the *LastModifiedUtc* property of the blob to the *IfModifiedSince* method, knowing that this condition could never be met and that you will deliberately fail, as depicted in the following code.

```
// Download blob content if newer than what we have:
try {
    blob.DownloadText(
        AccessCondition.GenerateIfModifiedSinceCondition(
            blob.Properties.LastModified.Value)); // Fails
}
catch (StorageException ex) {
    Console.WriteLine(String.Format("Failure: Status={0}({0:D}), Msg={1}",
        (HttpStatusCode)ex.RequestInformation.HttpStatusCode,
        ex.RequestInformation.HttpStatusMessage));
}
```

You can do the inverse of the previous example by reading a blob only if its contents have not been modified since a specified date using the *IfNotModifiedSince* static method of the *AccessCondition* class. You might do this as part of a process for archiving an older date. Here is the code for this.

```
// Download blob content if more than 1 day old:
try {
    blob.DownloadText(
        AccessCondition.GenerateIfNotModifiedSinceCondition(
            DateTimeOffset.Now.AddDays(-1))); // Fails
}
catch (StorageException ex) {
    Console.WriteLine(String.Format("Failure: Status={0}({0:D}), Msg={1}",
        (HttpStatusCode)ex.RequestInformation.HttpStatusCode,
        ex.RequestInformation.HttpStatusMessage));
}
```

Conditional updates

You can perform updates conditionally, too. For example, many applications require optimistic concurrency when updating data. You want to replace an existing blob's contents, but only if someone hasn't updated the blob since you last retrieved it. If the blob was updated by another party, consider your copy of the blob to be stale and handle it according to your application's business logic for a concurrency collision. You accomplish this by using the static *IfMatch* method of the *AccessCondition* class to conditionally perform an action only if the properties match. If no updates are made to the target blob, the *ETag* properties of two blobs are identical and the update succeeds. If an update has occurred to the targeted blob (for example, the *ETag* properties do not match), a *StorageClient-Exception* exception is thrown.

```
// Upload new content if the blob wasn't changed behind your back:
try {
    blob.UploadText("Succeeds",
        AccessCondition.GenerateIfMatchCondition(blob.Properties.ETag)); // Succeeds
}
catch (StorageException ex) {
    Console.WriteLine(String.Format("Failure: Status={0}({0:D}), Msg={1}",
        (HttpStatusCode)ex.RequestInformation.HttpStatusCode,
         ex.RequestInformation.HttpStatusMessage));
}
```

When contention is encountered in an optimistic concurrency scenario, the usual countermeasure is to catch the exception, notify the requesting user or application of the contention, and then offer the option of fetching a fresh copy of the data. Generally, this means that the user has lost his revisions and must reapply his edits to the fresh copy before re-attempting to save his changes.

Another common application requirement is to create a blob in storage, but only if the blob doesn't already exist. You can use the asterisk wildcard character to match on any value. In the following code, when no properties match anything (for example, the blob does not already exist), you proceed with uploading. If the blob already exists, a *StorageClientException* is thrown. Generally, in production code, you should catch this exception and handle the situation according to the specific requirements of your application.

```
// Upload your content if it doesn't already exist:
try {
    // Fails
    blob.UploadText("Fails", AccessCondition.GenerateIfNoneMatchCondition("*"));
}
catch (StorageException ex) {
    Console.WriteLine(String.Format("Failure: Status={0}({0:D}), Msg={1}",
        (HttpStatusCode)ex.RequestInformation.HttpStatusCode,
         ex.RequestInformation.HttpStatusMessage));
}
```

Blob leases

Windows Azure storage provides a locking mechanism called a *lease* for preventing multiple parties from attempting to write to the same blob. A *blob lease* provides exclusive write access to the blob. After a lease is acquired, a client must include the active lease ID with the write request. The client has a one-minute window from the time the lease is acquired to complete the write; however, the lease can be continuously renewed to extend this time indefinitely to meet your application's needs.

A lease request may be performed in one of four modes:

- **Acquire**   Request a new lease.

- **Renew**   Renew an existing lease.

- **Release**   Release the lease, which allows another client to immediately acquire a lease on the blob.

- **Break**   End the lease, but prevent other clients from acquiring a new lease until the current lease period expires.

Taking a lease on a blob can also be used as a very convenient and inexpensive locking semantic for other cloud operations. For example, one Windows Azure Cloud Services instance might take a lease on a blob as means of signaling other instances that the resource is busy. Other instances would then be required to check for the existence of a lease before proceeding with a competing operation. If a lock is present, the competing operation can be held in a loop until the blob lock is released. When used in this manner, the blob lease acts as a traffic light. The competing instances stop when the traffic light is red (for example, the lock is present) and proceed when it turns green (for example, the lock was removed).

The following HTTP *PUT* request demonstrates how to acquire a lease on a blob. The query string *comp=lease* sets up the operation. The action to be taken on the lease is transmitted via the x-ms-lease-action HTTP header, as the following example demonstrates.

```
PUT http://azureinsiders.blob.core.windows.net/demo/test.txt
    ?comp=lease&timeout=90 HTTP/1.1
x-ms-version: 2012-02-12
User-Agent: WA-Storage/2.0.0
x-ms-lease-action: acquire
x-ms-lease-duration: 30
x-ms-date: Wed, 26 Dec 2012 08:36:22 GMT
Authorization: SharedKey azureinsiders:YsBInVJ6NhkAIgkuUk9647JbpEthVnZR1WAOcYRM1Hc=
Host: azureinsiders.blob.core.windows.net
Content-Length: 0
```

In the following Windows Azure client library code, you call the *AcquireLease* method on a blob and then show the blob's contents in Internet Explorer to prove you can perform reads against blobs that have leases. Immediately after, you attempt to acquire a second lease on the same blob. Always wrap your attempts to acquire a lease inside of a try/catch block, and always confirm that the *WebException*'s status code is a Conflict status code, because the *WebException* could have been caused by any one of a number of possible conditions.

```
String leaseId = blob.AcquireLease(TimeSpan.FromSeconds(30), null);

// Succeeds: reads are OK while a lease is obtained
Process.Start("IExplore", blob.Uri.ToString()).WaitForExit();

// Try to acquire another lease:
try {
    leaseId = blob.AcquireLease(TimeSpan.FromSeconds(30), null);
}
catch (StorageException ex) {
    if ((HttpStatusCode)ex.RequestInformation.HttpStatusCode !=
        HttpStatusCode.Conflict) throw;
    Console.WriteLine(ex.RequestInformation.HttpStatusMessage);
}
```

You next demonstrate that the lease prevents writing to the blob until you supply a valid lease ID.

```
// Fails: Writes are not OK while a lease is held:
try {
    blob.UploadText("Can't upload while lease held without lease ID");
}
catch (StorageException ex) {
    if ((HttpStatusCode)ex.RequestInformation.HttpStatusCode !=
        HttpStatusCode.Conflict) throw;
    Console.WriteLine(ex.RequestInformation.HttpStatusMessage);
}
// Succeeds: Writes are OK if we specify a lease Id:
try {
    leaseId = blob.AcquireLease(TimeSpan.FromSeconds(30), null);
}
catch { } // Ensure we have the lease before doing the PUT
```

To release the lease on a blob via the RESTful API, simply execute another HTTP *PUT* against the blob's URI by using a query string parameter *comp=lease*, and set *x-ms-lease-action* to *Release*, as shown here.

```
PUT http://azureinsiders.blob.core.windows.net/demo/test.txt
    ?comp=lease&timeout=90 HTTP/1.1
x-ms-version: 2012-02-12
User-Agent: WA-Storage/2.0.0
x-ms-lease-id: a9053786-c96e-4bb9-8711-477fbd7fcb03
x-ms-lease-action: release
x-ms-date: Sun, 30 Dec 2012 02:29:22 GMT
Authorization: SharedKey azureinsiders:LJEakr84hNV6nStrTAgBzZdo3k5OGlHy3f2syVuRrEM=
Host: azureinsiders.blob.core.windows.net
Content-Length: 0
```

To release a blob using the Windows Azure client library, call the *ReleaseLease* method and pass in the lease ID, as shown in this code snippet.

```
blob.ReleaseLease(AccessCondition.GenerateLeaseCondition(leaseId));
Process.Start("IExplore", blob.Uri.ToString()).WaitForExit();
```

Finally, after you have released your lease on the blob, you can update its contents to demonstrate how the lease is no longer preventing writing to the blob. You bring the contents up in the browser to visually verify that the contents were updated.

```
blob.UploadText("Data uploaded while lease NOT held");
Process.Start("IExplore", blob.Uri.ToString()).WaitForExit();
```

Using block blobs

As you learned earlier in this chapter, block blobs segment your data into chunks, or blocks. The size of one of these chunks is 4 MB or smaller.

When you upload data using the block semantics, you must provide a block ID, which is stored with your data; the stream that you are uploading your data from; and an MD5 hash of your data that is used to verify the successful transfer but is not stored. Uploaded blocks are stored in an uncommitted state. After uploading all of the blocks and calling the *Commit* method, the uncommitted blobs become committed in an atomic transaction. There is a restriction that the final blob be no greater than 200 GB after it is committed. An exception is thrown if this value is exceeded. If you don't commit an uploaded blob within seven days, Windows Azure storage deletes them.

The block ID is an array of 64 bytes (or fewer) that is base64-encoded for transport over the HTTP protocol.

Another useful characteristic of block blobs is that they can be uploaded in parallel to increase throughput, providing you have unused CPU power and available network bandwidth.

In the following code, you create an array of three strings (*A*, *B*, and *C*) that represents three distinct single-character blocks of data that you want to place in blob storage. You encode this array of strings into a memory stream using UTF8 encoding and then, for every block, you call the *PutBlock* method, passing your block ID, the stream containing your data, and an MD5 hash of the data being put into blob storage.

Hashes must be calculated and blocks must be apportioned before they can be stored, so you will start with the Windows Azure client library code for this example, and then look at the RESTful representation of this code immediately thereafter.

```
// Put 3 blocks to the blob verifying data integrity
String[] words = new[] { "A ", "B ", "C " };
var MD5 = new MD5Cng();
for (Int32 word = 0; word < words.Length; word++) {
    Byte[] wordBytes = words[word].Encode(Encoding.UTF8);
```

```
      // Azure verifies data integrity during transport; failure=400 (Bad Request)
      String md5Hash = MD5.ComputeHash(wordBytes).ToBase64String();
      blockBlob.PutBlock(word.ToBlockId(), new MemoryStream(wordBytes), md5Hash);
}
```

Execution of the preceding code causes three HTTP *PUT* requests to be made against data storage—one for each of the three blocks containing the data *A*, *B* and *C*. The *comp=block* parameter controls the kind of blob you are updating, and the *blockid*=<blockid> (where the *<blockid>* represents a unique block identifier).

```
PUT http://azureinsiders.blob.core.windows.net/demo/MyBlockBlob.txt
    ?comp=block&blockid=MDAwMDA%3D&timeout=90 HTTP/1.1
x-ms-version: 2012-02-12
User-Agent: WA-Storage/2.0.0
Content-MD5: ZOO5/MV88bFp+O72x61VOg==
x-ms-date: Sun, 30 Dec 2012 03:02:12 GMT
Authorization: SharedKey azureinsiders:tM/FIZZnnzdb1fFIjgD+hb/wiHHOFyFvGN1JPx82TPo=
Host: azureinsiders.blob.core.windows.net
Content-Length: 2
Connection: Keep-Alive

A


HTTP/1.1 201 Created
Transfer-Encoding: chunked
Content-MD5: ZOO5/MV88bFp+O72x61VOg==
Server: Windows-Azure-Blob/1.0 Microsoft-HTTPAPI/2.0
x-ms-request-id: 34e2df15-088f-46e1-af4e-6c10ef390940
x-ms-version: 2012-02-12
Date: Sun, 30 Dec 2012 03:02:15 GMT


0


PUT http://azureinsiders.blob.core.windows.net/demo/MyBlockBlob.txt
    ?comp=block&blockid=MDAwMDE%3D&timeout=90 HTTP/1.1
x-ms-version: 2012-02-12
User-Agent: WA-Storage/2.0.0
Content-MD5: CUf4UWGwWRnZaUDz3hSFLg==
x-ms-date: Sun, 30 Dec 2012 03:02:14 GMT
Authorization: SharedKey azureinsiders:6ednOFFuqGuoe3qt9cmMtYD6OkLChpFFddBm3BEtx9k=
Host: azureinsiders.blob.core.windows.net
Content-Length: 2

B


HTTP/1.1 201 Created
Transfer-Encoding: chunked
Content-MD5: CUf4UWGwWRnZaUDz3hSFLg==
Server: Windows-Azure-Blob/1.0 Microsoft-HTTPAPI/2.0
x-ms-request-id: ca5790b6-d889-43d5-ab24-a21a21617fbf
x-ms-version: 2012-02-12
Date: Sun, 30 Dec 2012 03:02:16 GMT


0
```

```
PUT http://azureinsiders.blob.core.windows.net/demo/MyBlockBlob.txt
    ?comp=block&blockid=MDAwMDI%3D&timeout=90 HTTP/1.1
x-ms-version: 2012-02-12
User-Agent: WA-Storage/2.0.0
Content-MD5: Q600VNgdC/J0zJ/wCXMiQw==
x-ms-date: Sun, 30 Dec 2012 03:02:15 GMT
Authorization: SharedKey azureinsiders:uc4Ttlza/fqoi5lYtXpYKqbhTLQoeojDOnvAGFf50C8=
Host: azureinsiders.blob.core.windows.net
Content-Length: 2

C


HTTP/1.1 201 Created
Transfer-Encoding: chunked
Content-MD5: Q600VNgdC/J0zJ/wCXMiQw==
Server: Windows-Azure-Blob/1.0 Microsoft-HTTPAPI/2.0
x-ms-request-id: 90adf2d6-7ea9-4b58-90a9-41d23e47de36
x-ms-version: 2012-02-12
Date: Sun, 30 Dec 2012 03:02:18 GMT

0
```

All three uploaded blocks of your block blob remain in an uncommitted state until you call *Commit* on them. You can verify this by downloading a list of uncommitted block IDs using the *DownLoad-BlockList* method and passing in a filter of *Uncommitted*. Two other values in the *BlockListingFilter* enumeration—*All* and *Committed*—allow you to download a list of all blocks or only those blocks that have been committed, respectively.

```
Console.WriteLine("Blob's uncommitted blocks:");
foreach (ListBlockItem lbi in blockBlob.DownloadBlockList(BlockListingFilter.Uncommitted))
    Console.WriteLine("  Name={0}, Length={1}, Committed={2}",
        lbi.Name.FromBlockId(), lbi.Length, lbi.Committed);
// Fails
try {
    blockBlob.DownloadText();
}
catch (StorageException ex) {
    Console.WriteLine(String.Format("Failure: Status={0}({0:D}), Msg={1}",
        (HttpStatusCode)ex.RequestInformation.HttpStatusCode,
         ex.RequestInformation.HttpStatusMessage));
}
```

Executing the preceding code demonstrates that the three uploaded blobs all have an uncommitted status and any attempt to download the uncommitted blob will result in failure.

```
Blob's uncommitted blocks:
   Name=0, Size=2, Committed=False
   Name=1, Size=2, Committed=False
   Name=2, Size=2, Committed=False
Failure: Status=NotFound, Msg=The specified blob does not exist.
```

You can request a list of all uncommitted blobs directly by sending an HTTP *GET* request to the blob's URI, the query string parameter *comp=blocklist*, and *blocklisttype=Uncommitted*, as shown here.

```
GET http://azureinsiders.blob.core.windows.net/demo/MyBlockBlob.txt
    ?comp=blocklist&blocklisttype=Uncommitted&timeout=90 HTTP/1.1
x-ms-version: 2012-02-12
User-Agent: WA-Storage/2.0.0
x-ms-date: Sun, 30 Dec 2012 04:28:08 GMT
Authorization: SharedKey azureinsiders:zKdrwpdnKaQX8UKeq3COblqvMc3BDBhmmmDdWSuS4Wo=
Host: azureinsiders.blob.core.windows.net
```

You are not limited to placing blocks in storage one at a time, or even in the same order that you have them arranged. In fact, in some applications, it may even be desirable to upload the same block multiple times at different positions within the blob, or to completely change the order in which the blocks exist. Imagine scenarios in which blocks of data are reorganized based on sorting some element of their content.

```
// Commit the blocks in order (and multiple times):
blockBlob.PutBlockList(new[] { 0.ToBlockId(), 0.ToBlockId(), 1.ToBlockId(), 2.ToBlockId() });
// Succeeds
try {
    blockBlob.DownloadText();
}
catch (StorageException ex) {
    Console.WriteLine(String.Format("Failure: Status={0}({0:D}), Msg={1}",
        (HttpStatusCode)ex.RequestInformation.HttpStatusCode,
        ex.RequestInformation.HttpStatusMessage));
}

Console.WriteLine("Blob's committed blocks:");
foreach (ListBlockItem lbi in blockBlob.DownloadBlockList())
    Console.WriteLine("   Name={0}, Length={1}, Committed={2}",
        lbi.Name.FromBlockId(), lbi.Length, lbi.Committed);
```

Executing the preceding code commits the changes and produces the following results, confirming that the blobs are now all committed and that the *A* blob was committed twice.

```
Blob's committed blocks:
    Name=0, Size=2, Committed=True
    Name=0, Size=2, Committed=True
    Name=1, Size=2, Committed=True
    Name=2, Size=2, Committed=True
A A B C
```

As you might anticipate from the pattern that is emerging, you can request a list of all committed blobs directly by sending an HTTP *GET* request to the blob's URI and the query string parameter *comp=blocklist*, and *blocklisttype=Committed* as follows.

```
GET http://azureinsiders.blob.core.windows.net/demo/MyBlockBlob.txt
    ?comp=blocklist&blocklisttype=Committed&timeout=90 HTTP/1.1
x-ms-version: 2012-02-12
User-Agent: WA-Storage/2.0.0
x-ms-date: Sun, 30 Dec 2012 21:52:11 GMT
Authorization: SharedKey azureinsiders:AMEqUfAuSg6oub4/zz+aE5LB3S6qbXxSNLipOoCNOxs=
Host: azureinsiders.blob.core.windows.net
```

Blocks might represent discrete segments of data that are organized like scenes in a movie, where you want to delete some scenes and change the order of others. The block blob API supports this kind of functionality. You can delete blocks just by excluding their *BlockIDs* from the *BlockList* body of your request, and you can reorder your blocks by changing their order in the list. This is shown in the following HTTP request, which deletes block *0* and saves block *2* before block *1*. It may be a little hard to see this directly, because the *BlockIDs* are base64-encoded in the BlockList, but you can easily modify the sample code shown a little later to see how the body of the message is changed by the block order.

```
PUT http://azureinsiders.blob.core.windows.net/demo/MyBlockBlob.txt
    ?comp=blocklist&timeout=90 HTTP/1.1
x-ms-version: 2012-02-12
User-Agent: WA-Storage/2.0.0
x-ms-blob-content-type: application/octet-stream
Content-MD5: uO2OSdbs3agLOJthlv1b4w==
x-ms-date: Sun, 30 Dec 2012 22:03:32 GMT
Authorization: SharedKey azureinsiders:IcJMoA2vWMPVfWKOf2NzzpqwR5hi1JOuPB8poQef8D4=
Host: azureinsiders.blob.core.windows.net
Content-Length: 114
Connection: Keep-Alive

<?xml version="1.0" encoding="utf-8"?>
<BlockList>
    <Latest>MDAwMDI=</Latest>
    <Latest>MDAwMDE=</Latest>
</BlockList>
```

The following code snippet shows how you can delete blocks by excluding their *BlockIDs* when you call *PutBlockList using the Windows Azure client library*. In the following code snippet, you delete block *0* and your duplicate block *1*, and save block *2* before block *1*.

```
// You can change the block order & remove a block:
blockBlob.PutBlockList(new[] { 2.ToBlockId(), 1.ToBlockId() });
// Succeeds
try {
    blockBlob.DownloadText();
}
catch (StorageException ex) {
    Console.WriteLine(String.Format("Failure: Status={0}({0:D}), Msg={1}",
        (HttpStatusCode)ex.RequestInformation.HttpStatusCode,
        ex.RequestInformation.HttpStatusMessage));
}
```

After executing the preceding code, you can verify that block A was deleted and blob C appears before block B by executing an HTTP *GET* against the blob's URI, as shown here.

```
GET http://azureinsiders.blob.core.windows.net/demo/MyBlockBlob.txt?timeout=90 HTTP/1.1
x-ms-version: 2012-02-12
User-Agent: WA-Storage/2.0.0
x-ms-date: Mon, 31 Dec 2012 07:04:54 GMT
Authorization: SharedKey azureinsiders:NhZ/aPp3HEtB6tMyT1NMj4BD4LRvySi8YV5/1BfQAwk=
Host: azureinsiders.blob.core.windows.net
```

The full blob as committed is returned as the response to this request. You can see the *C B* content in the body of the message response.

```
HTTP/1.1 200 OK
Content-Length: 4
Content-Type: application/octet-stream
Last-Modified: Mon, 31 Dec 2012 07:04:53 GMT
Accept-Ranges: bytes
ETag: "0x8CFB53C446E71CD"
Server: Windows-Azure-Blob/1.0 Microsoft-HTTPAPI/2.0
x-ms-request-id: 3523b2a0-1069-4e01-8f7a-8210f4e60612
x-ms-version: 2012-02-12
x-ms-lease-status: unlocked
x-ms-lease-state: available
x-ms-blob-type: BlockBlob
Date: Mon, 31 Dec 2012 07:04:54 GMT

C B
```

When you upload a blob that is greater than 32 MB, the *Upload*Xxx operations automatically break your upload up into 4-MB blocks, upload each block with *PutBlock*, and then commit all blocks with the *PutBlockList* method. The block size can be changed by modifying the *WriteBlockSizeInBytes* property of your client proxy (for example, your instance of *CloudBlobClient*), as shown in the following commented code block.

```
// The client library can automatically upload large blobs in blocks:
// 1. Define size of "large blob" (range=1MB-64MB, default=32MB)
client.SingleBlobUploadThresholdInBytes = 32 * 1024 * 1024;

// 2. Set individual block size (range=1MB-4MB, default=4MB)
client.WriteBlockSizeInBytes = 4 * 1024 * 1024;

    // 3. Set # of blocks to simultaneously upload (range=1-64, default=# CPUs)
    client.ParallelOperationThreadCount = Environment.ProcessorCount;
```

Using page blobs

Page blobs add the features of random access and sparse population to the blob storage story, and they quintuple the maximum size from 200 MB to 1 terabyte. Page blobs were added to Windows Azure storage to enable development of the VHD virtual drive abstraction. They are also useful in fixed-length logging scenarios, where rolling overwrite of the oldest data in the log may be desired.

The sparse feature is nice because it allows you to allocate a storage amount up to 1 terabyte, but you are charged only for the pages that you place in the blob, no matter how much storage space you allocate. When reading and writing page blobs, you're required to read and write your data in page-sized chunks that begin on a page boundary.

In the following sample code, you create an array of 5 bytes (integers 1 through 5), and you write that data to page 0. Next, you create an array of 5 bytes (descending integers 5 through 1), and you write that data to page 2. There is no significance to the integers I selected for this example beyond demonstrating that you can read and write data in sparsely populated pages that begin on page boundaries.

```
const Int32 c_BlobPageSize = 512;
Console.Clear();
CloudBlobClient client = account.CreateCloudBlobClient();
CloudBlobContainer container = client.GetContainerReference("demo").EnsureExists();
CloudPageBlob pageBlob = container.GetPageBlobReference("MyPageBlob.txt");
pageBlob.DeleteIfExists();

// You must create a page blob specifying its size:
pageBlob.Create(10 * c_BlobPageSize);

Byte[] data = new Byte[1 * c_BlobPageSize];  // Must be multiple of page size

// Write some data to Page 0 (offset 0):
Array.Copy(new Byte[] { 1, 2, 3, 4, 5 }, data, 5);
pageBlob.WritePages(new MemoryStream(data), 0 * c_BlobPageSize); // Offset 0
// Write some data to Page 2 (offset 1024):
Array.Copy(new Byte[] { 5, 4, 3, 2, 1 }, data, 5);
pageBlob.WritePages(new MemoryStream(data), 2 * c_BlobPageSize); // Offset 1024

// Show committed pages:
foreach (PageRange pr in pageBlob.GetPageRanges())
    Console.WriteLine("Start={0,6:N0}, End={1,6:N0}", pr.StartOffset, pr.EndOffset);

// Read the whole blob (with lots of 0's):
using (var stream = new MemoryStream()) {
    pageBlob.DownloadToStream(stream);
    data = stream.GetBuffer();
}
Console.WriteLine("Downloaded length={0:N0}", data.Length);
Console.WriteLine(
    "  Page 0 data: " + BitConverter.ToString(data, 0 * c_BlobPageSize, 10));
Console.WriteLine(
    "  Page 1 data: " + BitConverter.ToString(data, 1 * c_BlobPageSize, 10));
Console.WriteLine(
    "  Page 2 data: " + BitConverter.ToString(data, 2 * c_BlobPageSize, 10));
```

At this point of execution, you have only two 512-byte pages in a 10-page, sparsely populated blob (pages 4–9 would look identical to pages 1 and 3). The first page blob starts at byte 0 and ends at byte 511, and the second one starts at byte 1024 and ends at byte 1535. When you loop through the pages of the blob and display the bytes that are in each page, you can see that pages 0 and 2 contain the bytes you uploaded, whereas pages 1, 3, and 4–10 all return zeros. You are being charged only for the two pages you stored, but the blob behaves as if all 10 pages were populated.

From this output, you might be tempted to think that uploading a page of zeros would be treated as a nonexistent page. Unfortunately, it would be incorrect to make such an assumption. A page must be cleared from the collection of pages in a blob in order for it to return to a nonexistent sparse state and for you to avoid being billed. You use the *ClearPages* method of the page blob in the code that follows to do this. Pages of zeros are considered part of the blob's official population, and you will be billed for their storage.

Over the network, the data is transmitted as HTTP *PUT* requests with the query string parameter *comp=page*, the HTTP header *x-ms-range* indicating the byte range, and *x-ms-page-write* indicating the type of operation being performed (*Update* in this example).

```
PUT http://azureinsiders.blob.core.windows.net/demo/MyPageBlob.txt
?comp=page&timeout=90 HTTP/1.1
x-ms-version: 2012-02-12
User-Agent: WA-Storage/2.0.0
x-ms-range: bytes=0-511
x-ms-page-write: Update
x-ms-date: Mon, 31 Dec 2012 07:45:32 GMT
Authorization: SharedKey azureinsiders:MLh8U/RxECpksvMuHdgzn2KD0Q6CSUH1ku4NJPb7MJI=
Host: azureinsiders.blob.core.windows.net
Content-Length: 512<unprintable data>
```

After writing the pages to blob storage, as shown in the preceding code, there are two 512-byte pages in a sparsely populated 5,120-byte page blob.

```
Start=0, End=511
Start=1024, End=1535
Downloaded length=5,120
   Page 0 data: 01-02-03-04-05-00-00-00-00-00
   Page 1 data: 00-00-00-00-00-00-00-00-00-00
   Page 2 data: 05-04-03-02-01-00-00-00-00-00
   Page 3 data: 00-00-00-00-00-00-00-00-00-00
```

You can continue modifying blobs by page. The following code shows reading a specific page range, clearing a set of pages, and then committing those changes.

```
// Read a specific range from the blob (offset 1024, 10 bytes):
using (var stream = new MemoryStream()) {
    pageBlob.DownloadRangeToStream(stream, 2 * c_BlobPageSize, 10);
    stream.Seek(0, SeekOrigin.Begin);
    data = new BinaryReader(stream).ReadBytes((Int32)stream.Length);
    Console.WriteLine("  Page 2 data: " + BitConverter.ToString(data, 0, 10));
}

// Clear a range of pages (offset 0, 512 bytes):
pageBlob.ClearPages(0, 512);

// Show committed pages:
foreach (PageRange pr in pageBlob.GetPageRanges())
    Console.WriteLine("Start={0,6:N0}, End={1,6:N0}", pr.StartOffset, pr.EndOffset);
```

After clearing the bytes in page 0 with the *ClearPages* method, only page 2 remains committed in this page blob. You use the *GetPageRanges* method to return a list of pages and then iterate over the result to prove that there is only one remaining with a starting position of 1,024 and an ending position of 1,535.

Blob snapshots

Blob storage supports a very powerful feature called snapshots. Like the name might imply, *snapshots* operate in a manner similar to photographs. You can take as many snapshots of a family member over time as you want. The resulting set of photographic snapshots form a chronology of the changes to your subject over time. Likewise, a snapshot in blob storage is a record of a blob's state at a particular point in time. To maintain efficient use of storage, Windows Azure storage stores only the delta between the previous version and the current version of the blob. Although snapshots may be deleted, they are immutable and provide an audit trail of the changes as well as a convenient mechanism for rolling back changes.

This powerful feature provides a rich and cost-effective versioning mechanism for your documents, images, and other artifacts. Consider the number of times that business documents such as sales orders, purchase orders, or contracts might be revised before being agreed to. Consider also the desire that business people may have to keep snapshots of those documents for use in mitigating disputes.

In the RESTful API of Windows Azure storage, snapshots are identified by using an opaque value supplied as a query string parameter to the blob's URI. Although the documentation states that this is an opaque value and can therefore be changed without notice, it sure looks a lot like a time stamp! The following shows an example.

```
http://.../cotnr/blob.dat?snapshot=2011-05-14T18:25:53.6230000Z
```

Creating the original blob

To create the blob in storage for this example, issue an HTTP *PUT* request against blob storage as follows.

```
PUT http://azureinsiders.blob.core.windows.net/demo/Original.txt?timeout=90 HTTP/1.1
x-ms-version: 2012-02-12
User-Agent: WA-Storage/2.0.0
x-ms-blob-type: BlockBlob
Content-MD5: vfup6ZfBEO5+wonANUivGw==
x-ms-date: Mon, 31 Dec 2012 08:13:20 GMT
Authorization: SharedKey azureinsiders:7NDtxB5cVOSveodezKGFTe8NFWXGgIHgs294Aq6IrdI=
Host: azureinsiders.blob.core.windows.net
Content-Length: 13

Original data
```

Windows Azure storage will respond with an HTTP status code of 201 (Created) to confirm the successful upload of your data.

```
HTTP/1.1 201 Created
Transfer-Encoding: chunked
Content-MD5: vfup6ZfBEO5+wonANUivGw==
Last-Modified: Mon, 31 Dec 2012 08:13:22 GMT
ETag: "0x8CFB545D5F2B219"
Server: Windows-Azure-Blob/1.0 Microsoft-HTTPAPI/2.0
x-ms-request-id: 579553cf-d37b-46aa-b1ed-8e4841993c02
x-ms-version: 2012-02-12
Date: Mon, 31 Dec 2012 08:13:20 GMT

0
```

You can perform this action using the Windows Azure client library by uploading contents into blob storage after acquiring a reference to the blob, as shown here.

```
// Create the original page blob (512 1s & 2s):
CloudBlob origBlob = container.GetBlobReference("Original.txt");
origBlob.UploadText("Original data");
```

Creating the blob's snapshot

The value of the *SnapshotTime* property contains the date and time the snapshot was taken. The following code retrieves the *SnapshotTime* value, which you can use to identify this specific blob snapshot later on.

```
PUT http://azureinsiders.blob.core.windows.net/demo/Original.txt
    ?comp=snapshot&timeout=90 HTTP/1.1
x-ms-version: 2012-02-12
User-Agent: WA-Storage/2.0.0
x-ms-date: Mon, 31 Dec 2012 08:13:20 GMT
Authorization: SharedKey azureinsiders:h164Br8QbritWbEiDG8OBnUjH8B/hxiFCQ1+ZIPqwRQ=
Host: azureinsiders.blob.core.windows.net
Content-Length: 0
```

Windows Azure responds to your snapshot request by returning another HTTP 201 (Created) status code similar to the following.

```
HTTP/1.1 201 Created
Transfer-Encoding: chunked
Last-Modified: Mon, 31 Dec 2012 08:13:22 GMT
ETag: "0x8CFB545D5F2B219"
Server: Windows-Azure-Blob/1.0 Microsoft-HTTPAPI/2.0
x-ms-request-id: 6e88ae98-a68a-46e5-a734-25a76a55e92e
x-ms-version: 2012-02-12
x-ms-snapshot: 2012-12-31T08:13:23.0482586Z
Date: Mon, 31 Dec 2012 08:13:21 GMT

0
```

You can perform the same action with the client library by calling the blob's *CreateSnapshot* method, which returns a cloud blob reference, and then caching the snapshot's *SnapshotTime* property (which returns the value of the HTTP *ETag* header).

```
// Create a snapshot of the original blob & save its timestamp:
CloudBlob snapshotBlob = origBlob.CreateSnapshot();
DateTime? snapshotTime = snapshotBlob.SnapshotTime;
```

You can prove that the snapshot cannot be updated by attempting to upload new data into it and noting that it fails.

```
// Try to write to the snapshot blob:
try { snapshotBlob.UploadText("Fails"); }
catch (ArgumentException ex) { Console.WriteLine(ex.Message); }
```

A similar attempt to upload data into the original blob, however, succeeds.

```
PUT http://azureinsiders.blob.core.windows.net/demo/Original.txt?timeout=90 HTTP/1.1
x-ms-version: 2012-02-12
User-Agent: WA-Storage/2.0.0
x-ms-blob-type: BlockBlob
Content-MD5: zgYkAjIEXVBppjaEcT9nLg==
x-ms-date: Mon, 31 Dec 2012 08:13:21 GMT
Authorization: SharedKey azureinsiders:sRxSV/eOIdHBsOHSQU6QMmfY1pMZl5LsqNPuQGaQkVs=
Host: azureinsiders.blob.core.windows.net
Content-Length: 8

New data

Resulting in another HTTP result status code of 201 (Created):

HTTP/1.1 201 Created
Transfer-Encoding: chunked
Content-MD5: zgYkAjIEXVBppjaEcT9nLg==
Last-Modified: Mon, 31 Dec 2012 08:13:23 GMT
ETag: "0x8CFB545D6138160"
Server: Windows-Azure-Blob/1.0 Microsoft-HTTPAPI/2.0
x-ms-request-id: f9e86330-6de5-402a-b592-0e65abb75c03
x-ms-version: 2012-02-12
```

```
Date: Mon, 31 Dec 2012 08:13:21 GMT

0
```

Of course, you can perform this same operation using the client library. You can also add code to perform a comparison of the two normal and snapshot blobs for additional verification.

```
// Modify the original blob & show it:
origBlob.UploadText("New data");
Console.WriteLine(origBlob.DownloadText());      // New data
Console.WriteLine();

// Show snapshot blob via original blob URI & snapshot time:
snapshotBlob = container.GetBlockBlobReference(
"Original.txt", snapshotTime);
Console.WriteLine(snapshotBlob.DownloadText());  // Original data


// Show all blobs in the container with their snapshots:
foreach (ICloudBlob b in
    container.ListBlobs(null, true, BlobListingDetails.Snapshots)) {
    Console.WriteLine("Uri={0}, Snapshot={1}", b.Uri, b.SnapshotTime);
}
```

Listing snapshots

If you're using snapshots, you might find it necessary in your application to obtain a list of all of the snapshots that exist for your blobs. To retrieve a list of all blobs in the container, issue an HTTP *GET* command against the resource, passing the query string parameters *restype=container&comp=list& include=snapshots&timeout=90.*

```
GET http://azureinsiders.blob.core.windows.net/demo
    ?restype=container&comp=list&include=snapshots&timeout=90 HTTP/1.1
x-ms-version: 2012-02-12
User-Agent: WA-Storage/2.0.0
x-ms-date: Mon, 31 Dec 2012 08:13:21 GMT
Authorization: SharedKey azureinsiders:xEkszk1RQ+WTGa7nfZfbP9QDQz8JWh7Fh7fPplxIvuE=
Host: azureinsiders.blob.core.windows.net

HTTP/1.1 200 OK
Transfer-Encoding: chunked
Content-Type: application/xml
Server: Windows-Azure-Blob/1.0 Microsoft-HTTPAPI/2.0
x-ms-request-id: 3f3d3919-aef4-4289-97c7-4fad8d655747
x-ms-version: 2012-02-12
Date: Mon, 31 Dec 2012 08:13:21 GMT

4D2
<?xml version="1.0" encoding="utf-8"?>
<EnumerationResults ContainerName="http://azureinsiders.blob.core.windows.net/demo">
  <Blobs>
    <Blob>
      <Name>Original.txt</Name>
```

```
    <Snapshot>2012-12-31T08:13:23.0482586Z</Snapshot>
    <Url>http://azureinsiders.blob.core.windows.net/demo/Original.txt
        ?snapshot=2012-12-31T08%3a13%3a23.0482586Z</Url>
    <Properties>
      <Last-Modified>Mon, 31 Dec 2012 08:13:22 GMT</Last-Modified>
      <Etag>0x8CFB545D5F2B219</Etag>
      <Content-Length>13</Content-Length>
      <Content-Type>application/octet-stream</Content-Type>
      <Content-Encoding />
      <Content-Language />
      <Content-MD5>vfup6ZfBE05+wonANUivGw==</Content-MD5>
      <Cache-Control />
      <BlobType>BlockBlob</BlobType>
    </Properties>
  </Blob>
  <Blob>
    <Name>Original.txt</Name>
    <Url>http://azureinsiders.blob.core.windows.net/demo/Original.txt</Url>
    <Properties>
      <Last-Modified>Mon, 31 Dec 2012 08:13:23 GMT</Last-Modified>
      <Etag>0x8CFB545D6138160</Etag>
      <Content-Length>8</Content-Length>
      <Content-Type>application/octet-stream</Content-Type>
      <Content-Encoding />
      <Content-Language />
      <Content-MD5>zgYkAjIEXVBppjaEcT9nLg==</Content-MD5>
      <Cache-Control />
      <BlobType>BlockBlob</BlobType>
      <LeaseStatus>unlocked</LeaseStatus>
      <LeaseState>available</LeaseState>
    </Properties>
  </Blob>
  </Blobs>
<NextMarker />
</EnumerationResults>
0
```

To retrieve a listing of blob snapshots in a container by using the Windows Azure client library, set an instance of the *BlobRequestOptions* class's *BlobListingDetails* property equal to *BlobListing-Details.Snapshots*, which is passed to the *ListBlobs* method of your blob container, as shown in the following code snippet.

```
// Show all blobs in the container with their snapshots:
foreach (ICloudBlob b in container.ListBlobs(null, true, BlobListingDetails.Snapshots))
{
    Console.WriteLine("Uri={0}, Snapshot={1}", b.Uri, b.SnapshotTime);
}
```

Running the preceding code produces the following output.

```
Original data
Uri=http://azureinsiders.blob.core.windows.net/demo/Original.txt,
    Snapshot=12/31/2012 8:13:23 AM +00:00
Uri=http://azureinsiders.blob.core.windows.net/demo/Original.txt, Snapshot=
Original data
```

As stated earlier, snapshots are an immutable record of your data taken at a given point in time. Snapshots, like photographs, may be read, copied, or deleted, but not altered. And just as you might produce an altered copy of an original photograph with a photo editing program, you can produce an altered copy of a blob with blob snapshots. Although you cannot update a blob snapshot, you can clone the snapshot to make another writeable blob that can then be modified. There is an efficiency implemented in the Windows Azure REST API through the use of an HTTP header. This efficiency allows creation of the snapshot clone to be done as a single transactional request; this avoids the requirement of one trip to fetch the source data and another to create the clone. To use this feature, the destination URI establishes the target resource to be updated, and the *x-ms-copy-source* header establishes the source of the data to be copied. The following HTTP *PUT* request shows an example of cloning the *Original.txt* blob to a blob called *Copy.txt*:

```
PUT http://azureinsiders.blob.core.windows.net/demo/Copy.txt?timeout=90 HTTP/1.1
x-ms-version: 2012-02-12
User-Agent: WA-Storage/2.0.0
x-ms-copy-source: http://azureinsiders.blob.core.windows.net/demo/Original.txt
    ?snapshot=2012-12-31T08%3A13%3A23.0482586Z
x-ms-date: Mon, 31 Dec 2012 08:13:21 GMT
Authorization: SharedKey azureinsiders:TEhQVnfZF/kLbbTVYCpzQlCn5UHrF9QRBzSWKBOohz8=
Host: azureinsiders.blob.core.windows.net
Content-Length: 0
```

Upon successful execution of the *PUT* operation, Windows Azure returns an HTTP status code 201 (Created).

```
HTTP/1.1 202 Accepted
Transfer-Encoding: chunked
Last-Modified: Mon, 31 Dec 2012 08:13:23 GMT
ETag: "0x8CFB545D63BA3D7"
Server: Windows-Azure-Blob/1.0 Microsoft-HTTPAPI/2.0
x-ms-request-id: 2b087f91-b3eb-4cc6-844f-b45e4de85aeb
x-ms-version: 2012-02-12
x-ms-copy-id: ebe42e0e-4094-4aff-a244-32a951f00562
x-ms-copy-status: success
Date: Mon, 31 Dec 2012 08:13:21 GMT

0
```

Using the Windows Azure client library, you can clone a snapshot of the blob by creating the target blob (in this case, *Copy.txt*), and then calling the *CopyFromBlob* method, passing an instance of the snapshot blob in as an argument. The following code demonstrates this technique.

```
// Create writable blob from the snapshot:
CloudBlockBlob writableBlob = container.GetBlockBlobReference("Copy.txt");
writableBlob.StartCopyFromBlob(snapshotBlob);
Console.WriteLine(writableBlob.DownloadText());
writableBlob.UploadText("Success");
Console.WriteLine(writableBlob.DownloadText());
```

Deleting snapshots

You can delete a blob and all of its snapshots, or you can delete individual snapshots from a blob; however, you are not allowed to delete a blob without also deleting all of its snapshots.

```
DELETE http://azureinsiders.blob.core.windows.net/demo/Original.txt?timeout=90 HTTP/1.1
x-ms-version: 2012-02-12
User-Agent: WA-Storage/2.0.0
x-ms-delete-snapshots: include
x-ms-date: Mon, 31 Dec 2012 08:13:21 GMT
Authorization: SharedKey azureinsiders:IAOrqcWDrjJUTBkM6jg+YKC6gLOCJvTTBVFai+wC8mQ=
Host: azureinsiders.blob.core.windows.net
```

Upon successful deletion of your blob and all of its snapshots, the Windows Azure storage service returns an HTTP status code 202 (Accepted) response.

```
HTTP/1.1 202 Accepted
Transfer-Encoding: chunked
Server: Windows-Azure-Blob/1.0 Microsoft-HTTPAPI/2.0
x-ms-request-id: f2c4f4a4-0319-4c27-a16a-e9bb28078fd6
x-ms-version: 2012-02-12
Date: Mon, 31 Dec 2012 08:13:21 GMT

0
```

When using the Windows Azure client library, snapshot deletion behavior is controlled by the *DeleteSnapshotsOption* property of an instance of the *BlobRequestOptions* class, which is passed as an argument to the *Delete* method of the blob to be deleted. An example of deleting a blob and its snapshots follows.

```
// DeleteSnapshotsOption: None (blob only; throws StorageException if snapshots exist),
// IncludeSnapshots, DeleteSnapshotsOnly
origBlob.Delete(DeleteSnapshotsOption.IncludeSnapshots);
```

Continuation tokens and blobs

A pagination mechanism for data that can be presented in a tabular format is often required because humans generally cannot digest more than a page of information at one time. Also, you want to ensure that the data being requested is appropriate for the query and not a mistake, because you are dealing with potentially massive databases in the cloud. It can take a lot of resources to compute and transmit billions of rows of data over the wire. Windows Azure must also take into account its own scalability; a large query can block or significantly impede many smaller queries, because those smaller queries may have to wait or compete for resources. *Continuation tokens*, as introduced in Chapter 4, allow Windows Azure storage to return a smaller subset of your data. A continuation token imposes upon you, however, to ask for subsequent pages of your data by passing you back a continuation token that you must then use to call back to retrieve subsequent pages of your query. Windows Azure storage refers to these pages of data as *segments*.

Blobs are not tabular data, so you do not have to anticipate continuation tokens when retrieving blobs; however, some of the API does return tabular data such as retrieving a list of blobs stored in a container. Because a container can have an unlimited number of entries, you should always anticipate that you may receive a continuation token back from any request that you make by calling an xxx-*Segmented* retrieval method.

```
Console.Clear();
CloudBlobClient client = account.CreateCloudBlobClient();

// ListContainers/BlobsSegmented return up to 5,000 items
const Int32 desiredItems = 5000 + 1000;   // Try to read more than the max

// Create a bunch of blobs (this takes a very long time):
CloudBlobContainer container = client.GetContainerReference("manyblobs");
container.EnsureExists();
for (Int32 i = 0; i < desiredItems; i++)
    container.GetBlockBlobReference(String.Format("{0:00000}", i)).UploadText("");

// Enumerate containers & blobs in segments
for (ContainerResultSegment crs = null; crs.HasMore(); ) {
    crs = client.ListContainersSegmented(
      null, ContainerListingDetails.None, desiredItems, crs.SafeContinuationToken());
    foreach (var c in crs.Results) {
        Console.WriteLine("Container: " + c.Uri);
        for (BlobResultSegment brs = null; brs.HasMore(); ) {
            brs = c.ListBlobsSegmented(null, true, BlobListingDetails.None,
                desiredItems, brs.SafeContinuationToken(), null, null);
            foreach (var b in brs.Results) Console.WriteLine("   Blob: " + b.Uri);
        }
    }
}
```

In the preceding code, the value of the *ContinuationToken* property of the *ResultSegment* will be either a continuation token or null when there are no more results to read. The following extension method, which is included in the Wintellect Azure Power Library, was used to simplify the programming model. It does this by supplying a Boolean indicator that controls exiting the for-loop when no more result segments are available.

```
public static BlobContinuationToken SafeContinuationToken(
        this ContainerResultSegment crs) {
    return (crs == null) ? null : crs.ContinuationToken;
}Blob request options
```

As used in the preceding code examples, instances of *BlobRequestOptions* may be passed as arguments to blob operations to augment the behavior of a request. The *BlobRequestOptions* class is an assortment of loosely related properties that are applicable during different kinds of operations. Only *Timeout* and *RetryPolicy* are used by all data access storage requests. Table 5-6 describes the properties of *BlobRequestOptions*.

TABLE 5-6 *BlobRequestOptions* properties and their impact on requests

BlobRequestOptions properties	**Impact on requests**
Timeout	Used for all blob operations. The timespan allowed for a given operation to complete before a timeout error condition, which is handled according to the *RetryPolicy* property. See Chapter 4 for more information.
RetryPolicy	Used for all blob operations. Controls the retry policy used when accessing data. See Chapter 4 for more information.
AccessCondition	Used only when performing conditional operations. Controls the conditions for selecting data based on an *ETag* value (for example, *If-Match*, *If-Non-Match*, *If-Modified-Since*, and *If-Not-Modified-Since*).
CopySourceAccessCondition	Used only when performing conditional copy operations on blobs. Controls the conditions for selecting data based on an *ETag* value (for example, *If-Match*, *If-Non-Match*, *If-Modified-Since*, and *If-Not-Modified-Since*).
DeleteSnapshotsOption	Used only when performing delete operations on blobs. *IncludeSnapshots* deletes the blob and all of its snapshots; *DeleteSnapshotsOnly* deletes the snapshots only (leaving the blob); *None*.
BlobListingDetails	Used only when performing blob list operations. Controls the data that is included in the list. Options include the following: *All* lists all available committed blobs, uncommitted blobs, and snapshots, and returns all metadata for those blobs. ■ *Metadata* retrieves blob metadata for each blob returned in the listing. ■ *None* lists only committed blobs and does not return blob metadata. ■ *Snapshots* lists committed blobs and blob snapshots. ■ *UncommittedBlobs* lists committed and uncommitted blobs.
UseFlatBlobListing	Used only when performing blob list operations.

Conclusion

The purpose of this chapter was to provide you with a thorough understanding of how to securely perform data operations against the blob storage service. You were first introduced to how primary data operations are accomplished against the two kinds of blobs supported by Windows Azure storage and the organizations container structure that encapsulates them. You learned how to navigate this structure as if it was a hierarchical directory using the storage API and about the metadata that can be used to augment them.

This chapter then explained the special high-value use of public anonymous containers for supplying Internet-addressable content to your applications. Finally, you learned about many advanced features, such as conditional operations, leases, Shared Access Signatures, Shared Access Policies, snapshots, and continuation tokens.

Tables

In this chapter, you learn about Windows Azure table storage. First, you examine the characteristics of this kind of data storage, including the kinds of real-world data and storage scenarios that lend themselves well to it. You then learn about the organizational structure of this type of storage, including the naming conventions and other rules that must be followed. You learn how to perform common create, read, update, and delete (CRUD) operations on table rows and tables and tackle security access, which allows CRUD operations to be performed only by authorized parties. Finally, you learn how to write applications for robustness and resiliency in the cloud.

Table basics

Windows Azure table storage provides a nonrelational, NoSQL-like database for storage and data operations on structured or semi-structured data. *Semi-structured* means that the data does not have to strictly conform to a given schema and that some variation is allowed (which you will see later in this chapter). The characteristics of table storage minimize some of the difficulties of achieving massive scalability objectives encountered in more traditional relational database systems. Achieving high-volume scalability is the primary goal of Windows Azure table storage.

A *table* can be viewed as a container that provides organizational structure to some quantity of entities, which may be of various types. Tables can automatically scale to accommodate up to 100 terabytes at the time of this writing. An *entity* can be viewed as a container that provides organizational structure to a quantity of related properties. It is a collection of properties that are similar to relational database columns. *Table containers* contain collections of entities that are similar to relational database rows. One of the primary differences between table entities and relational database rows, however, is that table entities can be of differing schemas in the same table, whereas relational database rows require strict adherence to a fixed schema. The properties of an entity are name-value pairs. Each entity can have up to 252 properties and 3 reserved mandatory properties.

Table storage structure

Figure 6-1 shows the hierarchical relationship between storage accounts, tables, and entities. A Windows Azure storage account encapsulates zero or more tables, and each table can in turn encapsulate a set of zero or more entities. Unlike the relational database model, though, in Windows Azure table storage, the entities in a single table may be of differing types. Note in Figure 6-1 how the customers and their orders are placed in one table (the *CustomerOrder* table), and the information about items is placed in another table (the *ItemInfo* table). You will see more about this mixing of schemas in a single table later in this chapter, in the section "Storing multiple entity types in a single table."

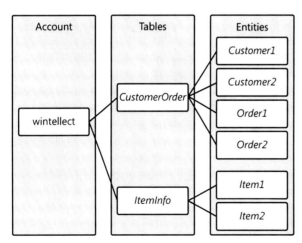

FIGURE 6-1 The table storage structure is a hierarchical relationship between storage accounts, tables, and entities.

To achieve Windows Azure performance objectives, tables frequently span multiple storage nodes. Figure 6-2 shows the *CustomerOrder* table being placed on Storage Node A and Storage Node B. The distribution of data across storage nodes is managed by Windows Azure storage and is based on the value of the *PartitionKey* property of each entity in the table. Entities that share the same *PartitionKey* value must be stored on the same storage node. They may not be distributed. Entities with different *PartitionKey* values may be optionally distributed to other storage nodes when necessary to meet performance objectives.

In Figure 6-2, both *CustomerOrder* and *ItemInfo* have a *PartitionKey* labeled *PartitionKey1*. Although they are both the first partition keys of their respective entities, these two partition keys are not the same. The diagram shows that at a specific moment in time, the third partition key for the *CustomerOrder* table is stored on the same storage node as the first partition key for the *ItemInfo* table. Of course, Windows Azure may shift and move these partition keys around to other storage nodes to adapt to the changing patterns of data use to meet performance objectives.

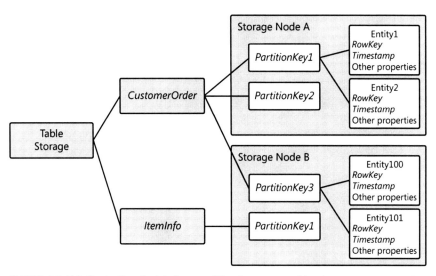

FIGURE 6-2 This illustration depicts how partition keys are used by storage management to automatically distribute entities to storage nodes in order to achieve performance objectives.

Table addressing

Table resources are located in data storage via URLs that match the following pattern:

http://<*account*>.table.core.windows.net/<*tablename*>

The <*account*> placeholder is the Windows Azure account name, and the <*tablename*> placeholder is the name of your table. A little later in this chapter, in the section "Table queries," you will see that the URL query string also supports extensive filtration and ordering features. When using the local development storage emulator, the URL pattern is slightly different from the previous pattern. The *hostname* becomes the IP address of the loopback adapter (that is, 127.0.0.1), to which the port number 10002 and the hardcoded literal account name *devstorageaccount1* are appended to form the complete base address, as depicted in the Storage Emulator window in Figure 6-3. The table name is appended to this base address to form the full URL of the table resource (for example, *http://127.0.0.1:10002/devstorageaccount1/MyTable*).

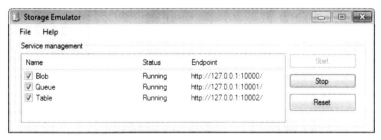

FIGURE 6-3 The endpoint IP address is shown in the Windows Azure Storage Emulator window.

Entity properties

As you learned earlier, a single entity can have a total of 255 properties. Three of these properties—*PartitionKey*, *RowKey*, and *Timestamp*—are reserved mandatory properties that every table schema must implement, but you are allowed to use the other 252 properties for your own purposes. Schemas you use in the same table are not required to share anything except the three mandatory fields.

Each entity is uniquely identified within a table by its primary key. The primary key is formed by concatenating the *PartitionKey* and the *RowKey*.

Entity partitions

A *partition* is a consecutive range of entities identified by a common *PartitionKey* value, which is unique within the table. Tables provide massively scalable storage by allowing the workload to be distributed over multiple storage nodes. The data architect must decide in advance how to best allocate data across multiple storage nodes to maximize performance. The partitioning process is performed automatically by Windows Azure table storage according to the data stored for each entity in its reserved *PartitionKey* property. Windows Azure table storage will not allocate a storage node for each partition; instead, it gathers performance metrics and then automatically moves data to new storage nodes only when necessary to achieve the Service Level Agreement (SLA) performance targets as described in Chapter 4, "Accessing Windows Azure data storage." To achieve SLA targets, a single storage node may serve as few as one partition, but Windows Azure storage will not unnecessarily allocate resources and will automatically scale back when demand for entities on a partition are below the thresholds.

PartitionKey

The *PartitionKey* is a string that may be up to 1,024 characters long and uniquely identifies a partition within a given table. Selecting a *PartitionKey* that is too broad and includes too many entities can hamper performance because Windows Azure storage will never allocate a single partition to more than one storage node. If the storage node serving your partition cannot service requests at the SLA level, performance suffers. Because all data in a partition is served by only one storage node, *PartitionKey* schemes that are too unique or granular can limit your ability to use an Entity Group Transaction (EGT) when you need atomicity, consistency, isolation, and durability (ACID) semantics, because all operations contained in an EGT must share a single *PartitionKey*. Also, schemes that are too unique or granular can impede the performance of data queries and reduce your ability to order your data without additional processing.

RowKey

The *RowKey* is a string that may be up to 1,024 characters long and allows an individual entity to be uniquely identified within a partition. When appended to the entity's *PartitionKey*, the combination forms the entity's *primary key*, which uniquely identifies an entity within its table.

Timestamp

The *Timestamp* property represents an entity's version and is used to implement optimistic concurrency. The value of this field is managed by Windows Azure table storage and may not be set by the client application.

Custom properties

The properties of an entity are name-type-value tuples, where the tuple type is one of the following:

- *String*
- *Byte* arrays
- Nullable and nonnullable:
  - *Guid*
  - *DateTime*
  - *Int32*
  - *Int64*
  - *Double*
  - *Boolean*

Entity Group Transactions

EGTs allow a set of storage operations against a single partition (for example, entities that exist in the same table and share a single *PartitionKey* value) to be executed as a single atomic unit of work with full ACID semantics. A failure to complete any one of the storage operations within the EGT will cause the entire group's operations to be rolled back. You are allowed to encapsulate as many as 100 storage operations in a single EGT as long as the total size of all storage operations to be performed is 4 megabytes (MB) or fewer.

Table and property naming rules

Tables and entities have several naming rules that you need to be aware of. A table name must be unique within a storage account and be between 3 and 63 (inclusive) mixed-case characters in length. This name is case-insensitive, which means that table uniqueness cannot be accomplished by merely varying the casing of letters within a name. For example, a table named *MyTable* is indistinguishable from a table named *mytable*. Property names of an entity can be mixed-case and between 1 and 25 (inclusive) characters in length. If you inadvertently violate any of these naming rules, you receive an HTTP 400 (Bad Request) error. More information about the naming rules is available at *http://msdn.microsoft.com/en-us/library/dd179338.aspx*.

Windows Azure client library table types

The Windows Azure client library takes advantage of the Open Data Protocol (OData) infrastructure already built into the Microsoft .NET Framework 4 Framework Class Library (FCL) through Windows Communication Foundation (WCF) Data Services. Although convenient in some ways because it takes advantage of existing knowledge and infrastructure, the reuse of a library not designed specifically for Windows Azure tables can also be frustrating in some areas. There are a lot of road blocks to be aware of and avoided because not all of the features supported by the library are available in Windows Azure. We'll get to those shortly.

Visualizing table entities

Table storage is capable of much faster performance than relational databases. One reason for this is that table storage doesn't have to support transactions across multiple tables. In a relational database, such transactions would frequently be a requirement to ensure referential integrity. If you added a new customer and its orders to your database but the operation could not be completed in its entirety, you might have customers without their corresponding orders; likewise, and without foreign key constraints, you might end up with orders that have no corresponding customers. This might lead you to erroneously conclude that you cannot store transactional data containing relations in Windows Azure table storage. What you need is a new way of looking at the problem.

Windows Azure table storage allows entities with differing schemas to be stored in the same table. This may seem like a bad idea at first, but later in this chapter, in the section "Storing multiple entity types in a single table," you will see why storing multiple entity types in a single table is a very important feature. As you learned earlier in the chapter, table storage provides the EGT feature, which allows all the mixed entities in a single table sharing a common *PartitionKey* to be operated upon atomically. Table 6-1 shows the data for multiple entity schemas being placed in a single Windows Azure *CustomerOrder* data storage table, which allows storing, retrieving, and updating customers and their associated orders. In Table 6-1, you'll see two customers, Jeff and Paul, plus two orders made by Jeff for milk and cereal.

TABLE 6-1 Sample contents of a *CustomerOrder* table that mixes customer schema with order schema in the same table

PartitionKey (1 KB string)	RowKey (1 KB string)	Timestamp (DateTime)	Entity kind	Name	City	Item	Quantity
Jeff	C_Jeff	012-08-27T17:47:26.4489137Z	Customer	Jeff Chia	Kirkland		
Paul	C_Paul	012-08-27T17:47:26.4489137Z	Customer	Paul Mehner	Olympia		
Jeff	O_Cereal	012-08-27T17:47:26.4489137Z	Order			Cereal	2
Jeff	O_Milk	012-08-27T17:47:26.4489137Z	Order			Milk	1

The three required properties are shown in the first three columns of Table 6-1, and recall that you are allowed 252 additional properties for your own schema definitions and that your schema must share only the three mandatory fields. In this example, customers have a name and a city but do not have items or quantities. Orders have items and quantities but do not have names or cities. Because you are storing mixed schema in the same table, a column has been allocated to store the kind of entity that each row represents, a *Customer* or an *Order*. In the following example, the *Int32* column named *KindCode* has a value of 0 (zero) representing a customer entity.

```
POST http://azureinsiders.table.core.windows.net/Demo()?timeout=90 HTTP/1.1
x-ms-version: 2012-02-12
User-Agent: WA-Storage/2.0.3
Accept: application/atom+xml,application/xml
Accept-Charset: UTF-8
MaxDataServiceVersion: 2.0;NetFx
DataServiceVersion: 2.0;
Content-Type: application/atom+xml;type=entry;charset=utf-8
x-ms-date: Mon, 14 Jan 2013 01:12:57 GMT
Authorization: SharedKeyLite azureinsiders:Ro2F/u//C85HgbkFhhB31es1NzrT1/lsKc5Lkvj8+Jw=
Host: azureinsiders.table.core.windows.net
Content-Length: 530

<?xml version="1.0" encoding="utf-8"?>
<entry xmlns=http://www.w3.org/2005/Atom
       xmlns:d=http://schemas.microsoft.com/ado/2007/08/dataservices
       xmlns:m="http://schemas.microsoft.com/ado/2007/08/dataservices/metadata">
    <id />
    <title />
    <updated>2013-01-14T01:12:57Z</updated>
    <author><name /></author>
    <content type="application/xml">
        <m:properties>
```

```
            <d:Name>Jeff</d:Name>
            <d:City>Seattle</d:City>
            <d:KindCode m:type="Edm.Int32">0</d:KindCode>
            <d:PartitionKey>Jeff</d:PartitionKey>
            <d:RowKey>C_Jeff</d:RowKey>
        </m:properties>
    </content>
</entry>
```

Table storage will respond to the HTTP *POST* request to create the entity by returning an HTTP status code 201 (Created) with a message payload that contains an echo of the entity just created. Notice in the following code that the entity in the response's *Timestamp* column has been updated to record when the entity was last updated. The *Timestamp* column is used for detection of version conflicts in optimistic concurrency scenarios, which you'll see later in this chapter, in the section "Table operation concurrency." Technically, according to the REST API documentation, the *Timestamp* column should be considered opaque by developers and subject to change. Given the ramifications of this data type changing, though, the possibility that the column will change seems extremely unlikely.

```
HTTP/1.1 201 Created
Cache-Control: no-cache
Transfer-Encoding: chunked
Content-Type: application/atom+xml;charset=utf-8
ETag: W/"datetime'2013-01-14T01%3A12%3A57.4464437Z'"
Location: http://azureinsiders.table.core.windows.net/Demo(PartitionKey='Jeff',RowKey='C_Jeff')
Server: Windows-Azure-Table/1.0 Microsoft-HTTPAPI/2.0
x-ms-request-id: 503c510c-7a5d-4ee5-9413-6e489d6b9c61
x-ms-version: 2012-02-12
Date: Mon, 14 Jan 2013 01:12:57 GMT

47B
<?xml version="1.0" encoding="utf-8" standalone="yes"?>
<entry xml:base=http://azureinsiders.table.core.windows.net/
    xmlns:d=http://schemas.microsoft.com/ado/2007/08/dataservices
    xmlns:m=http://schemas.microsoft.com/ado/2007/08/dataservices/metadata
    m:etag="W/&quot;datetime'2013-01-14T01%3A12%3A57.4464437Z'&quot;"
    xmlns="http://www.w3.org/2005/Atom">
    <id>
        http://azureinsiders.table.core.windows.net/Demo(PartitionKey='Jeff',RowKey='C_Jeff')
    </id>
    <title type="text"></title>
    <updated>2013-01-14T01:12:57Z</updated>
    <author>
        <name />
    </author>
    <link rel="edit" title="Demo" href="Demo(PartitionKey='Jeff',RowKey='C_Jeff')" />
    <category term="azureinsiders.Demo"
        scheme="http://schemas.microsoft.com/ado/2007/08/dataservices/scheme" />

    <content type="application/xml">
    <m:properties>
        <d:PartitionKey>Jeff</d:PartitionKey>
```

```
      <d:RowKey>C_Jeff</d:RowKey>
      <d:Timestamp m:type="Edm.DateTime">2013-01-14T01:12:57.4464437Z</d:Timestamp>
      <d:Name>Jeff</d:Name>
      <d:City>Seattle</d:City>
      <d:KindCode m:type="Edm.Int32">0</d:KindCode>
    </m:properties>
  </content>
</entry>
0
```

After successfully creating the customer entity *Jeff*, you *POST* another request to the table end-point to create the customer entity *Paul*, but because the message is nearly identical to the creation of the customer *Jeff*, *Paul* has been omitted for brevity.

You can update properties of an existing entity by sending the HTTP *MERGE* request to the table endpoint with a message body containing the updated properties. You may not recognize the HTTP *MERGE* verb because it is not defined in RFC 2616 but rather was introduced as part of the OData protocol. (You learn about the OData protocol later in this chapter in the section "The Table service and the Open Data Protocol.") The *PUT* verb defined in RFC 2616 defines a replace operation. The *MERGE* verb compares each property and performs individual property updates as necessary rather than replace the entire entity.

The parenthetical expression after the table name *Demo (PartitionKey='Jeff',RowKey='C_Jeff')*, shown in the following code, filters the selection to a single entity because the *PartitionKey* plus the *RowKey* combination is always guaranteed to be unique within a single table.

The response of successfully transmitting this message to the Table service endpoint is an HTTP status code 204 (No Content), as shown in the next HTTP response. This message lets you know that the operation was performed successfully but that there is no additional message beyond the HTTP status code and other headers.

```
HTTP/1.1 204 No Content
Cache-Control: no-cache
Content-Length: 0
ETag: W/"datetime'2012-08-27T21%3A32%3A05.0647473Z'"
Server: Windows-Azure-Table/1.0 Microsoft-HTTPAPI/2.0
x-ms-request-id: 4aec3673-e610-4501-a5f1-fc0eb9b0d816
x-ms-version: 2011-08-18
Date: Mon, 27 Aug 2012 21:32:04 GMT
```

Of course, you can accomplish this through the Windows Azure client library, as the following code demonstrates. The code is commented to point out key things to be aware of. The *Basics* method begins by accepting an instance of your storage account credentials object. You call the storage account's *CreateCloudTableClient* method to retrieve an instance of a proxy for communicating with table storage. Your data operations are all performed through a table operation context class that you obtain by calling the *GetTableReference* method of the *CloudTableClient* instance. You then call the specific CRUD methods that are exposed on an instance of the *TableOperation* class, and then pass the table operation instance to your table operation's context instance as an argument to one of its many *Execute* methods.

In the sample code, you add an entity for *Jeff* and an entity for *Paul* by creating an instance of the *TableOperation* class and calling the *Insert* method, passing in an instance of the customer entity for *Jeff*. The *TableOperation* instance is then passing that instance to the instance of *CloudTable*'s *Execute* method. This process is then repeated for *Paul*. No calls to the Windows Azure Table service were made by adding entities into the local instance of *CloudTable*. The *Execute* method of the *CloudTable* instance is called to start the marshaling of local entities to the Windows Azure Table service. Next, you execute two separate queries for the customers Jeff and Paul. Upon their successful retrieval, you execute Jeff's name, making it uppercase; delete any entity where the customer name property does not equal *Jeff*; and then save the changes back to table storage.

```
public static void Basics(CloudStorageAccount account) {
    Console.Clear();
    CloudTableClient client = account.CreateCloudTableClient();
    CloudTable ct = client.GetTableReference(c_tableName).Clear();

    // Create 2 insert table operations & execute them:
    var to = TableOperation.Insert(new CustomerEntity("Jeff", "C_Jeff") { Name = "Jeff", City =
"Seattle" });
    TableResult tr = ct.Execute(to);
    to = TableOperation.Insert(new CustomerEntity("Paul", "C_Paul") { Name = "Paul", City =
"Olympia" });
    tr = ct.Execute(to);

    foreach (var pk in new[] { "Jeff", "Paul" }) {
        // Read all entities where PartitionKey == pk
        TableQuery<CustomerEntity> query = new TableQuery<CustomerEntity> {
            FilterString = new FilterBuilder<CustomerEntity>(ce => ce.PartitionKey, CompareOp.
EQ, pk),
            SelectColumns = new[] { new PropertyName<CustomerEntity>(ce => ce.Name).ToString()
},
            TakeCount = null
        };

        foreach (var customer in ct.ExecuteQuery(query)) {
            Console.WriteLine(customer);
            if (customer.Name == "Jeff") {      // Update "Jeff"
                customer.Name = customer.Name.ToUpper();
                tr = ct.Execute(TableOperation.Replace(customer));
            }
            else {
                tr = ct.Execute(TableOperation.Delete(customer));  // Delete "Paul"
            }
        }
    }
}
```

Creating tables

To create a new table called *Demo* in your storage account, send an HTTP *POST* message with the following payload.

```
POST http://azureinsiders.table.core.windows.net/Tables()?timeout=90 HTTP/1.1
x-ms-version: 2012-02-12
User-Agent: WA-Storage/2.0.3
Accept: application/atom+xml,application/xml
Accept-Charset: UTF-8
MaxDataServiceVersion: 2.0;NetFx
DataServiceVersion: 2.0;
Content-Type: application/atom+xml;type=entry;charset=utf-8
x-ms-date: Mon, 14 Jan 2013 21:06:05 GMT
Authorization: SharedKeyLite azureinsiders:77r5yXkSnS1l1QvPkbeVzBMnJXX4tG9WXZSNWapC7A0=
Host: azureinsiders.table.core.windows.net
Content-Length: 407

<?xml version="1.0" encoding="utf-8"?>
<entry xmlns=http://www.w3.org/2005/Atom
    xmlns:d=http://schemas.microsoft.com/ado/2007/08/dataservices
    xmlns:m="http://schemas.microsoft.com/ado/2007/08/dataservices/metadata">
    <id />
    <title />
    <updated>2013-01-14T21:06:04Z</updated>
    <author>
      <name />
    </author>
    <content type="application/xml">
        <m:properties>
            <d:TableName>Demo</d:TableName>
        </m:properties>
    </content>
</entry>
```

Posting this message to the Table service endpoint creates the table named *Demo*, as indicated by the HTTP status code of 201 (Created) and its message body describing the table and its properties.

```
HTTP/1.1 201 Created
Cache-Control: no-cache
Transfer-Encoding: chunked
Content-Type: application/atom+xml;charset=utf-8
Location: http://azureinsiders.table.core.windows.net/Tables('Demo')
Server: Windows-Azure-Table/1.0 Microsoft-HTTPAPI/2.0
x-ms-request-id: f8e1e417-0f6e-4063-9f3e-ef9931ec140f
x-ms-version: 2012-02-12
Date: Mon, 14 Jan 2013 21:06:04 GMT
```

```
<?xml version="1.0" encoding="utf-8" standalone="yes"?>
<entry xml:base=http://azureinsiders.table.core.windows.net/
    xmlns:d=http://schemas.microsoft.com/ado/2007/08/dataservices
    xmlns:m=http://schemas.microsoft.com/ado/2007/08/dataservices/metadata
    xmlns="http://www.w3.org/2005/Atom">
    <id>http://azureinsiders.table.core.windows.net/Tables('Demo')</id>
    <title type="text"></title>
    <updated>2013-01-14T21:06:05Z</updated>
    <author>
        <name />
    </author>
    <link rel="edit" title="Tables" href="Tables('Demo')" />
        <category term="azureinsiders.Tables"
        scheme="http://schemas.microsoft.com/ado/2007/08/dataservices/scheme" />
    <content type="application/xml">
        <m:properties>
            <d:TableName>Demo</d:TableName>
        </m:properties>
    </content>
</entry>
0
```

Using the Windows Azure client library, you can create the *Demo* table programmatically using a single line of code by calling the *CreateCloudTableClient* method of the *CloudStorageAccount* instance.

```
CloudTableClient client = account.CreateCloudTableClient().ClearTable("Demo");
```

The Table service and the Open Data Protocol

Because the first XML web services were introduced over a decade ago in the Microsoft operating systems, developers have frequently designed and implemented their own data storage web services to perform typical CRUD operations. Over the years, patterns emerged, which eventually congealed into best practices that were later codified into Open Data Protocol (OData).

The Table service is a partial implementation of the OData protocol. Like the RESTful principles upon which the OData protocol is built, OData operates in a manner consistent with the way the web works. It builds upon existing web technologies such as HTTP, Plain-Old-XML (POX), Atom Publishing Protocol (AtomPub), and JavaScript Object Notation (JSON) to provide a common and unified set of protocols and procedures for applications, services, and data stores to exchange information. Entities are stored in locations identified by a URI over the HTTP transport and operated upon with standard HTTP verbs such as *GET*, *PUT*, *POST*, and *DELETE*. Additional information on the OData protocol can be found by visiting the documentation area of the OData website: *http://www.odata.org/documentation*.

The Windows Azure client library uses Atom exclusively as its over-the-wire format for performing data operations. The generic term *Atom* is often used to describe two different formats. The *Atom Syndication Format* (RFC 4287) is an XML schema used in the delivery of syndicated web content; *AtomPub* (RFC 5023) is a simple HTTP-based standard for creating and updating web resources and is based upon the RFC 4287 syndication format.

The following XML fragment is an example of serialization by the Windows Azure Table service of an entity using the AtomPub format.

```
<entry xml:base=http://wintellect.table.core.windows.net/
       xmlns:d="http://schemas.microsoft.com/ado/2007/08/dataservices"
       xmlns:m=http://schemas.microsoft.com/ado/2007/08/dataservices/metadata
       m:etag="W/&quot;datetime'2010-10-29T16%3A51%3A10.738767Z'&quot;"
       xmlns="http://www.w3.org/2005/Atom">
<id>
  http://wintellect.table.core.windows.net/demo(PartitionKey='Jeff',RowKey='C_Jeff')
</id>
  <title type="text"></title>
  <updated>2010-10-29T16:52:57Z</updated>
  <author> <name /> </author>
  <link rel="edit" title="demo" href="demo(PartitionKey='Jeff',RowKey='C_Jeff')" />
  <category term="wintellect.demo"
            scheme="http://schemas.microsoft.com/ado/2007/08/dataservices/scheme"/>
  <content type="application/xml">
    <m:properties>
        <d:PartitionKey>Jeff</d:PartitionKey>
        <d:RowKey>C_Jeff</d:RowKey>
        <d:Timestamp m:type="Edm.DateTime">2010-10-29T16:51:10.738767Z</d:Timestamp>
        <d:Kind>Customer</d:Kind>
        <d:Name>Jeffrey Richter</d:Name>
        <d:City>Seattle</d:City>
    </m:properties>
  </content>
</entry>
```

Serializing and deserializing entities with *CloudTable*

The Windows Azure client library provides a convenient object-oriented abstraction to aid the .NET developer in performing client-side operations against OData data sources. The v2.x Windows Azure client library builds on the functionality of the ODataLib library (*http://odata.codeplex.com/*), but you may also use the earlier WCF Data Services client library (formerly ADO.NET Data Services).

As you learned earlier, a table is used to store an entity's properties, which are tuples of name-type-value information. The *CloudTable* type allows data stored in an OData repository to be downloaded and deserialized into instances of managed .NET objects.

For outbound requests to update data, the *CloudTable* type serializes managed .NET objects into an Atom schema and uploads these name-type-value tuples, as shown in the *<content>* element of the message body in the following HTTP *POST*.

```
POST http://azureinsiders.table.core.windows.net/Demo HTTP/1.1
User-Agent: Microsoft ADO.NET Data Services
DataServiceVersion: 1.0;NetFx
MaxDataServiceVersion: 2.0;NetFx
x-ms-version: 2011-08-18
x-ms-date: Sat, 25 Aug 2012 15:12:01 GMT
Authorization: SharedKeyLite azureinsiders:uVKrGusRzN/LY/EzDeHvAIfiv1n6VgIVK+LhaFTBhlc=
Accept: application/atom+xml,application/xml
Accept-Charset: UTF-8
Content-Type: application/atom+xml
Host: azureinsiders.table.core.windows.net
Content-Length: 721
Connection: Keep-Alive
<?xml version="1.0" encoding="utf-8" standalone="yes"?>
<entry xmlns:d=http://schemas.microsoft.com/ado/2007/08/dataservices
    xmlns:m=http://schemas.microsoft.com/ado/2007/08/dataservices/metadata
    xmlns="http://www.w3.org/2005/Atom">
  <title />
  <author>
    <name />
  </author>
  <updated>2012-08-25T15:12:01.7549368Z</updated>
  <id />
  <content type="application/xml">
    <m:properties>
      <d:City>Seattle</d:City>
      <d:KindCode m:type="Edm.Int32">0</d:KindCode>
      <d:Name>Jeff</d:Name>
      <d:PartitionKey>Jeff</d:PartitionKey>
      <d:RowKey>C_Jeff</d:RowKey>
      <d:Timestamp m:type="Edm.DateTime">0001-01-01T00:00:00</d:Timestamp>
    </m:properties>
  </content>
</entry>
```

When an entity is being updated and the updated entity has properties not found in the original entity, those properties are appended to the entity by default. The resulting entity is downloaded again in the message response, as shown in the following code, and the in-memory managed .NET object's properties are updated to reflect the latest changes in the entity's state.

```
HTTP/1.1 201 Created
Cache-Control: no-cache
Transfer-Encoding: chunked
Content-Type: application/atom+xml;charset=utf-8
ETag: W/"datetime'2013-01-14T21%3A06%3A06.4433369Z'"
Location: http://azureinsiders.table.core.windows.net/Demo(PartitionKey='Jeff',RowKey='C_Jeff')
Server: Windows-Azure-Table/1.0 Microsoft-HTTPAPI/2.0
x-ms-request-id: d86895a2-587a-4e30-ab1e-779e03ab57a4
x-ms-version: 2012-02-12
Date: Mon, 14 Jan 2013 21:06:05 GMT

47B
<?xml version="1.0" encoding="utf-8" standalone="yes"?>
<entry xml:base=http://azureinsiders.table.core.windows.net/
    xmlns:d=http://schemas.microsoft.com/ado/2007/08/dataservices
    xmlns:m=http://schemas.microsoft.com/ado/2007/08/dataservices/metadata
    m:etag="W/&quot;datetime'2013-01-14T21%3A06%3A06.4433369Z'&quot;"
    xmlns="http://www.w3.org/2005/Atom">
    <id>
        http://azureinsiders.table.core.windows.net/Demo(PartitionKey='Jeff',RowKey='C_Jeff')
    </id>
    <title type="text"></title>
    <updated>2013-01-14T21:06:06Z</updated>
    <author>
    <name />
</author>
    <link rel="edit" title="Demo" href="Demo(PartitionKey='Jeff',RowKey='C_Jeff')" />
    <category term="azureinsiders.Demo"
        scheme="http://schemas.microsoft.com/ado/2007/08/dataservices/scheme" />

    <content type="application/xml">
    <m:properties>
      <d:PartitionKey>Jeff</d:PartitionKey>
      <d:RowKey>C_Jeff</d:RowKey>
      <d:Timestamp m:type="Edm.DateTime">2013-01-14T21:06:06.4433369Z</d:Timestamp>
      <d:Name>Jeff</d:Name>
      <d:City>Seattle</d:City>
      <d:KindCode m:type="Edm.Int32">0</d:KindCode>
    </m:properties>
  </content>
</entry>
0
```

Note When retrieving data from an OData repository, entities without a class property are ignored and discarded without notification. Likewise, a class property with no entity property is ignored by default. However, by setting the *IgnoreMissingProperties* property of the TSC to *false*, the default behavior can be altered so that an *InvalidOperationException* is thrown instead.

Data operation options

The *TableOperation* type supports the four basic CRUD operations of create, retrieve, update, and delete. It also supports an insert-and-merge and an insert-or-replace operation to efficiently handle inserts when the entity may already exist. The update operation can be performed either as an entire replacement of an existing entity or as a merge with an existing entity. The list of operations supported by the *TableOperation* type is shown in Table 6-2.

TABLE 6-2 *TableOperation* methods

Name	Description
Delete	Creates a table operation that will delete an entity from a table.
Insert	Creates a table operation that will insert a new entity into a table.
InsertOrMerge	Creates a table operation that will insert a new entity if it does not already exist, or will merge property changes with an existing entity.
InsertOrReplace	Creates a table operation that will insert a new entity if it does not already exist or will replace an entity that does.
Merge	Creates a table operation that will merge changes with an existing entity.
Replace	Creates a table operation that will replace an existing entity.
Retrieve	Creates a table operation that will retrieve an existing entity.

Table queries

Most applications use subsets of the data contained in a single table based on criteria that has been directly or indirectly supplied by a user. Unless you are calculating statistics on the aggregate of all data in the table, you probably will want to filter data to just a small subset matching your criteria. With the potential for billions of rows occupying terabytes of storage, transferring an entire table's data to the client is impractical unless the quantity of data is known to be small and unlikely to grow. Even when it might be practical, repetitively transferring large quantities of data unnecessarily can be very expensive. Ideally, the data storage service should perform as much filtration as possible so that only the data required by the application is transmitted over the network.

The OData Protocol provides a robust and standardized mechanism for passing data filtration parameters to an OData implementation such as the Windows Azure table storage service. OData opens up opportunities for knowledge reuse, allowing you to take what you know about your own custom WCF Data Service implementations (or other OData implementations) and apply it to the Windows Azure table storage service.

Table queries by primary key

The fastest and most efficient way to retrieve an entity is by specifying its primary key on the request. The following is an example of the URI syntax used to select entities from a table, given the entity's primary key. The *PartitionKey* with a value of *Jeff* and the comma-separated *RowKey* with a value *C_Jeff* are supplied immediately after the table name in parentheses.

```
http://azureinsiders.table.core.windows.net/Demo(PartitionKey='Jeff',RowKey='C_Jeff')
```

Table queries using the RESTful API

The *$filter* query string parameter option allows a subset of the entities in a table matching a predicate expression to be returned to the caller. The *$filter* value is case-sensitive to support expression evaluation in situations where case matching is required. The Table service is able to perform all the filtration processing on the service side of the wire, reducing the volume of data transmitted to satisfy the request and eliminating (or reducing) the wasted effort of discarding rows that do match the criteria on the client side of the wire. An example of using the *$filter* query parameter would look similar to the following.

```
http://azureinsiders.table.core.windows.net/Demo?$filter=Country eq 'Italy'
```

The complete contents of the *Demo* table are pared down by the Table service so that only those entities with a country of Italy are returned to the client.

The predicate expression for the *$filter* parameter accepts URI operators supplied in Table 6-3.

TABLE 6-3 OData URI expression operators

URI operator	Description	Example
Logical operators		
eq	Values are equal to each other.	/Demo?$filter=Country eq 'Italy'
ne	Values are not equal to each other.	/Demo?$filter=Country ne 'Italy'
gt	First value is greater than the second value.	/Demo?$filter=Price gt 100
ge	First value is greater than or equal to the second value.	/Demo?$filter=Price ge 100
lt	First value is less than the second value.	/Demo?$filter=Price lt 100
le	First value is less than or equal to the second value.	/Demo?$filter=Price le 100

URI operator	Description	Example
and	Expressions are logically and'd together.	/Demo?$filter=Price ge 100 and Price le 200
or	Expressions are logically or'd together.	/Demo?$filter=Price le 100 or Price le 200
not	Expressions are logically negated.	/Demo?$filter=Price le 100 not Description eq 'Tuna'
Arithmetic operators		
add	Adds a value to an operand.	/Demo?$filter=Price add 10 le 100
sub	Subtracts a value from an operand.	/Demo?$filter=Price sub 10 le 100
mul	Multiplies an operand by a value.	/Demo?$filter=Price mul 10 le 100
div	Divides an operand by a value.	/Demo?$filter=Price div 10 le 100
mod	Computes the modulo of an operand divided by a value.	/Demo?$filter=Price mod 2 eq 0
Grouping operators		
()	Precedence grouping of expressions.	/Demo?$filter=(Price ge 100) or (Price le 200)

If you require only the first portion of data matching your search criteria, you can further pare down the data returned from the Table service by appending *$top=n* to the query string, where *n* represents the number of entities that you want to return. If you are familiar with Transact-SQL, note that this parameter provides identical behavior to SQL's *TOP* clause.

Table queries using the Windows Azure client library

The following code examines methods of querying your data by using the Windows Azure client library. You'll see the impact that your query choices have on the URI and the *$filter* query string parameter described earlier in this chapter.

```
public static void QueryFilterStrings(CloudStorageAccount account) {
    Console.Clear();

    CloudTable ct = account.CreateCloudTableClient().GetTableReference(c_tableName);
    const String pk = "Jeff", rk = "C_Jeff";

    // Best performance: Query single entity via specific PK/RK
    // This syntax puts the PK & RK in the URL itself
    var q1 = new TableQuery {
        FilterString = new FilterBuilder<TableEntity>
            (te => te.PartitionKey, CompareOp.EQ, pk).And
                (te => te.RowKey, CompareOp.EQ, rk)
    };
    TableQuery tq1 = new TableQuery() { FilterString = q1.FilterString };
    var r1 = ct.ExecuteQuery(tq1).ToList();

    // and again using the TableOperation.Retrieve method

    var r1b = ct.Execute(TableOperation.Retrieve<TableEntity>(pk, rk)).Result;
```

```
//PK and RK in the FilterString
var q2 = new TableQuery {
    FilterString = new FilterBuilder<TableEntity>
        (te => te.PartitionKey, CompareOp.EQ, pk).And
            (te => te.RowKey, CompareOp.EQ, rk)
};
TableQuery tq2 = new TableQuery() { FilterString = q2.FilterString };
var r2 = ct.ExecuteQuery(tq2).ToList();

// Worst performance: Query against whole table because no PK or RK provided
var q3 = new TableQuery { FilterString = "City eq 'Redmond'" };
TableQuery tq3 = new TableQuery() { FilterString = q3.FilterString };
var r3 = ct.ExecuteQuery(tq3).ToList();

// medium performance: query a range of partition keys
var q4 = new TableQuery { FilterString = new FilterBuilder<TableEntity>
    (te => te.PartitionKey, RangeOp.IncludeLowerExcludeUpper, pk) };
TableQuery tq4 = new TableQuery() { FilterString = q4.FilterString };
var r4 = ct.ExecuteQuery(tq4).ToList();

String s;
TableQuery tq;
List<DynamicTableEntity> r;

s = TableQuery.GenerateFilterConditionForBool("ABoolean", "eq", true);
tq = new TableQuery { FilterString = s };
r = ct.ExecuteQuery(tq).ToList();

s = TableQuery.GenerateFilterConditionForBinary
("AByteArray", "eq", new Byte[] { 1, 2, 3, 4, 5 });
tq = new TableQuery { FilterString = s };
r = ct.ExecuteQuery(tq).ToList();

s = TableQuery.GenerateFilterConditionForDate("ADate", "eq", DateTimeOffset.Now);
tq = new TableQuery { FilterString = s };
r = ct.ExecuteQuery(tq).ToList();

s = TableQuery.GenerateFilterConditionForDouble("ADouble", "eq", 1.23);
tq = new TableQuery { FilterString = s };
r = ct.ExecuteQuery(tq).ToList();

s = TableQuery.GenerateFilterConditionForGuid("AGuid", "eq", Guid.NewGuid());
tq = new TableQuery { FilterString = s };
r = ct.ExecuteQuery(tq).ToList();

s = TableQuery.GenerateFilterConditionForInt("AnInt32", "eq", 123);
tq = new TableQuery { FilterString = s };
r = ct.ExecuteQuery(tq).ToList();

s = TableQuery.GenerateFilterConditionForLong("AnInt64", "eq", 321);
tq = new TableQuery { FilterString = s };
r = ct.ExecuteQuery(tq).ToList();
}
```

In the preceding code, query 1 supplies a *PrimaryKey* and a *RowKey* that uniquely identify the entity in table storage; this type of query offers the best performance. Query 1 uses the *AsTable-ServiceQuery* method, as shown in the next XML snippet.

```
// Query 1:
GET http://azureinsiders.table.core.windows.net/Demo(PartitionKey='PK',RowKey='RK')?timeout=90
HTTP/1.1
x-ms-version: 2012-02-12
User-Agent: WA-Storage/2.0.3
Accept: application/atom+xml,application/xml
Accept-Charset: UTF-8
MaxDataServiceVersion: 2.0;NetFx
x-ms-date: Tue, 15 Jan 2013 00:38:12 GMT
Authorization: SharedKeyLite azureinsiders:AAiPTMg4Hv2UOdUxR/swzZnYIy23AIGXjyibVAquK/w=
Host: azureinsiders.table.core.windows.net
```

When preparing the URI for transmission, the Windows Azure client library escapes special characters for transmission. This can lead to an exception being thrown by the library, because not all characters can be escaped. Generally, your *PrimaryKey* and *RowKey* properties will follow a known scheme, so you will know immediately if this condition impacts you. To work around the URI escape constraint, you must alter your request so that the *PrimaryKey* and *RowKey* are no longer a part of the URI. Query 2 is similar to query 1, except that by using *TableOperation.ExecuteQuery* instead of *TableOperation.Retrieve<TableEntity>*, the *PartitionKey* and *RowKey* are migrated out of the highly efficient URI and into the query string *$filter* parameter of the request. The resulting HTTP request looks as follows.

```
// Query 2:
GET http://azureinsiders.table.core.windows.net/Demo
    ?$filter=(PartitionKey%20eq%20'PK')%20and%20(RowKey%20eq%20'RK')%20&timeout=90 HTTP/1.1
x-ms-version: 2012-02-12
User-Agent: WA-Storage/2.0.3
Accept: application/atom+xml,application/xml
Accept-Charset: UTF-8
MaxDataServiceVersion: 2.0;NetFx
x-ms-date: Tue, 15 Jan 2013 00:57:32 GMT
Authorization: SharedKeyLite azureinsiders:QfDtSdQmKZdVOVg28gchqFIb8LjPR9wT/evb5eszXxo=
Host: azureinsiders.table.core.windows.net
```

Upon successful execution of this query, Windows Azure storage service returns the following response.

```
HTTP/1.1 200 OK
Cache-Control: no-cache
Transfer-Encoding: chunked
Content-Type: application/atom+xml;charset=utf-8
Server: Windows-Azure-Table/1.0 Microsoft-HTTPAPI/2.0
x-ms-request-id: 7dc2b880-d547-4015-9252-994fc6413a71
x-ms-version: 2012-02-12
Date: Tue, 15 Jan 2013 01:29:54 GMT
```

```
577
<?xml version="1.0" encoding="utf-8" standalone="yes"?>
<feed xml:base=http://azureinsiders.table.core.windows.net/
    xmlns:d=http://schemas.microsoft.com/ado/2007/08/dataservices
    xmlns:m=http://schemas.microsoft.com/ado/2007/08/dataservices/metadata
    xmlns="http://www.w3.org/2005/Atom">
  <title type="text">Demo7</title>
  <id>http://azureinsiders.table.core.windows.net/Demo</id>
  <updated>2013-01-15T01:29:54Z</updated>
  <link rel="self" title="Demo7" href="Demo" />
  <entry m:etag="W/&quot;datetime'2013-01-15T01%3A29%3A44.0274198Z'&quot;">
    <id>
        http://azureinsiders.table.core.windows.net/Demo(PartitionKey='Jeff',RowKey='C_Jeff')
    </id>
    <title type="text"></title>
    <updated>2013-01-15T01:29:54Z</updated>
    <author>
      <name />
    </author>
    <link rel="edit" title="Demo" href="Demo(PartitionKey='Jeff',RowKey='C_Jeff')" />
    <category term="azureinsiders.Demo"
        scheme="http://schemas.microsoft.com/ado/2007/08/dataservices/scheme" />
    <content type="application/xml">
      <m:properties>
        <d:PartitionKey>Jeff</d:PartitionKey>
        <d:RowKey>C_Jeff</d:RowKey>
        <d:Timestamp m:type="Edm.DateTime">2013-01-15T01:29:44.0274198Z</d:Timestamp>
        <d:City>Seattle</d:City>
        <d:KindCode m:type="Edm.Int32">0</d:KindCode>
        <d:Name>JEFF</d:Name>
      </m:properties>
    </content>
  </entry>
</feed>
0
```

Of course, you can query upon any property of the entity. In the next query, you will specify the *City* but not provide a *PartitionKey* or *RowKey* . This is the least efficient type of query, because every entity in the table must be scanned and evaluated for inclusion by using the *$filter* query string parameter. You should avoid this kind of query whenever possible. The request and response of this type of query are shown here.

```
// Query 3:
GET http://azureinsiders.table.core.windows.net/Demo?
$filter=City%20eq%20'Redmond'&timeout=90 HTTP/1.1
x-ms-version: 2012-02-12
User-Agent: WA-Storage/2.0.3
Accept: application/atom+xml,application/xml
Accept-Charset: UTF-8
MaxDataServiceVersion: 2.0;NetFx
x-ms-date: Tue, 15 Jan 2013 01:42:53 GMT
Authorization: SharedKeyLite azureinsiders:PF4xdTqBU2xNUaEo2UA5OS6T5HYTqPtJapXNcIqWoag=
Host: azureinsiders.table.core.windows.net
```

Upon successful execution of this query, Windows Azure storage service returns the following response.

```
HTTP/1.1 200 OK
Cache-Control: no-cache
Transfer-Encoding: chunked
Content-Type: application/atom+xml;charset=utf-8
Server: Windows-Azure-Table/1.0 Microsoft-HTTPAPI/2.0
x-ms-request-id: 82fbf522-fda5-422c-b363-f8b394d19eb6
x-ms-version: 2012-02-12
Date: Tue, 15 Jan 2013 01:42:53 GMT

20F
<?xml version="1.0" encoding="utf-8" standalone="yes"?>
<feed xml:base=http://azureinsiders.table.core.windows.net/
    xmlns:d=http://schemas.microsoft.com/ado/2007/08/dataservices
    xmlns:m=http://schemas.microsoft.com/ado/2007/08/dataservices/metadata
    xmlns="http://www.w3.org/2005/Atom">
  <title type="text">Demo</title>
  <id>http://azureinsiders.table.core.windows.net/Demo</id>
  <updated>2013-01-15T01:42:54Z</updated>
  <author>
    <name />
  </author>
  <link rel="self" title="Demo" href="Demo" />
</feed>
0
```

In some application scenarios, it may be desirable to select a range of entities sharing a set of partition keys. The usefulness of this technique will depend upon the scheme you chose for generating these keys and whether entities group together well into such processing ranges.

The request for query 4 demonstrates the ability to retrieve entities based on a range of *Partition-Key* values using range comparison codes (*eq, gt, ge, lt, le, ne*) in the *$filter* query string. This kind of query is moderate in performance.

```
GET http://azureinsiders.table.core.windows.net/Demo
    ?$filter=((PartitionKey%20ge%20'Jeff')%20and%20(PartitionKey%20lt%20'Jefg')%20)%20
    &timeout=90 HTTP/1.1
x-ms-version: 2012-02-12
User-Agent: WA-Storage/2.0.3
Accept: application/atom+xml,application/xml
Accept-Charset: UTF-8
MaxDataServiceVersion: 2.0;NetFx
x-ms-date: Tue, 15 Jan 2013 03:18:32 GMT
Authorization: SharedKeyLite azureinsiders:8BH5vlH9wSD2kPfJSkXpkx/V26k1YyY4LSQwNc3brb4=
Host: azureinsiders.table.core.windows.net
```

The following Windows Azure client library code produces this kind of request. Note that *Filter-Builder* is a class from the Wintellect Power Azure library, which is available as a NuGet package (*http://nuget.org*). The extension method merely simplifies the coding of *$filter* parameters.

```
// Query 4:
// medium performance: query a range of partition keys
```

```
var q4 = new TableQuery {
    FilterString = new FilterBuilder<TableEntity>
        (te => te.PartitionKey, RangeOp.IncludeLowerExcludeUpper, pk)
};
TableQuery tq4 = new TableQuery() { FilterString = q4.FilterString };
var r4 = ct.ExecuteQuery(tq4).ToList();
```

And to conclude, the code for query 6 demonstrates what the *$filter* looks like for other types of data such as *Boolean, Byte[], DateTime, Guid, Double,* and *String.*

```
// Query 5:
http://azureinsiders.table.core.windows.net/Demo()?$filter=
    (((((ABoolean eq true) and
    (AByteArray eq X'0102030405')) and
    (ADateTime lt datetime'2012-09-09T14:42:30.3110212Z')) and
    (AGuid eq guid'23af33b7-08f7-4bf1-9bb8-2da7d6402427')) and
    (ADouble ne null)) and (AString ne 'Foo')
```

When comparing strings in code with LINQ expressions, you should use the ==, !=, *Equals* and *CompareTo* methods of the *String* type.

Table entity ordering

The OData protocol provides a standardized mechanism for the client to pass data ordering information to the service so that the service can order the data before returning it to the caller. This is done using the *$orderby* query string; however, at the time of this writing, Windows Azure table storage does not offer a service-side ordering feature. Tables order entities in *PartitionKey/RowKey* order. As stated earlier, the *PartitionKey/RowKey* combination is the primary key of your table. Use the dominant and natural order of your data when designing your primary key scheme.

When you need to use a sort order that is not the primary key, you can select subsets of the data and perform the sorting on the client side of the wire. That may be more efficient in some scenarios than in others.

Another technique you can use is to create clone entities that you replicate your data to, where each entity's *PrimaryKey/RowKey* is altered to the appropriate sort order, as shown in Table 6-5. Because the primary key is always unique, a common practice is to store these cloned entities in the same table. In the example provided in Table 6-5, the customer rows have been cloned and the *RowKey* value represents either a *Name* or a *City*, designated by an *N_* or a *C_* prefix, respectively. To return the data in an order supported by the data, the caller must filter the data so that only the desired order is returned. If you want the data in City order, you filter the table to return only those rows where the *RowKey* begins with the letter C. If you want the data returned in Name order, you filter the table to return only those rows beginning with the letter N. The natural order supplied by the *PartitionKey/RowKey* ensures that the data is returned in the desired order.

Of course, this technique does not scale very well, because the volumes of data involved are multiplied by the number of required sort orders. Entities can become unsynchronized over time because of software defects or other failures, and there is a cost associated with storing redundant data because the number of sorts desired multiplies your storage requirements.

TABLE 6-5 Duplicate rows with alternative *RowKey* values for sorting entities

PartitionKey (1 KB string)	RowKey (1 KB string)	Timestamp (DateTime)	Entity type	Name	City	Item	Quantity
Jeff	N_Jeff	012-08-27T17:47:26.4489137Z	Customer	Jeff Chia	Kirkland		
Jeff	C_Kirkland	012-08-27T17:47:26.4489137Z	Customer	Jeff Chia	Kirkland		
Paul	N_Paul	012-08-27T17:47:26.4489137Z	Customer	Paul Mehner	Olympia		2
Paul	C_Olympia	012-08-27T17:47:26.4489137Z	Customer	Paul Mehner	Olympia		1

A variation on the cloning technique is to create separate entity definitions only for the primary key, arranged in the alternate sort order, and any additional properties that may be necessary to support the query. This technique is similar to the older databases based on file systems, where a separate file was used for each index made against data in the table.

In many application usage scenarios, the user chooses an entity from a list and operates on that entity. When the full data of that entity is required, that data can be retrieved by using a secondary request off of the primary table. The *choose from a list and then operate on the entity* paradigm is already a common pattern for web applications.

Sorting and redundant storage consume processing power and storage space, so try when possible to avoid sorting and use filtering instead. Reducing the size of data retrieved, and sorting your data on the client side, is often the fastest and most efficient technique. Applications often offer users an opportunity to change their sort order and filtering options, and this should be factored into your design.

Storing multiple entity types in a single table

Earlier in this chapter, you saw customers and orders being placed in the same table. Although this practice may violate everything you've learned about normalizing your data for a relational database, it is exactly how you want to approach Windows Azure table storage. As stated earlier in this chapter, Windows Azure table storage supports transactions called Entity Group Transactions, which cannot span multiple tables. To store customer data and all the customer's orders in a single transaction, you must store the data in a single table, and all entities must share the same *PartitionKey*. Doing so aids performance because it guarantees that all data will be on the same storage node and that multiple data retrievals will not be necessary to assemble the data from multiple tables. Scalability is also improved because all related data is transferred intact to the new storage node during load balancing. In large databases, especially those with high-availability or zero-down-time requirements, it may be impractical to update data to match new versions of the schema. The old and the new schemas can exist together side by side, and the consuming software has the responsibility of accounting for the possibility that the table has data that matches multiple schema definitions.

The Windows Azure client library defines a type called *TableServiceEntity* with the following definition.

```
namespace Microsoft.WindowsAzure.StorageClient {
    // Summary:
    //      Represents an entity in the Windows Azure Table service.
    [CLSCompliant(false)]
    public abstract class TableServiceEntity {
        // Summary:
        //      Initializes a new instance of the Microsoft.WindowsAzure.StorageClient.
TableServiceEntity
        //      class.
        protected TableServiceEntity();
        //
        // Summary:
        //      Initializes a new instance of the Microsoft.WindowsAzure.StorageClient.
TableServiceEntity
        //      class.
        //
        // Parameters:
        //   partitionKey:
        //      The partition key.
        //
        //   rowKey:
        //      The row key.
        protected TableServiceEntity(string partitionKey, string rowKey);

        // Summary:
        //      Gets or sets the partition key of a table entity.
        public virtual string PartitionKey { get; set; }
        //
        // Summary:
        //      Gets or sets the row key of a table entity.
        public virtual string RowKey { get; set; }
        //
        // Summary:
        //      Gets or sets the timestamp for the entity.
        public DateTime Timestamp { get; set; }
    }
}
```

To work with the *TableServiceContext* class, the derived *TableServiceEntity* class needs to have the required *DataServiceKey* attribute applied to it to define which properties are to be used as the *PartitionKey* and the *RowKey* of an entity. The Wintellect Power Azure Library includes the following class to supply the necessary attributes.

```
/// <summary>
/// Represents an entity in the Windows Azure Table service.
/// Use this as the base class of all XxxEntity classes to avoid explicitly
/// applying the DataServiceKey attribute to all of them.
/// </summary>
[DataServiceKey(new String[] { "PartitionKey", "RowKey" })]
```

```
    public class TableEntity : ITableEntity {
        /// <summary>
        /// Initializes a new instance of the Wintellect.WindowsAzure.StorageClient.TableEntity
class.
        /// </summary>
        public TableEntity() { }

        /// <summary>
        /// Initializes a new instance of the Wintellect.WindowsAzure.StorageClient.TableEntity
class.
        /// </summary>
        /// <param name="partitionKey">The partition key.</param>
        /// <param name="rowKey">The row key.</param>
        public TableEntity(String partitionKey, String rowKey) {
            PartitionKey = partitionKey;
            RowKey = rowKey;
        }

        /// <summary>
        /// Gets or sets the partition key of a table entity. For Windows Azure Diagnostic tables,
        /// the PartitionKey is the tick count of the time the event was recorded, padded to
        /// 19 digits with leading zeroes and rounded to the nearest minute.
        /// </summary>
        [WadFieldOrder(0)]
        public virtual String PartitionKey { get; set; }

        /// <summary>
        /// Gets or sets the row key of a table entity. For Windows Azure Diagnostic tables, the
        /// RowKey is of the format "Deployment___Role___RoleInstance___
AutoGeneratedOpaqueInteger"
        /// </summary>
        [WadFieldOrder(1)]
        public virtual String RowKey { get; set; }

        /// <summary>
        /// Gets or sets the timestamp for the entity.
        /// </summary>
        [WadFieldOrder(2)]
        public DateTime Timestamp { get; set; }

        public override String ToString() {
            return String.Format("PK={0}, RK={1}, Timestamp={2}",
                PartitionKey, RowKey, Timestamp);
        }
    }
```

The preceding code implements an interface called *ITableEntity*, which is used to generically describe the behavior of being a table entity (which consists of defining the *ParititionKey*, the *RowKey*,
and the *Timestamp* columns, as follows.

```
    public interface ITableEntity {
        /// <summary>
        /// Gets or sets the partition key of a table entity.
        /// </summary>
        String PartitionKey { get; set; }
```

```
/// <summary>
/// Gets or sets the row key of a table entity.
/// </summary>
String RowKey { get; set; }

/// <summary>
/// Gets or sets the timestamp for the entity.
/// </summary>
DateTime Timestamp { get; set; }
}
```

To facilitate the concept of different kinds of entities, the Windows Azure Power Library provides an abstract *KindTableEntity* class. The class also provides many helpful methods for working with tables that contain multiple kinds of entities, which are documented in the code that follows.

```
public interface IKindTableEntity<TEnum> :
    ITableEntity where TEnum : struct {
    Int32 KindCode { get; set; }
    TIKindEntity ToKind<TIKindEntity>() where TIKindEntity : IKindTableEntity<TEnum>;
    TIKindEntity ToObject<TIKindEntity>(TIKindEntity @object) where TIKindEntity :
    IKindTableEntity<TEnum>;
}

public abstract class KindTableEntity<TEnum> :
    TableEntity, IKindTableEntity<TEnum> where TEnum : struct {
    private const BindingFlags c_propertyBindingFlags =
        BindingFlags.Public | BindingFlags.Instance | BindingFlags.FlattenHierarchy;
    private static readonly Dictionary<Type, HashSet<String>> s_interfaceTypeToProperties =
        new Dictionary<Type, HashSet<String>>();

    public static void WritingEntityDelegate(Object sender, ReadingWritingEntityEventArgs e) {
        // Find all the properties in the XML
        var xmlPropertySet = e.Data.Descendants(
            TableEntityRaw.MetadataNamespace + "properties").ElementAt(0);

        // Get the value of the KindCode property & look up its kind name
        String kindCode =
            xmlPropertySet.Element(TableEntityRaw.DataServicesNamespace + "KindCode").Value;
        TEnum kind = GetKindFromCode(Int32.Parse(kindCode));

        // Find the interface from the kind name
        // (NOTE: assumes interface is defined in the same scope as the enum type itself)
        String typeNamePrefix = typeof(TEnum).FullName;
        typeNamePrefix =
            typeNamePrefix.Substring(0, typeNamePrefix.Length - typeof(TEnum).Name.Length);
        Type interfaceType =
            typeof(TEnum).Assembly.GetType(typeNamePrefix + "I" + kind.ToString() + "Entity");

        // Get the names of the interface's properties (and the implemented interfaces too)
        // The properties are cached to improve performance
        Monitor.Enter(s_interfaceTypeToProperties);
        HashSet<String> propsToKeep;
        if (!s_interfaceTypeToProperties.TryGetValue(interfaceType, out propsToKeep)) {
            propsToKeep = new HashSet<String>
                (interfaceType.GetProperties(c_propertyBindingFlags).Select(pi => pi.Name));
            foreach (var inheritedInterface in interfaceType.GetInterfaces())
```

```
                propsToKeep.UnionWith(inheritedInterface.GetProperties
                    (c_propertyBindingFlags).Select(pi => pi.Name));
            s_interfaceTypeToProperties.Add(interfaceType, propsToKeep);
        }
        Monitor.Exit(s_interfaceTypeToProperties);

        // Find the properties in the XML that are NOT interface properties & remove them
        var propsToRemove = xmlPropertySet.Elements().Where(element =>
            !propsToKeep.Contains(element.Name.LocalName));
        propsToRemove.Remove();
    }

    protected KindTableEntity() { }
    protected KindTableEntity(String partitionKey, String rowKey, TEnum kind) :
base(partitionKey, rowKey)
    {
        SetKind(kind);
    }

    public Int32 KindCode { get; set; }
    public void SetKind(TEnum value) { KindCode = (Int32)(Object)value; }
    private static TEnum GetKindFromCode(Int32 kindCode) { return (TEnum)(Object)kindCode; }
    public TEnum GetKind() { return GetKindFromCode(KindCode); }
    private String GetKindName() { return GetKind().ToString(); }

    public override String ToString() {
        return String.Format("{0}, Kind={1}", base.ToString(), GetKindName());
    }

    private void VailidateKindInterface<TIKindTableEntity>()
            where TIKindTableEntity : IKindTableEntity<TEnum> {
        if (!typeof(TIKindTableEntity).IsInterface)
            throw new InvalidOperationException("TIKindTableEntity must be an interface type");
        String interfaceName = "I" + GetKindName() + "Entity";
        if (typeof(TIKindTableEntity).Name != interfaceName)
            throw new InvalidCastException("This " + GetKindName() +
                " entity must be cast to an " + interfaceName);
    }

    public TIKindTableEntity ToKind<TIKindTableEntity>() where TIKindTableEntity :
        IKindTableEntity<TEnum> {
        VailidateKindInterface<TIKindTableEntity>();
        return (TIKindTableEntity)(Object)this;
    }

    // This method is useful for debugging; it is called when the 'union' type's ToString
    //   is called
    public TIKindTableEntity ToObject<TIKindTableEntity>(TIKindTableEntity @object)
            where TIKindTableEntity : IKindTableEntity<TEnum> {
        VailidateKindInterface<TIKindTableEntity>();
        if (!typeof(TIKindTableEntity).IsAssignableFrom(@object.GetType()))
            throw new InvalidCastException(String.Format("The {0} object must implement the {1}
                interface",
            @object.GetType(), typeof(TIKindTableEntity)));
```

```
        // Copy all interface properties from the union object to the nonunion object
        foreach (var p in typeof(TIKindTableEntity).GetProperties(c_propertyBindingFlags))
            p.SetValue(@object, p.GetValue(this, null), null);

        return @object;
    }
```

The following code creates a table called *demoKindTable* and populates it with two customers, *Paul* and *Jeff*, with two orders for *Jeff*. Next, the example code reads back all entities with a *Primary-Key* of *Jeff*, and then, based on the entity type being *Customer* or *Order*, the code casts the entity to its appropriate class.

```
public static void MultipleKinds(CloudStorageAccount account) {
    Console.Clear();
    CloudTable ct = account.CreateCloudTableClient().GetTableReference(
        "CustomerAndOrders").EnsureExists(true);
    // Add a single entity with one PartitionKey value
    ct.Execute(TableOperation.Insert(new CustomerEntity("Paul", "C_Paul") {
        Name = "Paul",
        City = "Olympia"
     }));

    // Add many entities sharing the same PartitionKey value
    TableBatchOperation tbo = new TableBatchOperation();
    tbo.Add(TableOperation.Insert(new CustomerEntity("Jeff", "C_Jeff") {
        Name = "Jeff",
        City = "Seattle"
    }));
    tbo.Add(TableOperation.Insert(new OrderEntity("Jeff", "O_Milk") {
        Item = "Milk",
        Quantity = 2
    }));
    tbo.Add(TableOperation.Insert(new OrderEntity("Jeff", "O_Cereal") {
        Item = "Cereal",
        Quantity = 1
    }));
    ct.ExecuteBatch(tbo);

    IEnumerable<DynamicTableEntity> jeffEntities = ct.ExecuteQuery(
        new TableQuery { FilterString =
            new FilterBuilder<TableEntity>(te => te.PartitionKey, CompareOp.EQ, "Jeff") });

    tbo = new TableBatchOperation();
    foreach (var e in jeffEntities) {
        switch ((EntityKindCodes)e.Properties["KindCode"].Int32Value) {
        // What kind of entity is this?
            case EntityKindCodes.Customer:
                var customer = new CustomerEntity(e.PartitionKey, e.RowKey) { ETag = e.ETag };
                customer.ReadEntity(e.Properties, null);
                customer.City = "Philadelphia";
                tbo.Add(TableOperation.Replace(customer));
                break;
            case EntityKindCodes.Order:
                var order = new OrderEntity(e.PartitionKey, e.RowKey) { ETag = e.ETag };
                order.ReadEntity(e.Properties, null);
                if (order.Item == "Milk") {
```

```
                    order.Quantity = 5;
                    tbo.Add(TableOperation.Replace(order));
                }
                break;
        }
    }
    ct.ExecuteBatch(tbo);
}

private static void ShowAllCustomersAndOrders(CloudTable ct) {
    // Query all customers & each customer's orders:
    var customerQuery = new TableQuery<CustomerEntity> {
        FilterString = new FilterBuilder<CustomerEntity>
            (ce => ce.KindCode, CompareOp.EQ, (Int32)EntityKindCodes.Customer)
    };
    var orderQuery = new TableQuery<OrderEntity> {
        FilterString = new FilterBuilder<OrderEntity>
            (oe => oe.KindCode, CompareOp.EQ, (Int32)EntityKindCodes.Order)
    };

    foreach (var ce in ct.ExecuteQuery(customerQuery)) {
        Console.WriteLine("Customer: " + ce);
        foreach (var oe in ct.ExecuteQuery(orderQuery)) Console.WriteLine("  Order: " + oe);
        Console.WriteLine();
    }
}
#region Table Entity Definitions: Application-specific types
        // 1. Define entity kinds in this enum, then define I(kind)Entity interfaces that derive
            from IKindTableEntity<EntityKinds>
private enum EntityKinds {
    // NOTE: Explicitly assign values to these symbols and never change them!
    Customer = 0,
    Order = 1
}

// 2. Define 1 interface per entity kind; add properties here
// NOTE: The name ('Customer') between 'I' & 'Entity' MUST match the kind string (enum field)
//    exactly
private interface ICustomerEntity : IKindTableEntity<EntityKinds> {
    String Name { get; set; }
    String City { get; set; }

    // Have this interface expose some of the inherited properties (but not the KindCode
        property):
    new String PartitionKey { get; set; }
    new String RowKey { get; set; }
    new DateTime Timestamp { get; set; }
}

// 2. Define 1 interface per kind of entity type; add properties here
// NOTE: The name ('Order') between 'I' & 'Entity' MUST match the kind string (enum field)
    exactly
private interface IOrderEntity : IKindTableEntity<EntityKinds> {
    String Item { get; set; }
    Int32? Quantity { get; set; }
```

```
        // Have this interface expose some of the inherited properties (but not the KindCode
            property):
        new String PartitionKey { get; set; }
        new String RowKey { get; set; }
        new DateTime Timestamp { get; set; }
    }


    // 3. Define 1 class per entity interface; derive from KindTableEntity & I(kind)Entity
    private sealed class CustomerEntity : KindTableEntity<EntityKinds>, ICustomerEntity {
        public CustomerEntity() : this(null, null) { }
        public CustomerEntity(String partitionKey, String rowKey) : base(partitionKey, rowKey,
                EntityKinds.Customer) { }
        public String Name { get; set; }
        public String City { get; set; }
        public override String ToString() {
            return String.Format("{0}, Name={1}, City={2}", base.ToString(), Name, City);
        }
    }


    // 3. Define 1 class per entity interface; derive from KindTableEntity & I(kind)Entity
    private sealed class OrderEntity : KindTableEntity<EntityKinds>, IOrderEntity {
        public OrderEntity() : this(null, null) { }
        public OrderEntity(String partitionKey, String rowKey) : base(partitionKey, rowKey,
                            EntityKinds.Order) { }
        public String Item { get; set; }
        public Int32? Quantity { get; set; }
        public override String ToString() {
            return String.Format("{0}, Item={1}, Quantity={2}", base.ToString(), Item, Quantity);
        }
    }


    // 4. Define 1 'union' class; derived from KindTableEntity & all
    //     the I(kind)Entity interfaces you want in the union
    private sealed class CustomerOrderEntity :
                            KindTableEntity<EntityKinds>, ICustomerEntity, IOrderEntity {
        // ICustomerEntity properties
        public String Name { get; set; }
        public String City { get; set; }

        // IOrderEntity properties
        public String Item { get; set; }
        public Int32? Quantity { get; set; }

        // This method is useful for debugging
        public override String ToString() {
            Object o = this;
            switch (this.GetKind()) {
                case EntityKinds.Customer: o = ToObject<ICustomerEntity>(new CustomerEntity()); break;
                case EntityKinds.Order: o = ToObject<IOrderEntity>(new OrderEntity()); break;
            }
            return o.ToString();
        }
    }
}
```

More information about using the *KindTableEntity* class from the Wintellect Power Azure Library
can be found at *http://www1.wintellect.com/resources/Details/46*.

Selecting good partition keys

A single server always processes all requests for a particular partition. This can create bottlenecks when the maximum capacity of a single server is reached and SLA targets cannot be achieved. To prevent such bottlenecks, attempt to select *PartitionKey* schemes that split entities across partitions. However, avoid being so random or granular that you lose the ability to use EGTs for data requiring ACID semantics, or you lose the natural ordering and grouping offered by a well-planned *PrimaryKey* scheme. Following this basic set of guidelines will help you to select a good *PrimaryKey* scheme:

- Identify the most dominant query that you will perform against your table and identify which properties will be used.

- Order your dominant properties by their relative importance to your applications.

- If the aggregated properties do not uniquely identify an entity, consider adding uniqueness. This uniqueness may be introduced as a sequence of numbers, letters, or even a GUID.

- If there is only one property in your dominant query, strongly consider making it your partition key.

- If there are two properties in your dominant query, consider making them the *PartitionKey* and *RowKey*.

- If you have more than two properties in your dominant query, consider organizing them into two groups, forming the *PartitionKey* and the *RowKey*.

Segmented queries and continuation tokens

A pagination mechanism for data that can be presented in a tabular format is often required because humans generally cannot digest more than a page of information at one time and service consumers generally scale better when data can be metered out to them over time. Also, you want to ensure that the data being requested is appropriate for the query and not a mistake, because you are dealing with potentially massive databases in the cloud. It can take a lot of resources to compute and transmit billions of rows of data over the wire. Windows Azure must also take into account its own scalability; a large query can block or significantly impede many smaller queries, because those smaller queries may have to wait or compete for resources. *Continuation tokens*, introduced in Chapter 4, allow Windows Azure storage to return a smaller subset of your data. You then pass back the continuation token to retrieve subsequent pages of your original query. Windows Azure storage refers to these pages of data as *segments*. Because the number of entities in a table is limited only by the storage limits on your account, you should always anticipate that you may receive a continuation token back from any request that you make.

In the following example, the *demoSegmented* table has 5,000 entities in it. To retrieve all of the entities in a table, issue an HTTP *GET* request against the table's URL.

```
GET http://azureinsiders.table.core.windows.net/demoSegmented?timeout=90 HTTP/1.1
x-ms-version: 2012-02-12
User-Agent: WA-Storage/2.0.3
Accept: application/atom+xml,application/xml
Accept-Charset: UTF-8
MaxDataServiceVersion: 2.0;NetFx
x-ms-date: Tue, 15 Jan 2013 06:48:42 GMT
Authorization: SharedKeyLite azureinsiders:ZiVRpLBkmRV4yaTuct0AChGwYR0oSTPnnWyCDcOmGnQ=
Host: azureinsiders.table.core.windows.net
```

Upon successful execution, the Table service will return an Atom feed containing the first segment of entities in the table. Because there is a limit of 1,000 entities per request, the response is guaranteed to be segmented. For brevity, only the first and last items of the 1,000 items in the first segment of the response are included here. The *x-ms-continuation-NextPartitionKey* and *x-ms-continuation-NextRowKey* HTTP headers provide a hash of the data necessary to make a subsequent call to the service to retrieve the next segment of data satisfying the query.

```
HTTP/1.1 200 OK
Cache-Control: no-cache
Transfer-Encoding: chunked
Content-Type: application/atom+xml;charset=utf-8
Server: Windows-Azure-Table/1.0 Microsoft-HTTPAPI/2.0
x-ms-request-id: e4bb558b-de4a-4527-9fee-79f5e8b44b65
x-ms-version: 2012-02-12
x-ms-continuation-NextPartitionKey: 1!4!UEs-
x-ms-continuation-NextRowKey: 1!12!Q3VzdDAxMDAw
Date: Tue, 15 Jan 2013 06:48:43 GMT

D63CE
<?xml version="1.0" encoding="utf-8" standalone="yes"?>
<feed xml:base=http://azureinsiders.table.core.windows.net/
    xmlns:d=http://schemas.microsoft.com/ado/2007/08/dataservices
    xmlns:m=http://schemas.microsoft.com/ado/2007/08/dataservices/metadata
    xmlns="http://www.w3.org/2005/Atom">
  <title type="text">demoSegmented</title>
  <id>http://azureinsiders.table.core.windows.net/demoSegmented</id>
  <updated>2013-01-15T06:48:43Z</updated>
  <link rel="self" title="demoSegmented" href="demoSegmented" />
  <entry m:etag="W/&quot;datetime'2013-01-15T06%3A48%3A21.0353344Z'&quot;">
    <id>http://azureinsiders.table.core.windows.net/demoSegmented(PartitionKey='PK',RowKey='Cu
st00000')</id>
    <title type="text"></title>
    <updated>2013-01-15T06:48:43Z</updated>
    <author>
      <name />
    </author>
    <link rel="edit" title="demoSegmented" href="demoSegmented(PartitionKey='PK',RowKey='Cu
st00000')" />
    <category term="azureinsiders.demoSegmented" scheme="http://schemas.microsoft.com/
ado/2007/08/dataservices/scheme" />
    <content type="application/xml">
      <m:properties>
        <d:PartitionKey>PK</d:PartitionKey>
        <d:RowKey>Cust00000</d:RowKey>
        <d:Timestamp m:type="Edm.DateTime">2013-01-15T06:48:21.0353344Z</d:Timestamp>
```

```
          <d:KindCode m:type="Edm.Int32">0</d:KindCode>
        </m:properties>
      </content>
    </entry>

. . . . . . . . . . items 1-998 deleted for brevity . . . . . . . . .
    <entry m:etag="W/&quot;datetime'2013-01-15T06%3A48%3A35.3497657Z'&quot;">
      <id>http://azureinsiders.table.core.windows.net/demoSegmented(PartitionKey='PK',RowKey='Cu
st02299')</id>
      <title type="text"></title>
      <updated>2013-01-15T06:48:45Z</updated>
      <author>
        <name />
      </author>
      <link rel="edit" title="demoSegmented" href="demoSegmented(PartitionKey='PK',RowKey='Cu
st02299')" />
      <category term="azureinsiders.demoSegmented" scheme="http://schemas.microsoft.com/
ado/2007/08/dataservices/scheme" />
      <content type="application/xml">
        <m:properties>
          <d:PartitionKey>PK</d:PartitionKey>
          <d:RowKey>Cust02299</d:RowKey>
          <d:Timestamp m:type="Edm.DateTime">2013-01-15T06:48:35.3497657Z</d:Timestamp>
          <d:KindCode m:type="Edm.Int32">0</d:KindCode>
        </m:properties>
      </content>
    </entry>
</feed>
0
```

Cross-table consistency

When applicable, your application is responsible for maintaining consistency across multiple tables. This can lead to increased complexity in writing your application. You may consider some strategies for improving the resiliency and reliability of your application, such as using queues to orchestrate work. Queues (discussed in Chapter 7, "Queues") have a built-in retry mechanism. When your *PartitionKey* matches on all the entities to be operated on, you can also use an EGT. Often in highly scalable environments, writing compensation code is more convenient. Instead of rolling back a data operation when an error occurs, *compensation code* moves forward. In the same way that a transaction is never deleted in accounting, an offsetting entry is made to preserve the audit trail. A compensation works like an offsetting accounting entry.

In some cases where the cleanup code starts to litter your application code, you may need to implement an orphan collector. An *orphan collector* is a process that runs in the background or on a periodic schedule to sweep the table of any data suffering from a violation of referential integrity. Orphan collectors can also be notification-driven, where an application informs the collector of an error, stimulating the collector into action. Of course, such orphan collectors typically save and log the data they collect for future integration.

Table operation concurrency

As with most data storage, there is sometimes contention when performing mutually exclusive data operations on the same entity. There are a variety of strategies for handling contention, ranging from an all-controlling exclusive lock to the noninterfering, anything goes, last-update-wins approach. By default, Windows Azure table storage uses a more middle-of-the-road optimistic concurrency, where the assumption is made that most of the data operations can be performed without conflict or the extremely heavy hand of taking an exclusive lock on the data.

Optimistic concurrency

Optimistic concurrency is the most popular concurrent update style for ensuring data consistency. It provides a nice balance between data consistency with a generally nominal impact on performance and scalability. You assume that most updates will succeed without contention, and you pay the performance penalty for resolving update conflicts only when they occur. When contention is high, the model breaks down, and it is better to consider either a pessimistic concurrency model or a last-in-wins model.

Optimistic concurrency is implemented by the Windows Azure Table service by using an *If-Match* HTTP header. The client is expected to send this header with every request to support concurrency checking. The *If-Match* header is used by the service to determine whether the data has been modified since it was last retrieved.

In the example that follows, the *If-Match* header has a value of *W/"datetime'2012-08-28T03%3A24%3A11.8035978Z'"*.

```
PUT http://azureinsiders.table.core.windows.net/Demo
    (PartitionKey='Jeff',RowKey='Richter')?timeout=90 HTTP/1.1
x-ms-version: 2012-02-12
User-Agent: WA-Storage/2.0.3
Accept: application/atom+xml,application/xml
Accept-Charset: UTF-8
MaxDataServiceVersion: 2.0;NetFx
If-Match: W/"datetime'2013-01-15T08%3A21%3A11.7643291Z'"
DataServiceVersion: 2.0;
Content-Type: application/atom+xml;type=entry;charset=utf-8
x-ms-date: Tue, 15 Jan 2013 08:21:29 GMT
Authorization: SharedKeyLite azureinsiders:b23XFc2IS5+BG4VS3Ue+M1BoGpxV591avP9p62WrOfQ=
Host: azureinsiders.table.core.windows.net
Content-Length: 595

<?xml version="1.0" encoding="utf-8"?>
<entry xmlns=http://www.w3.org/2005/Atom
    xmlns:d=http://schemas.microsoft.com/ado/2007/08/dataservices
    xmlns:m=http://schemas.microsoft.com/ado/2007/08/dataservices/metadata
    m:etag="W/&quot;datetime'2013-01-15T08%3A21%3A11.7643291Z'&quot;">
    <id />
    <title /><updated>2013-01-15T08:21:29Z</updated>
    <author>
    <name />
```

```
        </author>
        <content type="application/xml">
        <m:properties>
            <d:Name>Jeff</d:Name>
            <d:City>Alpha</d:City>
            <d:KindCode m:type="Edm.Int32">0</d:KindCode>
            <d:PartitionKey>Jeff</d:PartitionKey>
            <d:RowKey>Richter</d:RowKey>
        </m:properties>
    </content>
</entry>
```

If the value of the *If-Match* header does not match the current data, the Windows Azure Table service returns an HTTP status code of 412 (Precondition Failed), as shown in the following sample response.

```
HTTP/1.1 412 Precondition Failed
Cache-Control: no-cache
Transfer-Encoding: chunked
Server: Windows-Azure-Table/1.0 Microsoft-HTTPAPI/2.0
x-ms-request-id: 7c03f3d1-c29d-4fa8-aa3f-bca881dc4ddd
x-ms-version: 2012-02-12
Date: Tue, 15 Jan 2013 08:21:10 GMT

176
<?xml version="1.0" encoding="utf-8" standalone="yes"?>
<error xmlns="http://schemas.microsoft.com/ado/2007/08/dataservices/metadata">
  <code>UpdateConditionNotSatisfied</code>
  <message xml:lang="en-US">The update condition specified in the request was not satisfied.
    RequestId:7c03f3d1-c29d-4fa8-aa3f-bca881dc4ddd
    Time:2013-01-15T08:21:11.3273858Z
  </message>
</error>
0
```

The Windows Azure client library can be used to better encapsulate the work of preparing and managing currency, as shown in the following sample code.

```
public static void OptimisticConcurrency(CloudStorageAccount account) {
    Console.Clear();
    // Preparation: Clear the table and add a customer to it
    CloudTableClient client = account.CreateCloudTableClient();
    CloudTable ct = client.GetTableReference(c_tableName).Clear();
    ct.Execute(TableOperation.Insert(new CustomerEntity("Jeff", "Richter")
     { Name = "Jeff", City = "Seattle" }));

    // 1st client queries the entity, updates it, & saves it back
    ThreadPool.QueueUserWorkItem(o => OptimisticUpdatePattern(client, "Alpha"));

    // 2nd client also queries the entity, updates it, & saves it back
    OptimisticUpdatePattern(client, "Beta");

    ShowFirstEntity(client, c_tableName);
}
```

```
private static void OptimisticUpdatePattern(CloudTableClient client, String newCity) {
    const String title = "Optimistic Concurrency Pattern";
    CloudTable ct = client.GetTableReference(c_tableName);

    // Read the first entity from the table:
    CustomerEntity ce = ct.ExecuteQuery(new TableQuery<CustomerEntity>()).First();
    ce.City = newCity;    // Change a property's value
    while (true) {
        try {
            MessageBox.Show(
                String.Format("NewCity={0}\r\nETag={1}\r\nHit OK to save changes", newCity,
ce.ETag),
                title, MessageBoxButtons.OK);
            Debugger.Break();
            ct.Execute(TableOperation.Replace(ce));
            break;    // No exception, success!
        }
        catch (StorageException ex) {
            if ((HttpStatusCode)ex.RequestInformation.HttpStatusCode != HttpStatusCode.
PreconditionFailed)
                throw;
            MessageBox.Show(
                String.Format("Failed to save {0}\r\nHit OK to try again", newCity),
                title, MessageBoxButtons.OK);
            // Reread the entity to update its ETag; the changed props don't change because of
PreserveChanges
            ce = (CustomerEntity)ct.Execute(TableOperation.Retrieve<CustomerEntity>
                (ce.PartitionKey, ce.RowKey)).Result;
        }
    }
}
```

Last update wins

Another strategy for handling data concurrency is to simply allow the last update to overwrite any existing updates that may have been made since the data was retrieved. Although this technique is the least used, there are use-cases for which this approach is satisfactory and sometimes even superior. If all the application cares about is the most recent consistent version of the data, a significant amount of overhead can be avoided in concurrency violation detection, avoidance, and recovery.

In the following code, you create a customer entity and use the instance of *DataServiceContext* to save the customer to Windows Azure table storage. In the next segment of code, you retrieve the customer that you created and then update the customer's *City* property to *Alpha*. To simulate multiple users updating in sequence, you create a new data context object, detach the customer object from the first context, and then attach it to the second. To trick date/time comparison into understanding that the data has been updated, you set the *ETag* to an asterisk just before calling *UpdateObject* on the context. You create yet another *DataServiceContext* and repeat the process, this time changing the *City* to *Beta*. The data has been changed in your in-memory copies, but not in Windows Azure table storage. Calling *UpdateObject* only notifies the data contexts that the data has been changed; it does not actually perform the update. To commit the in-memory changes of the first modified data context, you call its *SaveChangesWithRetries* method and use the *ShowFirstEntity* method to retrieve the customer, verifying that the city was changed to *Alpha*. Next, you call the second data context's *SaveChangesWithRetries* method followed by the *ShowFirstEntity* method to retrieve the result and show that the city is now *Beta* instead of *Alpha*. Note that in an optimistic concurrency scenario, the second update would have resulted in a concurrency violation error.

```
public static void LastUpdateWins(CloudStorageAccount account) {
    Console.Clear();
    // Preparation: Clear the table and add a customer to it
    CloudTableClient client = account.CreateCloudTableClient();
    var ct = client.GetTableReference(c_tableName).Clear();
    ct.Execute(TableOperation.Insert(
        new CustomerEntity("Jeff", "Richter") { Name = "Jeff", City = "Seattle" }));

    // Last update always wins
    CustomerEntity ce1 = ct.ExecuteQuery(
        new TableQuery<CustomerEntity> { FilterString = String.Empty }).First();
    ce1.City = "Alpha";
    ce1.ETag = "*";    // "*" ETag matches whatever ETag the entity in the table has

    CustomerEntity ce2 = ct.ExecuteQuery(
        new TableQuery<CustomerEntity> { FilterString = String.Empty }).First();

    ce2.City = "Beta";
    ce2.ETag = "*";    // "*" ETag matches whatever ETag the entity in the table has
    ct.Execute(TableOperation.Replace(ce1));  // Last update wins
    ShowFirstEntity(client, c_tableName);

    ct.Execute(TableOperation.Replace(ce2));  // Last update wins
    ShowFirstEntity(client, c_tableName);
}

private static void ShowFirstEntity(CloudTableClient client, String tableName) {
    Console.WriteLine(client.GetTableReference(tableName).ExecuteQuery(
        new TableQuery<CustomerEntity>()).First());
}
```

Pessimistic concurrency

A pessimistic concurrency model is not directly supported by Windows Azure storage services, but one technique for creating your own is to take a lease on a blob and use that lease to represent a lock on an entity (or range of entities). Your code must first check for the existence of a blob lease before allowing the table entity to be modified, and your code must also release the lease when the pending operation has been completed in order to allow other callers to perform their own operations.

Pessimistic locking schemes are significantly slower than optimistic or last-win schemes because of the overhead involved in managing the locks and the delay in not being able to assume that the operation will succeed without checking first.

Conclusion

In this chapter, you learned about Windows Azure table storage. First, you examined the characteristics of this kind of data storage, including the kinds of real-world data and storage scenarios that lend themselves well to it. You then learned about the organizational structure of this type of storage, including the naming conventions and other rules that must be followed. You explored how to perform CRUD operations on table rows and tables and the importance of being able to save multiple types of entities in the same table.

Queues

In this chapter:

This chapter introduces queue storage and what it is used for. You will learn about the critical characteristics of queue storage, such as the way messages are processed and its impact on idempotency.

Queue storage overview

Queues provide a very reliable mechanism for asynchronous message transmission and delivery, but not permanent data storage. Their primary use is to allow computational resources such as web servers, business services, and other applications in the cloud to communicate reliably with each other. Queue service offers up to seven days of message durability, but the queue service does not provide indefinite durable data storage like blob and table storage does.

The number of queues that can be created in a storage account, and the number of messages that can be placed in an individual queue, is unlimited. The practical limit, however, is governed by the 100-terabyte storage capacity of the account. Data operations against queues are authenticated using the Windows Azure storage account keys. Figure 7-1 shows the hierarchical relationship between storage accounts, queues, and messages.

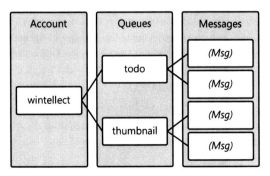

FIGURE 7-1 The hierarchical message queue structure relates accounts, queues, and messages.

The size of each individual message can be up to 64 kilobytes (KB). This limit implies that your application's architecture is designed to push lots of small messages through quickly to improve scalability and not handle larger sized messages. If your requirements call for larger sized messages, you can batch your messages up and store them in a blob, placing the URI to the batch blob onto the message queue instead of the actual messages. When the recipient receives the message from the queue, it can merely retrieve the data from the blob and, upon successful completion of the work, delete both the blob and queued message. If you use such a technique, you will have to come up with mechanisms for dealing with the occasionally orphaned blobs.

Messages are not guaranteed to be delivered in a strict First-In-First-Out (FIFO) manner. In fact, under some conditions, a message can be delivered more than one time. This is discussed later in this chapter in the section "Retrieving messages from a queue."

After seven days, any unprocessed messages still in a queue will be automatically purged. So although Windows Azure storage queues are durable, the guarantee on message delivery is limited to one week. This is not unreasonable in most business application scenarios; typically you want your queues to drain quickly to level out processing and distribute the work load evenly across the available message recipients such as Windows Azure worker roles. Leveling out the work over time will generally save you money because you'll be able to purchase only the amount of resources necessary to handle the average volume of work rather than peak capacity.

Business use cases

Queues are a simple yet very effective technology for addressing a wide range of common business requirements, such as the availability of services, leveling out the work to be performed over time, handling disjointed work, distributing the workload, and loosely coupling message consumers with message producers.

Availability

Keeping a dependent application functioning while the services that the application depends on are unavailable is often desirable, and in many circumstances, even required. Services and other data processing applications may be offline for periods of time for software upgrades, routine maintenance, and system failures. In many communication scenarios in which movement may impact reliability, as is the case with a mobile device or computers located on automobiles, ships, airplanes, and trains, the mobile computer or device might be temporarily out of range of a radio transmitter, or the radio communications may be unreliable or intermittent. Queues ensure guaranteed delivery of your messages by durably persisting them until they can be delivered. Even though Windows Azure storage queues do not offer an unlimited guarantee, because messages that are not delivered within seven days are automatically purged, this durability constraint still offers more than enough time for the vast majority of software application scenarios.

If your messages are in danger of being purged because they're nearing the seven-day age threshold and you need more time, you can pull them off the head of the queue and immediately place them back on the tail, thus rotating all the messages in the queue and extending their lifetime by another seven days.

Load leveling

The backlog of work on a server is seldom evenly distributed throughout the hours of a day. Over time, servers experience peaks and valleys in their backlog of work to be performed. When peak workload is attained, the arrival of any additional work will cause service failures.

You can address peak workloads by purchasing an adequate amount of resource capacity to handle a peak workload during its longest duration. To ensure service availability, you need to make your hardware purchasing decisions on the worst-case scenario, so include a little extra horsepower to handle contingencies. This means that during nonpeak operations, the extra capacity that you purchased will not be used. With load leveling, any work in excess of the resource capacity during peak demand is captured and delayed until adequate resources are available to process the request. Queuing allows you to design your application and make resource purchasing decisions based on average loads rather than on maximum loads, saving you money.

Disjointed work

Some kinds of workflows can be decomposed into smaller constituent tasks that may be run in parallel. Queuing enables a high degree of parallelism and resource apportionment. The parallelism can dramatically improve throughput and increase the availability of your services. This may require you to architect your application to take advantage of the parallelism Windows Azure offers you. Architectures that work well for an on-premise application may not take full advantage of its parallelism and dynamic scalability.

Long-running work

Some types of work take a relatively long amount of time to complete, creating a bottleneck that ties up front-end resources. Queues allow the client submitting the work to be freed up immediately while the work waits for resources and completes processing.

Distributed work

Queues enable Windows Azure web role virtual machines to offload processing onto worker role virtual machines. This greatly improves scalability because an appropriate number of virtual machines can be assigned to each queue to service the workload independent of the workload in other queues.

In heterogeneous scenarios, queues may be useful in passing messages between different platforms and languages—for example, a Java application on a UNIX machine might pass messages to a Microsoft .NET application running on a Windows-based device that is using queues as a means of providing security and transportation. The schema of the message is the basis for the contract between the two systems.

Queues can also be used as an election system. When a message is deposited in a message queue, the first receiver to process the message becomes the one elected to perform a task.

Publish/subscribe messaging

Publish/subscribe is a messaging pattern comprising message senders (called *publishers*) and message receivers (called *subscribers*). The publishers send messages to an unknown number of subscribers. The number of subscribers can vary between zero and a number bound only by resource availability. The message receivers subscribe only to the published messages of senders who have messages the receivers are interested in receiving. Their interest in receiving messages is highly variable and contingent upon many factors such as time of day, location of the consumer (he or she may be mobile), and resource consumption.

Receivers register with the messaging infrastructure their interest in particular topics and content. When a message sender publishes a message to an outgoing queue, the message is propagated to all receiving subscribers based on their registered criteria.

The entire publish/subscribe model is loosely coupled. Subscribers and publishers have no formal relationship with each other. Publishers send messages without concern for subscribers, and subscribers receive messages without concern for the message publishers. Many applications benefit from the parallelism and loose coupling characteristics of the publish/subscribe model.

Windows Azure queue storage supports implementations of all of the preceding business use cases except publish/subscribe. If you need publish/subscribe functionality, you may want to investigate the Windows Azure Service Bus queues as an option.

Queue addressing

Message queues are located in data storage URLs that match the following pattern.

> *http://*<account>*.queue.core.windows.net/*<queuename>/<messagename>

The *<account>* placeholder is the Windows Azure account name, *<queuename>* is the name you gave the queue when it was created, and *<messagename>* is the name of an individual message being stored in that queue.

The URL pattern is slightly different for the local development storage emulator. The hostname becomes the IP address of the loopback adapter (that is, 127.0.0.1), to which the port number 10001 and the hardcoded literal account name *devstorageaccount1* are appended, to form the complete base address. This is depicted in the Storage Emulator window shown in Figure 7-2. The queue name and message name are appended to this base address to form the full URL to a message, for example:

http://127.0.0.1:10001/devstorageaccount1/myqueue/mymessage)

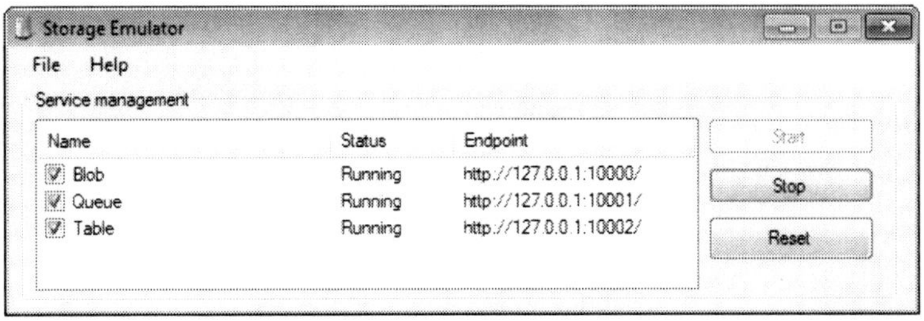

FIGURE 7-2 The endpoint addresses are shown in the Windows Azure Storage Emulator window.

Creating a message queue

Messages require organization and infrastructure, to ensure that they arrive at their final destination in a relatively predictable fashion. Message queues are an infrastructure through which messages travel. Except when errors, timeouts, or other conditions interfere, messages are typically delivered to their recipients on a First-In-First-Out basis. Windows Azure does not offer delivery guarantees, because messages may be delivered in any order and to multiple recipients. Messages are not even guaranteed to be delivered at all, because messages that have languished too long in a queue are silently deleted without being delivered. With these message delivery disclaimers having been identified, it is still useful to have knowledge of conditions that are typical of your application and its environment when planning your infrastructure. In other words, if you know that your application's operational characteristics might require hours or days to process queued messages during peak times because you have long-running tasks that must be performed for each message, you might add more computational capacity to handle the message backlog at strategic times to prevent any chance that messages might become stale before they are processed.

To create a new message queue, send an appropriately constructed HTTP *PUT* message to the URI where you want the message queue created. The following example creates a message queue called *demo* in the *azureinsiders* namespace.

```
PUT http://azureinsiders.queue.core.windows.net/demo?timeout=90 HTTP/1.1
x-ms-version: 2012-02-12
User-Agent: WA-Storage/2.0.0
x-ms-date: Sun, 25 Nov 2012 21:44:32 GMT
Authorization: SharedKey azureinsiders:svakOk/40lL1E6HCHNSS8xF+3OCU3x1PgJbllEvdlHw=
Host: azureinsiders.queue.core.windows.net
Content-Length: 0
```

Upon successful execution, Windows Azure storage will respond by sending you back an HTTP 201 status code indicating that the message queue resource was successfully created, as shown in the following example.

```
HTTP/1.1 201 Created
Transfer-Encoding: chunked
Server: Windows-Azure-Queue/1.0 Microsoft-HTTPAPI/2.0
x-ms-request-id: 7bd71974-27eb-4e02-a33b-192b5b91b23c
x-ms-version: 2012-02-12
Date: Sun, 25 Nov 2012 21:44:30 GMT
0
```

The message queue named *demo* can also be created by using the Windows Azure client library with the following code, as provided in the *QueuePatterns* class.

```
private static CloudQueue CreateQueue(CloudQueueClient client) {
    CloudQueue queue = client.GetQueueReference("demo").EnsureExists(true);
    return queue;
}
```

Queue naming rules

You should be aware of several naming rules for queues and messages. A queue name must be between 3 and 63 (inclusive) characters in length; start with a letter or number; and contain only lowercase letters, numbers, and the hyphen. All letters used in blob container names must be lowercase.

If you violate any of these naming rules, you receive an HTTP 400 (Bad Request) status code from the data storage service, resulting in a *StorageClientException* being thrown if you are accessing data storage by using the Windows Azure client library. Additional information about the naming rules for queues can be found at the following URL: *http://msdn.microsoft.com/en-us/library/dd179349.aspx*.

Posting a message into a queue

To post a message into a message queue for delivery to a message recipient, you send an HTTP POST request to the message queue's base URI address, to which you append the literal *messages* suffix. The body of the message is the payload to be placed in the message queue for delivery to the message recipient.

```
POST http://azureinsiders.queue.core.windows.net/demo/messages?messagettl=345600&timeout=90 HTTP/1.1
x-ms-version: 2012-02-12
User-Agent: WA-Storage/2.0.0
messagettl: 345600
x-ms-date: Sun, 25 Nov 2012 21:59:29 GMT
Authorization: SharedKey azureinsiders:THixAW61ZEWHtWmVCHEHeZp28cGhc3fD8fs//3IJYX4=
Host: azureinsiders.queue.core.windows.net
Content-Length: 105
```

```
<?xml version="1.0" encoding="utf-8"?>
<QueueMessage>
    <MessageText>TXNnQQ==</MessageText>
</QueueMessage>
```

Upon successful execution, Windows Azure storage will respond by returning an HTTP 201 status code, which indicates that the message was successfully created in the message queue, as shown in the following example.

```
HTTP/1.1 201 Created
Transfer-Encoding: chunked
Server: Windows-Azure-Queue/1.0 Microsoft-HTTPAPI/2.0
x-ms-request-id: 51853324-de1c-47ae-9407-0af6995a9a4b
x-ms-version: 2012-02-12
Date: Sun, 25 Nov 2012 22:19:42 GMT
0
```

Timeout values controlling a message's time to live, visibility, and time to be processed may all be supplied as *querystring* parameters, as shown in Table 7-1.

TABLE 7-1 *Querystring* parameters for message posting

Parameter	Value	Effect
messagettl	Integer seconds	Optional. Identifies the amount of time a message is allowed to live in the queue before being purged by Windows Azure data storage. This value cannot be less than zero or exceed the maximum message life (seven days at the time of this book's writing). The default is the maximum message life, currently 604,800 seconds (seven days). Although the parameter is optional to the API, the Windows Azure client library supplies a default value of 604,800 seconds (or seven days).
timeout	Integer seconds	Optional. Identifies the amount of time, in seconds, allowed for the queuing service to process the request. This value cannot be less than zero and the default at the time of this book's writing was 30 seconds. Although the parameter is optional to the API, the Windows Azure client library automatically supplies a default value of 90 seconds for this parameter, overriding the REST API default value of 30 seconds.
visibilitytimeout	Integer seconds	Optional. Identifies the amount of time, in seconds, allowed before the message will become visible in the queue again if it has not been deleted by the message consumer.

Messages can also be placed into a queue by using the Windows Azure client library, as shown in the following sample code.

```
private static void AddMessages(CloudQueue queue) {
    // Add 2 messages to a queue:
    var timeToLive = TimeSpan.FromDays(4);
    queue.AddMessage(new CloudQueueMessage("MsgA"), timeToLive);
    queue.AddMessage(new CloudQueueMessage("MsgB"), timeToLive);
}
```

Retrieving messages from a queue

Retrieving messages from a queue is done by simply sending an HTTP GET request to the message queue's base URI address, which you append the literal /*messages* suffix to.

```
GET http://azureinsiders.queue.core.windows.net/demo/messages?
    numofmessages=32&visibilitytimeout=5&timeout=90 HTTP/1.1
x-ms-version: 2012-02-12
User-Agent: WA-Storage/2.0.0
x-ms-date: Sun, 25 Nov 2012 22:43:58 GMT
Authorization: SharedKey azureinsiders:KFmWSeej/U4yYKA34hku5OACx+zx9AvXLCEuyT7FyB4=
Host: azureinsiders.queue.core.windows.net
Connection: Keep-Alive
```

Upon successful execution, Windows Azure data storage will respond by sending you an HTTP 200 status code and a message body consisting of the queued messages. The following response shows two messages being returned and includes additional metadata about each message.

```
HTTP/1.1 200 OK
Transfer-Encoding: chunked
Content-Type: application/xml
Server: Windows-Azure-Queue/1.0 Microsoft-HTTPAPI/2.0
x-ms-request-id: 86314925-37a1-49be-a7d7-31029fafe2fe
x-ms-version: 2012-02-12
Date: Sun, 25 Nov 2012 22:43:58 GMT

360
?<?xml version="1.0" encoding="utf-8"?>
<QueueMessagesList>
  <QueueMessage>
    <MessageId>7c02d548-ffe2-42d9-bc44-6867776f60f2</MessageId>
    <InsertionTime>Sun, 25 Nov 2012 22:19:44 GMT</InsertionTime>
    <ExpirationTime>Thu, 29 Nov 2012 22:19:44 GMT</ExpirationTime>
    <DequeueCount>1</DequeueCount>
    <PopReceipt>AgAAAEAAAAAAAAAYgyzXl7LzQE=</PopReceipt>
    <TimeNextVisible>Sun, 25 Nov 2012 22:44:03 GMT</TimeNextVisible>
    <MessageText>TXNnQQ==</MessageText>
  </QueueMessage>
  <QueueMessage>
    <MessageId>c0405546-b4c6-4a07-b199-0303495c38eb</MessageId>
    <InsertionTime>Sun, 25 Nov 2012 22:19:53 GMT</InsertionTime>
    <ExpirationTime>Thu, 29 Nov 2012 22:19:53 GMT</ExpirationTime>
    <DequeueCount>1</DequeueCount>
    <PopReceipt>AgAAAEAAAAAAAAAYgyzXl7LzQE=</PopReceipt>
    <TimeNextVisible>Sun, 25 Nov 2012 22:44:03 GMT</TimeNextVisible>
    <MessageText>TXNnQg==</MessageText>
  </QueueMessage>
</QueueMessagesList>
0
```

You can augment your message request by specifying a number of parameters, provided in Table 7-2, that control the number of messages retrieved at one time, how long to wait for the messages to be retrieved, and how long the messages should remain invisible to other potential recipients.

TABLE 7-2 *Querystring* parameters for message retrieval

Parameter	Value	Effect
numofmessages	Integer messages	Optional. Identifies the number of messages to retrieve at one time, between 1 and 32 (inclusive). When fewer messages are visible than the number specified, all visible messages are returned. If *numofmessages* isn't specified, the message queue returns one message by default.
timeout	Integer seconds	Optional. Identifies the amount of time, in seconds, allowed for the queuing service to process the request. This value cannot be less than zero, and the default at the time of this book's writing was 30 seconds. Although the parameter is optional to the API, the Windows Azure client library automatically supplies a default value of 90 seconds for this parameter, overriding the REST API default value of 30 seconds.
visibilitytimeout	Integer seconds	Optional. Identifies the amount of time, in seconds, allowed before the message will become visible in the queue again if it is not deleted by the message consumer.

> **Note** The default *visibilitytimeout* is 30 seconds for Windows Azure, but the default *visibilitytimeout* when using the client library is 90 seconds. The client library overrides the 30-second default of Windows Azure storage service by always sending a *visibilitytimeout querystring* parameter of 90 seconds when a *visibilitytimeout* has not been specified.

Messages can also be retrieved from a queue by a consumer by using the Windows Azure client library, as shown in the next code example. The queue's *GetMessage* method retrieves a specified number of messages from the queue, and the default is 32.

The *visibilityTimeout* parameter controls the amount of time before the message becomes visible in the queue again if the message is not deleted. This time span is added to the current time to compute the *TimeNextVisible* property of each message returned by the service. The default *visibilityTimeout* is 30 seconds, but the value used in the example has been arbitrarily reduced to 5 seconds to simulate a message processing failure. You'll learn more about this later in the chapter in the section "Poison messages and handling."

```
private static void RetrieveMessages(CloudQueue queue) {
    // Consumers process messages:
    var visibilityTimeout = TimeSpan.FromSeconds(5); // Max=7 days
    Int32 demo = 0;
    while (true) {
        const Int32 c_MaxMsgsToGet = 32;
        var msgs = queue.GetMessages(c_MaxMsgsToGet, visibilityTimeout);
        if (msgs.Count() == 0) {
            Thread.Sleep(1000);  // IMPORTANT: Balance cost with latency
            continue;
```

```
        }
        foreach (CloudQueueMessage cqm in msgs) {
            Console.WriteLine(QueueMessageToString(cqm)); // For demo
            if (cqm.DequeueCount < 3) {
                // Process message here...
            }
            else {
                // Log poison msg to fix code here...
            }
            if (demo == 1) queue.SafeDeleteMessage(cqm);
        }
        if (demo++ == 1) break;
        Console.WriteLine();
    }
}
```

As shown in Table 7-3, each message contains additional information useful in its handling, such as when it was placed on the queue, when it should be discarded, how many times it has been consumed, who the current owner of the message is, and when it will become visible to other potential consumers again.

TABLE 7-3 Message response properties

Property	Description
MessageId	The *MessageId* is a GUID that uniquely identifies the message.
InsertionTime	The date and time that the message was originally placed on the queue.
ExpirationTime	The date and time that the message expires. When the current time relative to the time as known by the Windows Azure storage service exceeds this value, the message is marked for deletion and will no longer be visible to message consumers. After this date and time, any outstanding *PopReceipts* held by consumers are considered expired, and the message may no longer be updated or deleted. Small differences in clock times between machines will cause variability in the actual expiry of messages.
DequeueCount	The number of times this message has been removed from the queue. The *DequeueCount* property is incremented by one each time the message is received by a new consumer. The value of this property should be checked first by the consumer to ensure that the message is not a poison message (one that has been dequeued an excessive number of times as defined by the application).
PopReceipt	An opaque value that is calculated and dispatched for every message recipient. The last *PopReceipt* issued identifies the message's current owner, who is the only recipient allowed to update or delete the message. If the message is not retrieved and deleted by a more recent message consumer after the message becomes visible in the queue again, the original *PopReceipt* can be still be used to update or delete the message. Attempts to use an expired *PopReceipt* results in an HTTP 400 (Bad Request) status code with additional information about the error in the body of the response.
TimeNextVisible	The time that the message should become visible in the queue again after it is retrieved by a message consumer but before the message consumer deletes it. This value is calculated by Windows Azure storage service by adding the value of the *visibilitytimeout querystring* parameter (or the visibility timeout default of 30 seconds) to the time the message was retrieved. You should anticipate that the consuming owner of the message will either update or delete the message before *TimeNextVisible* is reached.
MessageText	The message contents as they were placed in the message. The message text must be capable of being UTF-8 encoded. To meet the encoding requirement, the Windows Azure client library base64 encodes this data.

Note The default *visibilitytimeout* is 30 seconds for Windows Azure, but the default *visibilitytimeout* when using the client library is 90 seconds. The client library overrides the 30-second default by always sending a *visibilitytimeout querystring* parameter of 90 seconds to the Windows Azure storage service unless a specific value is supplied in code.

Pop receipts

A *pop receipt* is an opaque value that is calculated as an extra element of each message retrieved from a queue. This receipt is used to prove current ownership for subsequent data operations against the message, such as updating or deleting the message. Because a message may be dispatched to more than one message consumer, the pop receipt serves as proof that its bearer is the current owner. If a consumer attempts to perform a data operation against a message with an invalid pop receipt, the queue service will respond with an HTTP status code of 440 (Bad Request), including additional information notifying you that the pop receipt was invalid.

Pop receipts are valid until one of these four events occurs:

- The pop receipt's message expires (for example, the current date and time exceed the expiry date of the message).

- The message is deleted by using the most recently issued pop receipt. Whenever a message is deleted, all pop receipts issued for that message are invalid.

- Another message consumer dequeues the message again. When a new consumer dequeues the message, all previously issued pop receipts become invalid. This condition occurs when the current date and time exceeds the message's *TimeNextVisible* element.

- The message is updated. Whenever a message is updated, a new pop receipt is generated and returned with the message.

If the message has already been deleted from the queue, the queue service will respond with an HTTP status code of 404 (Not Found).

Peek messages

You can examine messages in the queue without consuming them by using the *peekonly* attribute with a value of *true*. The only difference between retrieving a message and peeking at a message is the inclusion of the *peekonly querystring* parameter in the request, as illustrated in the following code.

```
GET http://azureinsiders.queue.core.windows.net/demo/messages?
    peekonly=true&numofmessages=32&timeout=90 HTTP/1.1
x-ms-version: 2012-02-12
User-Agent: WA-Storage/2.0.0
x-ms-date: Mon, 26 Nov 2012 04:49:34 GMT
Authorization: SharedKey azureinsiders:79rhRtWUw6D9CROGDJCj8r546m+zg9aHjICNp3ZkAeA=
Host: azureinsiders.queue.core.windows.net
```

Sending the preceding message to the queue service returns the messages in the queue without processing them and without making them invisible to other consumers. Additional information about each message is also returned, such as the time the message was placed in the queue, the message's calculated expiration time, and how many times the message has been dequeued. The number of times a message has been dequeued can be useful in determining whether a message is poisoning the queue. If a message is poisoning the queue, the message requires special handling to be removed from the queue to avoid slowing the rate by which other messages get processed.

```
HTTP/1.1 200 OK
Transfer-Encoding: chunked
Content-Type: application/xml
Server: Windows-Azure-Queue/1.0 Microsoft-HTTPAPI/2.0
x-ms-request-id: bcbe9e6d-a598-44cb-8b33-b71b44bc9487
x-ms-version: 2012-02-12
Date: Mon, 26 Nov 2012 04:49:35 GMT

276
?<?xml version="1.0" encoding="utf-8"?>
<QueueMessagesList>
  <QueueMessage>
    <MessageId>e4edecae-bd13-4793-a5ff-378ba65a3640</MessageId>
    <InsertionTime>Mon, 26 Nov 2012 04:49:33 GMT</InsertionTime>
    <ExpirationTime>Fri, 30 Nov 2012 04:49:33 GMT</ExpirationTime>
    <DequeueCount>0</DequeueCount>
    <MessageText>TXNnQQ==</MessageText>
  </QueueMessage>
  <QueueMessage>
    <MessageId>c4352d27-71fa-44aa-aa50-bfb0ef9ec4c6</MessageId>
    <InsertionTime>Mon, 26 Nov 2012 04:49:33 GMT</InsertionTime>
    <ExpirationTime>Fri, 30 Nov 2012 04:49:33 GMT</ExpirationTime>
    <DequeueCount>0</DequeueCount>
    <MessageText>TXNnQg==</MessageText>
  </QueueMessage>
</QueueMessagesList>
```

Messages can also be peeked at in a queue by using the Windows Azure client library, as shown in the following sample code.

```
private static void PeekMessages(CloudQueue queue) {
    const Int32 c_MaxMsgsToGet = 32;
    Console.WriteLine("Peek the messages:");
    foreach (var cqm in queue.PeekMessages(c_MaxMsgsToGet))
        Console.WriteLine(QueueMessageToString(cqm));
    Console.WriteLine();
}
```

Retrieving metadata

The primary piece of metadata about each queue is the approximate message count, which can be retrieved by sending an HTTP *HEAD* request to the message queue URI with a *comp=metadata querystring* parameter.

```
HEAD http://azureinsiders.queue.core.windows.net/demo?comp=metadata&timeout=90 HTTP/1.1
x-ms-version: 2012-02-12
User-Agent: WA-Storage/2.0.0
x-ms-date: Sun, 25 Nov 2012 22:41:24 GMT
Authorization: SharedKey azureinsiders:jI7k2PKh783MluA7oxBG2GK8RL1U2bhQa/5GApP30w4=
Host: azureinsiders.queue.core.windows.net
Connection: Keep-Alive
```

   Upon successful execution, Windows Azure data storage will respond by sending you an HTTP 200 status code and other message headers, including the *x-ms-approximate-message-count* header, as shown here.

```
HTTP/1.1 200 OK
Transfer-Encoding: chunked
Server: Windows-Azure-Queue/1.0 Microsoft-HTTPAPI/2.0
x-ms-request-id: f56244df-8409-4c3a-8b9a-90c6f6c916a0
x-ms-version: 2012-02-12
x-ms-approximate-messages-count: 2
Date: Sun, 25 Nov 2012 22:41:23 GMT
```

Deleting messages

After your consuming application successfully completes processing a message, you'll need to delete that message before it becomes visible again and gets dispatched to another consumer. If the message is dispatched before your consuming application gets an opportunity to delete it, the application will not be allowed to delete it because the message's pop receipt will no longer be the current one. To avoid unnecessary charges for wasted resources, extend the time you use for the *visibilitytimeout querystring* parameter that you're using for message retrieval.

   To delete a message from a queue, you send an HTTP DELETE request to the message's URI, matching the following pattern and including the message's pop receipt value as a *querystring* parameter.

```
http://<account>.queue.core.windows.net/<queue>messages<message-id>?popreceipt=<popreceipt>
```

The following is an example of an HTTP request to delete a message.

```
DELETE http://azureinsiders.queue.core.windows.net/demo/messages/
    c4352d27-71fa-44aa-aa50-bfb0ef9ec4c6?
    popreceipt=AgAAAAEAAAAAAAAANOWDwZPLzQE%3D&timeout=90 HTTP/1.1
x-ms-version: 2012-02-12
User-Agent: WA-Storage/2.0.0
x-ms-date: Mon, 26 Nov 2012 05:06:06 GMT
Authorization: SharedKey azureinsiders:OMn/QDRQO76mJ/hZ7As6nOE+SnupBTnt7SdHqa5vChs=
Host: azureinsiders.queue.core.windows.net
```

If the message deletion request is successful, the queue service responds with an HTTP status code of 204 (No Content), as shown in the following response.

```
HTTP/1.1 204 No Content
Content-Length: 0
Server: Windows-Azure-Queue/1.0 Microsoft-HTTPAPI/2.0
x-ms-request-id: 40562f87-b202-40c6-a12e-505b04cc0ac5
x-ms-version: 2012-02-12
Date: Mon, 26 Nov 2012 05:06:07 GMT
```

Messages can also be deleted by using the Windows Azure client library by calling a message's *DeleteMessage* method. To write robust code, you should catch the possible *StorageException* that may be thrown if the message has already been deleted or you are no longer in possession of the most recent pop receipt for the message. When you catch a *StorageException*, you must then check the exception's *RequestInformation* property's *HttpStatusCode* property to ensure that it is an *HttpStatusCode.NotFound* error. If it is an *HttpStatusCode.NotFound* error, you can assume the message was already deleted and safely ignore the exception. If the *HttpStatusCode* is not an *HttpStatusCode.NotFound* though, then you should assume it is some other condition and re-throw the exception. Writing this kind of code around every message delete operation would be repetitive and painful. The following code shows how to create an extension method called *SafeDeleteMessage* to encapsulate the exception handling pattern.

```
public static void SafeDeleteMessage(this CloudQueue queue, String messageId, String popReceipt)
{
    try { queue.DeleteMessage(messageId, popReceipt); }
    catch (StorageException e) {
        RequestResult rr = e.RequestInformation;
        if ((rr.HttpStatusCode == (Int32) HttpStatusCode.NotFound) &&
          (rr.ExtendedErrorInformation.ErrorMessage == QueueErrorCodeStrings.MessageNotFound)) {
            // pop receipt must be invalid;
            // ignore or log (so that we can tune the visibility timeout)
        } else throw; // Not the error we were expecting
    }
}
```

Poison messages and handling

Periodically, a message may not be able to be processed by a consumer. This is often because of an error condition such as erroneous data, a programming defect, or an environmental condition. In a few application scenarios, you may not have to successfully complete message processing, in which case the exception may be caught and the message deleted from the queue during error handling.

Deleting a message that cannot be processed is not usually desired. When an unhandled exception occurs, the message becomes visible again on the queue and the next consumer retrieves the message. When this occurs, the *DequeueCount* property of the message is incremented, allowing the consumer to know how many times a message has been dequeued without deletion. A message that has been dequeued multiple times is considered a *poison message*. It is clogging the arteries of your infrastructure by keeping good messages from being processed, because consumers continue to waste resources processing the poison message.

As a best practice, consumers should always check the *DequeueCount* property to ensure that its value is within a reasonable range. When the value is unacceptably high, the message should be treated as a poison message and handled appropriately. In many messaging infrastructures, a dead letter queue is created for messages that cannot be processed by an application. Upon detection of a poison message, your code could create a clone of the message in your application's dead letter queue and then delete the original message from its source queue. As an alternative to the dead letter queue, you might save poison messages in blobs that you place in a blob container you have created for that purpose. You could also create an entity in table storage if you preferred.

Consider the code earlier in this chapter in the section "Retrieving messages from a queue," in which you retrieve a batch of messages and then wait a period of time before proceeding by placing your thread to sleep for an appropriate amount of time. What is appropriate for your application will depend largely upon your goal of message processing performance after considering the estimated cost of its acquirement. You are balancing your costs of performance with latency of message processing. If the code did not pause briefly by putting its executing thread to sleep or otherwise occupy itself by performing some other work for a period of time, the code would immediately make another request of the server for more messages, and if there were no messages, the code would hit the server again. In short, you would be relentlessly demanding more messages from the service, and you would be paying for each transaction to tell you only that there was nothing to process. Thrashing on a message queue by continuously hitting it in a tight loop can be an effective way of squeezing out a small amount of additional message throughput; however, you will be wasting CPU time, network bandwidth, storage service resources answering nonoperational requests, and money for fees associated with these overhead transactions. It is even possible that you might degrade throughput rather than improve it. If this is of concern to you, you should conduct performance tests with your application in the cloud under anticipated workloads to fine tune the period you wait between checks for additional messages to process.

As you begin to process the messages in the code that follows, you retrieve them from the queue in a *foreach* loop and immediately check that each message's *DequeueCount* property is not greater than the value you established, in this case *2*. In most cases, a value of *1* would be too small, because that would imply that no retries are allowed, but conversely, a value that is too high would result in unnecessarily wasting resources. If the *DequeueCount* is within range, you process the message, but if it is out of range, you handle the condition by moving it to a dead letter queue, blob storage, table storage, or some other kind of storage such as a SQL Azure table.

One more operation in the following code needs explanation. The *SafeDeleteMessage* method wraps handling of *PopReceipt* to ensure that the correct message gets deleted from the queue. You'll learn more about the *PopReciept* in the next section of this chapter.

```
while (true) {
    var msgs = queue.GetMessages(c_MaxMsgsToGet, visibilityTimeout);
    if (msgs.Count() == 0) {
        Thread.Sleep(1000);  // IMPORTANT: Balance cost with latency
        continue;
    }
    foreach (CloudQueueMessage cqm in msgs) {
        Console.WriteLine(QueueMessageToString(cqm)); // For demo
        if (cqm.DequeueCount < 3) {
            // Process message here...
        }
        else {
            // Log poison msg to fix code here...
        }
        if (demo == 1) queue.SafeDeleteMessage(cqm);
    }
    if (demo++ == 1) break;
    Console.WriteLine();
}
```

If you attempt to update or delete a message in the queue with an outdated pop receipt, you will receive a response with an HTTP status code of 400 indicating that one of the query parameters (your pop receipt in this case) was outside of the permissible range.

```
HTTP/1.1 400 One of the query parameters specified in the request URI is outside the
permissible range.
Proxy-Connection: Keep-Alive
Connection: Keep-Alive
Content-Length: 455
Via: 1.1 TK5-PRXY-22
Date: Wed, 02 May 2012 19:37:23 GMT
Content-Type: application/xml
Server: Windows-Azure-Queue/1.0 Microsoft-HTTPAPI/2.0
x-ms-request-id: 6a03526c-ca2c-4358-a63a-b5d096988533
x-ms-version: 2011-08-18

<?xml version="1.0" encoding="utf-8"?>
    <Error>
        <Code>OutOfRangeQueryParameterValue</Code>
        <Message>One of the query parameters specified in the request URI is outside the
permissible range.
```

```
        RequestId:6a03526c-ca2c-4358-a63a-b5d096988533
        Time:2012-05-02T19:37:24.2438463Z
    </Message>
    <QueryParameterName>numofmessages</QueryParameterName>
    <QueryParameterValue>0</QueryParameterValue>
    <MinimumAllowed>1</MinimumAllowed>
    <MaximumAllowed>32</MaximumAllowed>
</Error>
```

Deleting a message queue

Creating or deleting queues is not that common. Generally, queues get set up to send messages between roles to facilitate scalability and separation of concerns. The queue is created and deleted, when necessary, as a maintenance task separate from the applications that create and consume messages. For example, often this functionality is placed in an application installer or in an application's administrative tools. When a queue is deleted, all messages that may be in the queue are deleted, too. If this is an important consideration to you, you will need to implement a mechanism for stopping senders from creating new messages until the consumers can drain the queue to an empty state. The queue will become immediately unavailable; however, the deletion itself happens asynchronously, so there may be some variable period of time (usually several seconds to a minute or two) where you will not be allowed to create a queue with the same name. Attempts to create a queue with the same name as one that is still in the process of being deleted will result in an HTTP 409 response indicating a conflict. If your code needs to delete and immediately recreate a queue, consider a strategy that uses a unique queue name, or introduce a delay and retry the procedure as provided in the sample code that accompanies this book. The following HTTP request shows how to delete a message queue.

```
DELETE http://azureinsiders.queue.core.windows.net/demo?timeout=90 HTTP/1.1
x-ms-version: 2012-02-12
User-Agent: WA-Storage/2.0.0
x-ms-date: Tue, 04 Dec 2012 00:51:13 GMT
Authorization: SharedKey azureinsiders:12CLGtMSxQCS6um456Onyv4nWiy7j2hxZfjOwstM+BU=
Host: azureinsiders.queue.core.windows.net
```

Upon successful execution of your request, Windows Azure storage service responds with an HTTP status code of 204 (No Content), which is your confirmation that the queue was deleted, as shown here.

```
HTTP/1.1 204 No Content
Content-Length: 0
Server: Windows-Azure-Queue/1.0 Microsoft-HTTPAPI/2.0
x-ms-request-id: e20fe807-b240-4139-8f93-570e3f20fafc
x-ms-version: 2012-02-12
Date: Tue, 04 Dec 2012 00:51:14 GMT
```

The queue can be deleted using the Windows Azure client library by calling the queue's delete method.

```
queue.Delete();
```

Conclusion

The purpose of this chapter was to provide you with a thorough understanding of how to securely perform data operations against the queuing storage service. You were introduced to many of the business cases for queuing. You learned how to create queues and place messages on the tail of the queue, and then you learned how to consume those messages from the head of the queue. This chapter then explained how the Windows Azure storage service makes a message invisible to other consumers until the consumer either deletes the message or the message's invisibility timeout expires, allowing other consumers to receive the message. You also learned how error conditions can create poison messages and how to check each message's *DeQueueCount* property to ensure that a message is not a poison message. Options for dealing with poison messages when they occur were explored. Finally, you learned how to delete a message queue.

Analytics, logging, and transaction metrics

This chapter introduces you to Windows Azure Storage Analytics. You will learn how to collect and analyze Windows Azure data management service consumption logs and metrics for blobs, tables, and queues. With the data you collect, you can analyze storage usage to improve the design of your applications and their access patterns to Windows Azure Storage as well as debug many usage scenarios.

Request logging

The request logging feature of the Storage Analytics service records successfully authenticated requests made against blob, table, and queue storage, as well as anonymous requests made against blob storage. The logging feature is enabled through the portal, which is depicted in Figure 8-1.

Logs are stored in a hidden block blob container named *$logs*. This container is automatically created for you when you enable Storage Analytics on a storage account and cannot be deleted. As explained in Chapter 5, "Blobs," the *$* prefix indicates that client tools should treat the containers as hidden. Thus, the *$logs* container is hidden by convention, but apart from that, it is the same as any other blob container and is accessible using the application programming interfaces (APIs). The blobs themselves, however, can only be read or deleted, which prevents mischievous tampering of the data.

In Figure 8-1, you see how to control logging of read, write, and delete operations on blobs, tables, and queues from the Logging section of the configure screen. You can also see how the number of days that you want to retain the data can be set. A setting of 0 (zero) provides unlimited logging until the 20-gigabyte (GB) limit on the account is reached. Because logging data can accumulate very rapidly, set your retention policy to something reasonable for your requirements.

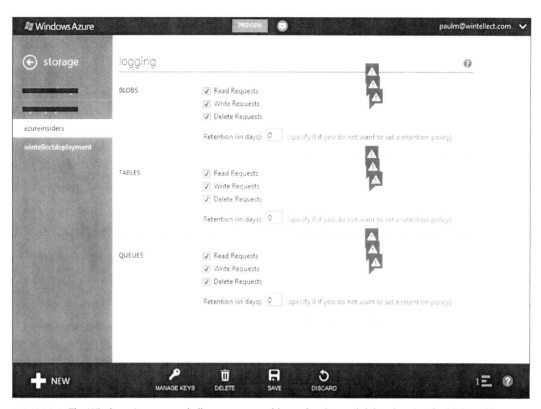

FIGURE 8-1 The Windows Azure portal allows you to enable read, write, and delete logging for blobs, tables, and queues, as well as establish a data retention policy for logging.

Most tools for viewing storage, including Microsoft Visual Studio, do not show containers beginning with $ (and you do not even have the option to show them); however, those containers are fully accessible via the RESTful API and through the Windows Azure client library.

By executing the following HTTP *GET* request against the *$logs* container URI, you can retrieve a list of all logs that have been collected.

```
GET http://azureinsiders.blob.core.windows.net/$logs?
    restype=container&comp=list&maxresults=1000&timeout=90 HTTP/1.1
x-ms-version: 2011-08-18
User-Agent: WA-Storage/1.6.0
x-ms-date: Sat, 21 Jul 2012 19:38:10 GMT
Authorization: SharedKey azureinsiders:06/NA+/4MPR3+YQnUaQ5/Yse54OkyjKGCA4ZbOqy2No=
Host: azureinsiders.blob.core.windows.net
Connection: Keep-Alive
```

The data is returned to you in the response as an *EnumerationResults* similar to the following.

```
HTTP/1.1 200 OK
Transfer-Encoding: chunked
Content-Type: application/xml
Server: Windows-Azure-Blob/1.0 Microsoft-HTTPAPI/2.0
x-ms-request-id: 44f51baa-5aca-43d3-b8c4-0b188342bb10
```

```
x-ms-version: 2011-08-18
Date: Sat, 21 Jul 2012 19:38:16 GMT
290D
<?xml version="1.0" encoding="utf-8"?>
<EnumerationResults ContainerName="http://azureinsiders.blob.core.windows.net/$logs">
  <MaxResults>1000</MaxResults>
  <Blobs>
    <Blob>
      <Name>blob/2012/07/19/0600/000000.log</Name>
      <Url>http://azureinsiders.blob.core.windows.net/$logs/blob/2012/07/19/0600/000000.log</Url>
      <Properties>
        <Last-Modified>Thu, 19 Jul 2012 06:51:11 GMT</Last-Modified>
        <Etag>0x8CF339204329DC8</Etag>
        <Content-Length>18604</Content-Length>
        <Content-Type>application/octet-stream</Content-Type>
        <Content-Encoding />
        <Content-Language />
        <Content-MD5 />
        <Cache-Control />
        <BlobType>BlockBlob</BlobType>
        <LeaseStatus>unlocked</LeaseStatus>
      </Properties>
    </Blob>
    <Blob> data truncated for brevity </Blob>
  </Blobs>
  <NextMarker />
</EnumerationResults>
```

In the preceding response to your request for a list of logs stored in the *$logs* blob container, the *Url* element of each blob listed in the *EnumerationResults* defines the location of a block blob containing logging information. The URL adheres to the following naming scheme by using the definitions provided in Table 8-1.

<service name>/*<YYYY>*/*<MM>*/*<DD>*/*<hhmm>*/*<Counter>*.log

TABLE 8-1 Segments of blob names containing logging data

Segment	Purpose
service name	Type of data being logged: blob, table, or queue.
YYYY	Four-digit number denoting the year that the log was made.
MM	Two-digit number denoting the month that the log was made.
DD	Two-digit number denoting the date that the log was made.
hh	Two-digit number denoting the hour, in 24-hour UTC format, that the log was made. This is the starting hour for the logs contained within the blob.
mm	Two-digit number denoting the starting minute for all the logs. (In the current version, this is always 00, but minutes have been reserved for possible future use.)
Counter	A six-digit zero-based counter. Multiple logs may be generated within an hour.

Logging in a high-volume distributed environment presents many challenges. Multiple storage nodes servicing the same request, the skew of clocks on servers, and the sheer volume of data being logged are all factors. The naming scheme for logs was designed to provide some level of efficiency in dealing with many of these challenges. It is important to note, though, that log entries can be recorded out of order. Long-running tasks are recorded upon their completion.

Additional metadata about each log can be obtained by appending the *include=metadata* query string parameter to the HTTP request.

If you are using the Windows Azure client library, you can iterate through the contents of the blob container *$logs* and then download the metadata about each blob by using the *FetchAttributes* method, as shown in the following code snippet.

```
public static void AnalyticsLogs(CloudStorageAccount account) {
    CloudBlobClient client = account.CreateCloudBlobClient();
    CloudBlobContainer c = client.GetContainerReference("$logs");
    for (BlobResultSegment brs = null; brs.HasMore(); ) {
        brs = c.ListBlobsSegmented(null, true, BlobListingDetails.None, 1000, brs.
SafeContinuationToken(), null, null);
        foreach (var b in brs.Results) {
            Console.WriteLine(" " + b.Uri);
            CloudBlockBlob blob = c.GetBlockBlobReference(b.Uri.ToString());
            blob.FetchAttributes();
            foreach (String key in blob.Metadata.Keys) {
                Console.WriteLine("\t{0}={1}", key, blob.Metadata[key]);
            }
        }
    }
}
```

Execution of the preceding code will produce the following output, which includes the URL of each blob and the five attributes described in Table 8-2.

```
http://azureinsiders.blob.core.windows.net/$logs/blob/2012/07/20/0400/000000.log
        StartTime=2012-07-20T04:19:44.1682549Z
        EndTime=2012-07-20T04:23:19.3206064Z
        LogType=read,write,delete
        LogVersion=1.0
        Opaque1=18950260600
http://azureinsiders.blob.core.windows.net/$logs/blob/2012/07/20/0400/000001.log
        StartTime=2012-07-20T04:33:26.9576275Z
        EndTime=2012-07-20T04:33:36.2645580Z
        LogType=read
        LogVersion=1.0
        Opaque1=19699789890
http://azureinsiders.blob.core.windows.net/$logs/blob/2012/07/20/0600/000000.log
        StartTime=2012-07-20T06:30:13.2831211Z
        EndTime=2012-07-20T06:32:23.5270955Z
        LogType=read
        LogVersion=1.0
        Opaque1=28073321296
http://azureinsiders.blob.core.windows.net/$logs/blob/2012/07/20/0600/000001.log
        StartTime=2012-07-20T06:39:10.0536200Z
        EndTime=2012-07-20T06:39:12.0582550Z
        LogType=read,write,delete
        LogVersion=1.0
        Opaque1=28777134253
```

TABLE 8-2 Log metadata attribute values

Element	Purpose
LogType	A comma-separated list of read, write, and delete permissions indicating the type of log.
StartTime	The minimum value of entries contained in the log.
EndTime	The maximum value of entries contained in the log.
LogVersion	The version of the log's format. Version 1.0 was current at the time of this writing. The *LogVersion* metadata value provides a mechanism for future versions of the log format to be programmatically consumed and processed.

When retrieving a list of blobs via the RESTful API, as shown earlier in this section on logging, you can include in the response the metadata elements in Table 8-2 by adding the *include=metadata* parameter to the request URI. This is useful when identifying which logs have occurred during a specific time range for processing.

```
GET http://azureinsiders.blob.core.windows.net/$logs?
    restype=container&comp=list&include=metadata&maxresults=1000&timeout=90 HTTP/1.1
x-ms-version: 2011-08-18
User-Agent: WA-Storage/1.6.0
x-ms-date: Sat, 21 Jul 2012 19:38:10 GMT
Authorization: SharedKey azureinsiders:06/NA+/4MPR3+YQnUaQ5/Yse54OkyjKGCA4ZbOqy2No=
Host: azureinsiders.blob.core.windows.net
Connection: Keep-Alive
```

Note Duplicate log records may exist in logs generated for the same hour. You can locate them by searching for duplicate *RequestId* and *Operation* numbers.

Metrics

Transaction and capacity statistics are gathered and stored by the Storage Analytics service. Metrics data can be used in the analysis of storage usage patterns to do the following:

■ Improve the performance or reliability of an application that uses the data stored in storage services.

■ Adapt your storage architecture to meet the changing needs of your applications.

■ Diagnose certain kinds of trouble in your client application such as the cause of frequent or periodic timeouts.

You can activate storage account metrics through the Windows Azure portal storage management Monitoring section of the configure screen, as shown in Figure 8-2.

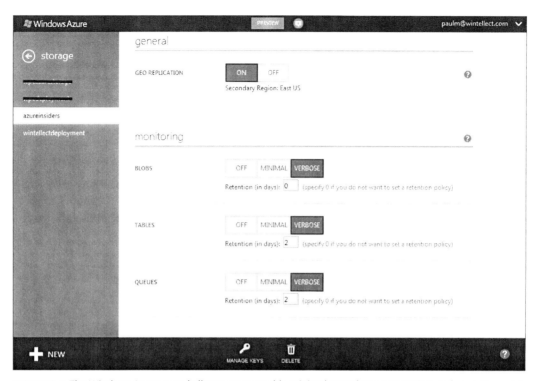

FIGURE 8-2 The Windows Azure portal allows you to enable minimal or verbose transaction and capacity metrics of blob, table, and queue activities, as well as establish a data retention policy for the collected results.

Transaction and capacity metrics are recorded in hidden storage tables, identified in the following list. These tables correspond to the type of storage being metered (blob, table, and queue). Transaction data is captured at both the operation level (*GET*, *PUT*, *POST*, and so on) and the storage service level. At the time of this writing, capacity data was captured only at the storage service level for blobs (but not for tables and queues). The following four tables are automatically created when metrics are enabled:

- **$MetricsTransactionsBlob**   Transaction metrics for blobs

- **$MetricsTransactionsTable**   Transaction metrics for tables

- **$MetricsTransactionsQueue**   Transaction metrics for queues

- **$MetricsCapacityBlob**   Capacity metrics for blobs

Like the *$logs* blob container, these metrics tables are automatically created when Storage Analytics are enabled for your storage account. They are accessed via the namespace of the storage account by using the URI pattern for tables (introduced in Chapter 6, "Tables").

```
http://<accountname>.table.core.windows.net/Tables("<$MetricsTableName>")
```

In Figure 8-2, you saw how to control the capture of transaction and capacity data for blobs, tables, and queues. You can also set the number of days that you want to retain the captured data. A setting of 0 provides unlimited logging until the 20-GB limit on the account is reached. Because logging data can accumulate very rapidly, set your retention policy to something reasonable for your requirements.

You can see the results of the captured data in a graphical format in the Dashboard view, shown in Figure 8-3.

FIGURE 8-3 The Dashboard view shows the captured data in an efficient graphical format.

There are nine metrics that may be monitored from the Windows Azure management portal, which consists of the following three sets of parameters for each storage type (blob, table, and queue):

- **Availability**   Service availability for blobs, tables and queues

- **Successful Percentage**   Ratio of requests completed successfully for blobs, tables, and queues

- **Total Requests**   Total storage requests made for blobs, tables and queues

Transaction metrics

To retrieve all the transaction metrics data for a specified storage type, issue an HTTP *GET* request against the appropriate metrics table storage URI. The following code shows transaction metrics for blob storage.

```
GET http://azureinsiders.table.core.windows.net/$MetricsTransactionsBlob() HTTP/1.1
User-Agent: Microsoft ADO.NET Data Services
DataServiceVersion: 1.0;NetFx
MaxDataServiceVersion: 2.0;NetFx
x-ms-version: 2011-08-18
x-ms-date: Mon, 30 Jul 2012 05:49:28 GMT
Authorization: SharedKeyLite azureinsiders:swdO3wVtHOqFBG3QWnVI2hL+8uwataeFEEKavFTF66A=
Accept: application/atom+xml,application/xml
Accept-Charset: UTF-8
Host: azureinsiders.table.core.windows.net
Connection: Keep-Alive
```

Upon its successful execution, the preceding request will return a list of all of the metrics collected for the blob. Of course, you can narrow the selection by providing additional section criteria, as shown here.

```
HTTP/1.1 200 OK
Cache-Control: no-cache
Transfer-Encoding: chunked
Content-Type: application/atom+xml;charset=utf-8
Server: Windows-Azure-Table/1.0 Microsoft-HTTPAPI/2.0
x-ms-request-id: a732028b-19c0-47f6-adcf-67810974362c
x-ms-version: 2011-08-18
Date: Mon, 30 Jul 2012 05:49:29 GMT

25073A
<?xml version="1.0" encoding="utf-8" standalone="yes"?>
<feed
    xml:base="http://azureinsiders.table.core.windows.net/"
    xmlns:d="http://schemas.microsoft.com/ado/2007/08/dataservices"
    xmlns:m="http://schemas.microsoft.com/ado/2007/08/dataservices/metadata"
    xmlns="http://www.w3.org/2005/Atom">
  <title type="text">$MetricsTransactionsBlob</title>
  <id>http://azureinsiders.table.core.windows.net/$MetricsTransactionsBlob</id>
  <updated>2012-07-30T05:49:30Z</updated>
  <link rel="self" title="$MetricsTransactionsBlob" href="$MetricsTransactionsBlob" />
  <entry m:etag="W/&quot;datetime'2012-07-19T06%3A19%3A49.3893856Z'&quot;">
    <id>http://azureinsiders.table.core.windows.net/$MetricsTransactionsBlob(
    PartitionKey='20120719T0500',RowKey='system%3BAll')</id>
    <title type="text"></title>
    <updated>2012-07-30T05:49:30Z</updated>
    <author>
      <name />
    </author>
    <link rel="edit" title="$MetricsTransactionsBlob"
        href="$MetricsTransactionsBlob(PartitionKey='20120719T0500',RowKey='system%3BAll')" />
    <category term="azureinsiders.$MetricsTransactionsBlob"
        scheme="http://schemas.microsoft.com/ado/2007/08/dataservices/scheme" />
```

```xml
<content type="application/xml">
  <m:properties>
    <d:PartitionKey>20120719T0500</d:PartitionKey>
    <d:RowKey>system;All</d:RowKey>
    <d:Timestamp m:type="Edm.DateTime">2012-07-19T06:19:49.3893856Z
    </d:Timestamp>
    <d:TotalRequests m:type="Edm.Int64">0</d:TotalRequests>
    <d:TotalBillableRequests m:type="Edm.Int64">0</d:TotalBillableRequests>
    <d:TotalIngress m:type="Edm.Int64">0</d:TotalIngress>
    <d:TotalEgress m:type="Edm.Int64">0</d:TotalEgress>
    <d:Availability m:type="Edm.Double">100</d:Availability>
    <d:AverageE2ELatency m:type="Edm.Double">0</d:AverageE2ELatency>
    <d:AverageServerLatency m:type="Edm.Double">0</d:AverageServerLatency>
    <d:PercentSuccess m:type="Edm.Double">0</d:PercentSuccess>
    <d:PercentSuccessOutsideSLA
      m:type="Edm.Double">0</d:PercentSuccessOutsideSLA>
    <d:PercentThrottlingError
      m:type="Edm.Double">0</d:PercentThrottlingError>
    <d:PercentTimeoutError m:type="Edm.Double">0</d:PercentTimeoutError>
    <d:PercentServerOtherError
      m:type="Edm.Double">0</d:PercentServerOtherError>
    <d:PercentClientOtherError
      m:type="Edm.Double">0</d:PercentClientOtherError>
    <d:PercentAuthorizationError
      m:type="Edm.Double">0</d:PercentAuthorizationError>
    <d:PercentNetworkError m:type="Edm.Double">0</d:PercentNetworkError>
    <d:Success m:type="Edm.Int64">0</d:Success>
    <d:AnonymousSuccess m:type="Edm.Int64">0</d:AnonymousSuccess>
    <d:SASSuccess m:type="Edm.Int64">0</d:SASSuccess>
    <d:SuccessOutsideSLA m:type="Edm.Int64">0</d:SuccessOutsideSLA>
    <d:AnonymousSuccessOutsideSLA
      m:type="Edm.Int64">0</d:AnonymousSuccessOutsideSLA>
    <d:SASSuccessOutsideSLA m:type="Edm.Int64">0</d:SASSuccessOutsideSLA>
    <d:ThrottlingError m:type="Edm.Int64">0</d:ThrottlingError>
    <d:AnonymousThrottlingError
      m:type="Edm.Int64">0</d:AnonymousThrottlingError>
    <d:SASThrottlingError m:type="Edm.Int64">0</d:SASThrottlingError>
    <d:ClientTimeoutError m:type="Edm.Int64">0</d:ClientTimeoutError>
    <d:AnonymousClientTimeoutError
      m:type="Edm.Int64">0</d:AnonymousClientTimeoutError>
    <d:SASClientTimeoutError m:type="Edm.Int64">0</d:SASClientTimeoutError>
    <d:ServerTimeoutError m:type="Edm.Int64">0</d:ServerTimeoutError>
    <d:AnonymousServerTimeoutError
      m:type="Edm.Int64">0</d:AnonymousServerTimeoutError>
    <d:SASServerTimeoutError m:type="Edm.Int64">0</d:SASServerTimeoutError>
    <d:ClientOtherError m:type="Edm.Int64">0</d:ClientOtherError>
    <d:AnonymousClientOtherError
      m:type="Edm.Int64">0</d:AnonymousClientOtherError>
    <d:SASClientOtherError m:type="Edm.Int64">0</d:SASClientOtherError>
    <d:ServerOtherError m:type="Edm.Int64">0</d:ServerOtherError>
    <d:AnonymousServerOtherError
      m:type="Edm.Int64">0</d:AnonymousServerOtherError>
    <d:SASServerOtherError m:type="Edm.Int64">0</d:SASServerOtherError>
    <d:AuthorizationError m:type="Edm.Int64">0</d:AuthorizationError>
    <d:AnonymousAuthorizationError
      m:type="Edm.Int64">0</d:AnonymousAuthorizationError>
```

```
            <d:SASAuthorizationError m:type="Edm.Int64">0</d:SASAuthorizationError>
            <d:NetworkError m:type="Edm.Int64">0</d:NetworkError>
            <d:AnonymousNetworkError m:type="Edm.Int64">0</d:AnonymousNetworkError>
            <d:SASNetworkError m:type="Edm.Int64">0</d:SASNetworkError>
        </m:properties>
    </content>
</entry>
```

You can use the Windows Azure client library to retrieve your metric data using the following code.

```
namespace Wintellect.WindowsAzure.Metrics {
    public class MetricsTransactionBlobEntity : TableEntity {
        public String Time { get; set; }
        public String AccessTypeTransactionType { get; set; }
        public long TotalIngress { get; set; }
        public long TotalEgress { get; set; }
        public long TotalRequests { get; set; }
        public long TotalBillableRequests { get; set; }
        public long Availability { get; set; }
        public Double AverageE2ELatency { get; set; }
        public Double AverageServerLatency { get; set; }
        public Double PercentSuccess { get; set; }
        public Double PercentThrottlingError { get; set; }
        public Double PercentTimeoutError { get; set; }
        public Double PercentServerOtherError { get; set; }
        public Double PercentClientOtherError { get; set; }
        public Double PercentAuthorizationError { get; set; }
        public Double PercentNetworkError { get; set; }
        public long Success { get; set; }
        public long AnonymousSuccess { get; set; }
        public long SASSuccess { get; set; }
        public long ThrottlingError { get; set; }
        public long AnonymousThrottlingError { get; set; }
        public long SASThrottlingError { get; set; }
        public long ClientTimeoutError { get; set; }
        public long AnonymousClientTimeoutError { get; set; }
        public long SASClientTimeoutError { get; set; }
        public long ServerTimeoutError { get; set; }
        public long AnonymousServerTimeoutError { get; set; }
        public long SASServerTimeoutError { get; set; }
        public long ClientOtherError { get; set; }
        public long SASClientOtherError { get; set; }
        public long AnonymousClientOtherError { get; set; }
        public long ServerOtherError { get; set; }
        public long AnonymousServerOtherError { get; set; }
        public long SASServerOtherError { get; set; }
        public long AuthorizationError { get; set; }
        public long AnonymousAuthorizationError { get; set; }
        public long SASAuthorizationError { get; set; }
        public long NetworkError { get; set; }
        public long AnonymousNetworkError { get; set; }
        public long SASNetworkError { get; set; }
    }
}
```

```
public static void AnalyticsBlobMetrics(CloudStorageAccount account) {
    CloudTableClient client = account.CreateCloudTableClient();
    CloudTable ct = client.GetTableReference("$MetricsTransactionsBlob");
    var query = new TableQuery<MetricsTransactionBlobEntity>();

    Int32 count = 0;
    var qr = ct.ExecuteQuery(query);
    foreach (var entity in qr) {
        Console.WriteLine("PK={0}, RK={1}, TS={2}", entity.PartitionKey, entity.RowKey,
entity.Timestamp);
        count++;
    }
    Console.WriteLine("Blob Transactions={0}", count);
    Console.WriteLine();
}
```

Execution of the preceding code will produce the following formatted output. You can include any fields from the schema that you might need. The default *ToString()* implementation includes the primary key, row key, and the timestamp, as shown here.

```
PK=20120724T0500, RK=system;All, TS=7/24/2012 6:23:16 AM
PK=20120724T0500, RK=user;All, TS=7/24/2012 6:23:16 AM
PK=20120724T0600, RK=system;All, TS=7/24/2012 7:21:22 AM
PK=20120724T0600, RK=user;All, TS=7/24/2012 7:21:24 AM
PK=20120724T0700, RK=system;All, TS=7/24/2012 8:23:01 AM
PK=20120724T0700, RK=user;All, TS=7/24/2012 8:23:00 AM
PK=20120724T0800, RK=system;All, TS=7/24/2012 9:22:46 AM
PK=20120724T0800, RK=user;All, TS=7/24/2012 9:22:45 AM
PK=20120724T0900, RK=system;All, TS=7/24/2012 10:19:56 AM
PK=20120724T0900, RK=user;All, TS=7/24/2012 10:19:57 AM
PK=20120724T1000, RK=system;All, TS=7/24/2012 11:21:59 AM
PK=20120724T1000, RK=user;All, TS=7/24/2012 11:21:58 AM
PK=20120724T1100, RK=system;All, TS=7/24/2012 12:21:28 PM
PK=20120724T1100, RK=user;All, TS=7/24/2012 12:21:27 PM
PK=20120724T1200, RK=system;All, TS=7/24/2012 1:22:22 PM
PK=20120724T1200, RK=user;All, TS=7/24/2012 1:22:22 PM
PK=20120724T1300, RK=system;All, TS=7/24/2012 2:22:59 PM
PK=20120724T1300, RK=user;All, TS=7/24/2012 2:22:59 PM
PK=20120724T1400, RK=system;All, TS=7/24/2012 3:18:44 PM
PK=20120724T1400, RK=user;All, TS=7/24/2012 3:18:44 PM
PK=20120724T1500, RK=system;All, TS=7/24/2012 4:28:54 PM
PK=20120724T1500, RK=user;All, TS=7/24/2012 4:28:53 PM
PK=20120724T1600, RK=system;All, TS=7/24/2012 5:21:48 PM
PK=20120724T1600, RK=user;All, TS=7/24/2012 5:21:50 PM
PK=20120724T1700, RK=system;All, TS=7/24/2012 6:22:19 PM
PK=20120724T1700, RK=user;All, TS=7/24/2012 6:22:19 PM
PK=20120724T1800, RK=system;All, TS=7/24/2012 7:19:44 PM
PK=20120724T1800, RK=user;All, TS=7/24/2012 7:19:44 PM
PK=20120724T1900, RK=system;All, TS=7/24/2012 8:20:14 PM
PK=20120724T1900, RK=user;All, TS=7/24/2012 8:20:13 PM
PK=20120724T2000, RK=system;All, TS=7/24/2012 9:20:57 PM
PK=20120724T2000, RK=user;All, TS=7/24/2012 9:20:58 PM
PK=20120724T2100, RK=system;All, TS=7/24/2012 10:20:43 PM
PK=20120724T2100, RK=user;All, TS=7/24/2012 10:20:43 PM
Entities in TSC=585
```

Capacity metrics

To retrieve all of the capacity metrics for blob storage, issue an HTTP *GET* request against the capacity metrics table storage URI. The following code shows capacity metrics for blob storage.

```
GET http://azureinsiders.table.core.windows.net/$MetricsCapacityBlob() HTTP/1.1
User-Agent: Microsoft ADO.NET Data Services
DataServiceVersion: 1.0;NetFx
MaxDataServiceVersion: 2.0;NetFx
x-ms-version: 2011-08-18
x-ms-date: Tue, 31 Jul 2012 04:43:41 GMT
Authorization: SharedKeyLite azureinsiders:8lvIQ1mY4sHqz5n9t7t/PjFYqv1T9Dqv2/V59vJtJpI=
Accept: application/atom+xml,application/xml
Accept-Charset: UTF-8
Host: azureinsiders.table.core.windows.net
Connection: Keep-Alive
```

The preceding request will return an Atom feed of the capacity entries related to blob storage. An Atom feed is a schema often used by blogging engines to publish posts in a stream of posts which are typically related by an overall topic. The Open Data Protocol (OData) protocol builds upon the Atom Publishing Protocol (AtomPub) as a means of querying and updating data in a RESTful manner. More information about the OData specification is available at the following link. OData is also covered thoroughly in Chapter 6.

http://www.odata.org

Table storage is an implementation of the OData protocol, and the preceding request will return an Atom feed similar to the following.

```
HTTP/1.1 200 OK
Cache-Control: no-cache
Transfer-Encoding: chunked
Content-Type: application/atom+xml;charset=utf-8
Server: Windows-Azure-Table/1.0 Microsoft-HTTPAPI/2.0
x-ms-request-id: 83834cc8-9769-4f5c-85e6-e61b17467b41
x-ms-version: 2011-08-18
Date: Tue, 31 Jul 2012 04:43:42 GMT

65EA
<?xml version="1.0" encoding="utf-8" standalone="yes"?>
<feed xml:base="http://azureinsiders.table.core.windows.net/"
    xmlns:d="http://schemas.microsoft.com/ado/2007/08/dataservices"
    xmlns:m="http://schemas.microsoft.com/ado/2007/08/dataservices/metadata"
    xmlns="http://www.w3.org/2005/Atom">
  <title type="text">$MetricsCapacityBlob</title>
  <id>http://azureinsiders.table.core.windows.net/$MetricsCapacityBlob</id>
  <updated>2012-07-31T04:43:43Z</updated>
  <link rel="self" title="$MetricsCapacityBlob" href="$MetricsCapacityBlob" />
  <entry m:etag="W/&quot;datetime'2012-07-20T01%3A21%3A42.8534297Z'&quot;">
    <id>http://azureinsiders.table.core.windows.net/$MetricsCapacityBlob(
    PartitionKey='20120720T0000',RowKey='analytics')</id>
    <title type="text"></title>
    <updated>2012-07-31T04:43:43Z</updated>
```

```
    <author>
      <name />
    </author>
    <link rel="edit" title="$MetricsCapacityBlob"
    href="$MetricsCapacityBlob(PartitionKey='20120720T0000',RowKey='analytics')" />
    <category term="azureinsiders.$MetricsCapacityBlob"
    scheme="http://schemas.microsoft.com/ado/2007/08/dataservices/scheme" />
    <content type="application/xml">
      <m:properties>
        <d:PartitionKey>20120720T0000</d:PartitionKey>
        <d:RowKey>analytics</d:RowKey>
        <d:Timestamp m:type="Edm.DateTime">2012-07-20T01:21:42.8534297Z</d:Timestamp>
        <d:Capacity m:type="Edm.Int64">29472</d:Capacity>
        <d:ContainerCount m:type="Edm.Int64">1</d:ContainerCount>
        <d:ObjectCount m:type="Edm.Int64">3</d:ObjectCount>
      </m:properties>
    </content>
  </entry>
  <entry m:etag="W/&quot;datetime'2012-07-20T01%3A21%3A41.5663217Z'&quot;">
    <id>http://azureinsiders.table.core.windows.net/$MetricsCapacityBlob(
    PartitionKey='20120720T0000',RowKey='data')</id>
    <title type="text"></title>
    <updated>2012-07-31T04:43:43Z</updated>
    <author>
      <name />
    </author>
    <link rel="edit" title="$MetricsCapacityBlob"
    href="$MetricsCapacityBlob(PartitionKey='20120720T0000',RowKey='data')" />
    <category term="azureinsiders.$MetricsCapacityBlob"
    scheme="http://schemas.microsoft.com/ado/2007/08/dataservices/scheme" />
    <content type="application/xml">
      <m:properties>
        <d:PartitionKey>20120720T0000</d:PartitionKey>
        <d:RowKey>data</d:RowKey>
        <d:Timestamp m:type="Edm.DateTime">2012-07-20T01:21:41.5663217Z</d:Timestamp>
        <d:Capacity m:type="Edm.Int64">852653</d:Capacity>
        <d:ContainerCount m:type="Edm.Int64">2</d:ContainerCount>
        <d:ObjectCount m:type="Edm.Int64">6003</d:ObjectCount>
      </m:properties>
    </content>
  </entry>
```

In Chapter 6, you learned about the rich and extensive querying capabilities provided by the OData protocol. You can use the techniques that you learned to filter the data returned by your query to match specific search criteria.

Of course, you can use the Windows Azure client library as before to retrieve your capacity data by using the following code.

```
public class MetricsCapacityBlobEntity : TableEntity {
    public long Capacity { get; set; }
    public long ContainerCount { get; set; }
    public long ObjectCount { get; set; }
}
```

```
public static void AnalyticsCapacityBlob(CloudStorageAccount account) {
    CloudTableClient client = account.CreateCloudTableClient();
    CloudTable ct = client.GetTableReference("$MetricsCapacityBlob");
    TableQuery<MetricsCapacityBlobEntity> query = new TableQuery
<MetricsCapacityBlobEntity>();
    Int32 count = 0;
    var qr = ct.ExecuteQuery(query);
    foreach (var entity in qr) {
        Console.WriteLine("PK={0}, RK={1}, TS={2}, Cap={3}, CC={4}, OC={5}",
            entity.PartitionKey, entity.RowKey, entity.Timestamp, entity.Capacity,
            entity.ContainerCount, entity.ObjectCount);
        count++;
    }
    Console.WriteLine("Blob Transactions={0}", count);
    Console.WriteLine();
}
```

Execution of the preceding code will produce the following formatted output, which shows the *PrimaryKey*, *RowKey*, *Timestamp*, *Capacity*, *ContainerCount*, and *ObjectCount* fields.

```
PK=20120720T0000, RK=analytics, TS=7/20/2012 1:21:42 AM, Cap=29472, CC=1, OC=3
PK=20120720T0000, RK=data, TS=7/20/2012 1:21:41 AM, Cap=852653, CC=2, OC=6003
PK=20120721T0000, RK=analytics, TS=7/21/2012 1:19:52 AM, Cap=74180, CC=1, OC=16
PK=20120721T0000, RK=data, TS=7/21/2012 1:19:52 AM, Cap=852491, CC=2, OC=6002
PK=20120722T0000, RK=analytics, TS=7/22/2012 1:21:49 AM, Cap=84658, CC=1, OC=22
PK=20120722T0000, RK=data, TS=7/22/2012 1:21:50 AM, Cap=852898, CC=2, OC=6004
PK=20120723T0000, RK=analytics, TS=7/23/2012 1:22:34 AM, Cap=60886, CC=1, OC=24
PK=20120723T0000, RK=data, TS=7/23/2012 1:22:30 AM, Cap=852898, CC=2, OC=6004
PK=20120724T0000, RK=analytics, TS=7/24/2012 1:20:54 AM, Cap=52531, CC=1, OC=14
PK=20120724T0000, RK=data, TS=7/24/2012 1:20:55 AM, Cap=852898, CC=2, OC=6004
PK=20120725T0000, RK=analytics, TS=7/25/2012 1:20:33 AM, Cap=42053, CC=1, OC=8
PK=20120725T0000, RK=data, TS=7/25/2012 1:20:33 AM, Cap=852898, CC=2, OC=6004
PK=20120726T0000, RK=analytics, TS=7/26/2012 1:19:20 AM, Cap=58, CC=1, OC=0
PK=20120726T0000, RK=data, TS=7/26/2012 1:19:20 AM, Cap=852898, CC=2, OC=6004
PK=20120727T0000, RK=analytics, TS=7/27/2012 1:21:52 AM, Cap=58, CC=1, OC=0
PK=20120727T0000, RK=data, TS=7/27/2012 1:21:52 AM, Cap=852898, CC=2, OC=6004
PK=20120728T0000, RK=analytics, TS=7/28/2012 1:19:24 AM, Cap=58, CC=1, OC=0
PK=20120728T0000, RK=data, TS=7/28/2012 1:19:25 AM, Cap=852898, CC=2, OC=6004
PK=20120729T0000, RK=analytics, TS=7/29/2012 1:19:38 AM, Cap=58, CC=1, OC=0
PK=20120729T0000, RK=data, TS=7/29/2012 1:19:38 AM, Cap=852898, CC=2, OC=6004
PK=20120730T0000, RK=analytics, TS=7/30/2012 1:22:07 AM, Cap=37485, CC=1, OC=4
PK=20120730T0000, RK=data, TS=7/30/2012 1:22:07 AM, Cap=852122, CC=2, OC=6000
PK=20120731T0000, RK=analytics, TS=7/31/2012 1:22:26 AM, Cap=38185, CC=1, OC=5
PK=20120731T0000, RK=data, TS=7/31/2012 1:22:26 AM, Cap=852066, CC=1, OC=6000
Entities in TSC=24
```

Enabling the analytics services via the REST interface

Request logging and metrics can be enabled or disabled via the RESTful API by sending an HTTP *PUT* message to the blob, table, or queue endpoint. The following message turns on logging for all delete, read, and write operations, as well as for metrics. Metrics and logging are both set to have a three-day retention policy.

```
PUT http://azureinsiders.blob.core.windows.net/?restype=service&comp=properties HTTP/1.1
x-ms-version: 2011-08-18
x-ms-date: Tue, 27 Aug 2011 04:28:19 GMT
Authorization: SharedKey azureinsiders:06/NA+/4MPR3+YQnUaQ5/Yse54OkyjKGCA4ZbOqy2No=
Host: azureinsiders.blob.core.windows.net
Connection: Keep-Alive
<?xml version="1.0" encoding="utf-8"?>
<StorageServiceProperties>
    <Logging>
        <Version>1.0</Version>
        <Delete>true</Delete>
        <Read>true</Read>
        <Write>true</Write>
        <RetentionPolicy>
            <Enabled>true</Enabled>
            <Days>3</Days>
        </RetentionPolicy>
    </Logging>
    <Metrics>
        <Version>1.0</Version>
        <Enabled>true</Enabled>
        <IncludeAPIs>false</IncludeAPIs>
        <RetentionPolicy>
            <Enabled>true</Enabled>
            <Days>3</Days>
        </RetentionPolicy>
    </Metrics>
</StorageServiceProperties>
```

A successful processing of your request will result in an HTTP Status 202 (Accepted) being returned, to confirm that your update was successful.

```
HTTP/1.1 202 Accepted
Connection: Keep-Alive
Transfer-Encoding: chunked
Date: Tue, 27 Aug 2011 04:28:20 GMT
Server: Windows-Azure-Table/1.0 Microsoft-HTTPAPI/2.0
x-ms-request-id: cb939a31-0cc6-49bb-9fe5-3327691f2a30
x-ms-version: 2011-08-18
```

Conclusion

Windows Azure Storage Analytics provides you with a convenient method for collecting and analyzing logging data and metrics for blobs, tables, and queues, as well as for debugging many usage scenarios. This allows you to analyze your storage usage patterns to improve the performance or reliability of applications that use the data stored in storage services, or to adapt your storage architecture to meet the changing needs of applications that rely upon data storage. This analysis data can also be useful in diagnosing certain kinds of application trouble, such as frequent or periodic timeouts.

Index

Symbols and numbers

C

About the author

PAUL MEHNER has been a software developer, architect, project manager, consultant, speaker, mentor, instructor, and entrepreneur for more than three decades. He is cofounder of the South Sound .NET User Group, one of the oldest recorded .NET user groups in the world, and was one of the earliest committee members of the International .NET Association (INETA). He also works for Wintellect as a Senior Consultant and Trainer.

Currently, Paul specializes in cloud computing on the Windows Azure platform, Service Oriented Architectures, Security Token Servers, Windows Communication Foundation, Windows Identity Foundation, and Windows Workflow Foundation. Prior to being reborn as a .NET protagonist in 2000, Paul's experience included more than 20 years supporting many flavors of the UNIX operating system. Paul began his early computing career in 1977 on a homebuilt breadboard computer with 256 bytes of RAM, 12 toggle switches, 9 light-emitting diodes, and an RCA CDP1802 microprocessor.

What do you think of this book?

We want to hear from you!
To participate in a brief online survey, please visit:

microsoft.com/learning/booksurvey

Tell us how well this book meets your needs—what works effectively, and what we can do better. Your feedback will help us continually improve our books and learning resources for you.

Thank you in advance for your input!

CPSIA information can be obtained at www.ICGtesting.com
Printed in the USA
BVOW001004170613

323508BV00009B/266/P